Southern Literary Studies

THE ART OF WALKER PERCY

THE ART OF WALKER PERCY

Stratagems for Being

Edited by
Panthea Reid Broughton

Louisiana State University Press
Baton Rouge and London

Designer: Patricia Douglas Crowder
Typeface: VIP Aster
Typesetter: LSU Press
Printer: Thomson-Shore, Inc.
Binder: John Dekker & Sons, Inc.

LIBRARY OF CONGRESS CATALOGING IN PUBLICATION DATA

The Art of Walker Percy: Stratagems for Being

    (Southern literary studies)
    1. Percy, Walker, 1916–   —Criticism and interpretation—Addresses, essays, lectures.   I. Broughton, Panthea Reid.   II. Series.
PS3566.E6912Z87   813'.5'4   78–27494
ISBN 0–8071–0560–0

For Walker

CONTENTS

ACKNOWLEDGMENTS AND ABBREVIATIONS

A NUMBER OF PEOPLE have been very helpful in the production of this book. Chief among them is my husband, John Irwin Fischer, without whose wise counsel this project would never have been completed. I'd also like to thank Louis Rubin, Les Phillabaum, Beverly Jarrett, Martha Hall, and Christine Cowan.

My thanks to the College of Arts and Sciences at Louisiana State University for funds to cover typing expenses, and to the *Southern Review* and the *Southern Literary Journal* for permission to reprint the essays by, respectively, Cleanth Brooks and Thomas LeClair. My grateful acknowledgment also goes to Alfred A. Knopf and Farrar, Straus, and Giroux for permission to quote from the works of Walker Percy. Citations to these books are included parenthetically in the essays that follow and are abbreviated as follows:

Mg   *The Moviegoer*. New York: Farrar, Straus & Giroux, 1967, Noonday Edition.

LG   *The Last Gentleman*. New York: Farrar, Straus & Giroux, 1966, Noonday Edition.

LR   *Love in the Ruins: The Adventures of a Bad Catholic at a*

Time Near the End of the World. Farrar, Straus & Giroux, 1971.

MB *The Message in the Bottle: How Queer Man Is, How Queer Language Is, and What One Has to Do with the Other*. New York: Farrar, Straus, & Giroux, 1975.

Ll *Lancelot*. New York: Farrar, Straus & Giroux, 1977.

On the Stratagem of this Book

WHEN WALKER PERCY was writer-in-residence at Louisiana State University in 1974–1975 he occupied a position peculiarly appropriate to him; he was *in* yet not *of* the English department. I think that position was emblemized by his office arrangements: for one semester he had an office that once had been Cleanth Brooks's; for the second semester he had an office in a new building occupied principally by mathematicians and philosophers. He seemed accessible in the first but, I think, happier in the second. Actually, Percy was to be surprisingly accessible and somehow inaccessible at one time. No one was more surprised than Jerry Kennedy, of the English department, when Walker Percy agreed to speak to a sophomore class about *The Moviegoer*; all Kennedy had to do was ask. But of course, Percy the private man could not so readily be called upon.

That combination of accessibility and inaccessibility in Percy did as much as anything to provoke this book. I remember the first letter I wrote to him from Virginia where I was then teaching. I outlined what I'm afraid was a rather simplistic interpretation of his fiction. He replied, kindly, that I was basically right but that "it's more complicated than that." Since then I have been trying to decipher those complications. And I think a great part of Percy's appeal to others is that they can at once know that they are "on to" what he's saying and that he is more complicated than they know.

There seems very little to prevent readers from being on to Percy. The kinds of liberties he takes with the novel form are never extreme enough to baffle or confuse. His style is winningly lucid; his wit is sharp but never vitriolic. Bill Godshalk tells me that of all the novels studied in his graduate seminar at the University of Cincinnati, the students' unanimous favorite was *Love in the Ruins*; they "loved" Percy's novel and had the most "joyous" time of the year discussing it. Certainly Percy's characters are the sort of folk everyone recognizes. One of my students once said to me that living his life felt like playing out a script written by Walker Percy. And, judging from Percy's standings on the best-seller lists, I gather that general readers, too, identify with Percy's characters and situations.

The philosophically or religiously oriented reader also finds Percy's work enormously appealing. Bill Poteat says that after reading the questions Percy poses at the beginning of "The Delta Factor," honors philosophy students at Duke virtually dismissed all other philosophical inquiry because they were convinced that only Walker Percy was asking the *real* questions. Although those students found pleasure in Percy's questioning, other readers find comfort in what they take to be Percy's unquestioning orthodoxy. I know of a man who reputedly does not believe much in "the Christ thing" himself, but who goes to mass regularly to pray that Walker Percy does not lose his faith. Certainly readers at differing levels of sophistication can see in Percy recognizable ideational frameworks—among them Christianity, existentialism, and stoicism. And critics can make telling comparisons between Percy's fiction and his nonfiction, reading the former as illustrations, or what Lewis Lawson has called "indirect communications," of the latter; thus they may see either fiction or nonfiction as an easily translatable explication of the other.

Percy's work, then, by tempting readers to identify with his people and to recognize his ideas, creates a large and enthusiastic public following. Nevertheless, that work defies whatever attempts readers may make to see it as transparent. It is always "more complicated than that"; for Percy's fiction and nonfiction have a curious baffling quality that eludes all but the most scrupulously thoughtful and sensitive of readers.

I am pleased to have such readers as authors of the essays in this collection. Some of these writers are quite young; others are preeminently well-established critics. Each is a Walker Percy fan; yet each knows how complicated Percy really is. And so their essays, written explicitly for this collection, suggest how much can be revealed about Percy's art when it is treated with the serious attention it deserves. The book offers the angles of vision of a structuralist, a mythologist, and a philosopher, as well as those of more traditional literary critics and theorists. Its scope includes *explication* and eschatology. In articles short and long, analytical and interpretative, the book assesses the charms, the achievements, the strengths, and the weaknesses of Percy's art. Implicit in the book is a desire that it will find an audience not only in Percy fans and Percy students but in Walker Percy himself.

Although all but two of the essays in this collection focus primarily upon one of Percy's five books, each offers insights helpful in understanding the entire canon. It is possible to see these essays in terms of topics: Percy and the South; Percy's fictional technique; Percy on language; Percy's use of certain philosophical and religious concepts. But it is probably more appropriate and more fruitful to classify these essays by kind rather than by topic.

Thornton and Lawson provide basic readings of Percy's two most recent books *The Message in the Bottle* and *Lancelot*.

Luschei, Vauthier, and Godshalk approach the first three novels through technical analysis. Luschei suggests that Percy borrows certain techniques of film making for writing *The Moviegoer* and makes them not only technical devices but thematic metaphors. Vauthier studies the patterns of pronoun reference in *The Last Gentleman* to establish how the narrative strategy itself shifts during the course of that novel and to suggest something of the thematic implications of that shift. Godshalk examines the impact of point of view upon the structure and meaning of *Love in the Ruins*. Other essays concentrate upon the traditions out of which Percy consciously writes: Webb treats *The Moviegoer* in terms of regional, particularly New Orleans, fiction and in terms of Percy's debt to Kierkegaard. Hobbs shows that Binx's progress in *The Moviegoer* is structured according to Kierkegaard's three stages on life's way. Pindell explains how the imagination of home works in *The Last Gentleman* to orient Will Barrett to the phenomenal and to render him receptive to the numenous. Kennedy studies *Love in the Ruins* in terms of philosophical dualism. Dowie sees in *Lancelot* a reversal of the Christian quest. And Brooks sees in all Percy's work a distrust of gnosticism that parallels the perspective of Eric Voegelin. The essays by LeClair, Poteat, Spivey, and myself, which too treat Percy's work in the light of particular traditions, also insist upon assessing Percy's achievement. My own essay on *The Last Gentleman* considers how that dualistic vision that Percy deplores nevertheless shapes his own way of seeing. LeClair suggests that an unwillingness to experiment with language and with what he terms an existential aesthetic limits the effectiveness of *Love in the Ruins*. Poteat shows how Percy's language theory, significant as it is, approaches but does not break through certain conceptual barriers. And Spivey's essay suggests that the one remaining challenge for Percy the novelist is to experience and portray a genuine encounter with the archetype of the shadow. My brief descriptive statements cannot adequately indicate the scope and depth of these essays, but they can at least suggest something of the range of stratagems employed in *The Art of Walker Percy* to "get at" the important yet curious work which is Walker Percy's.

The concept of stratagems itself is Percy's. In "The Loss of the Creature" he distinguishes between less authentic stratagems and those that succeed, at least for the moment, in "providing access to being" (*MB*, 51). In that essay Percy suggests that we can gain access to being only if we are taken by surprise and therefore can circumvent the "symbolic complex" with which a given experience has been invested (*MB*, 47). Thus if we are presented a dogfish to dissect when we expected a sonnet to interpret (or vice versa) we may be startled into actually experiencing it. Similarly if we get lost on the way to the Grand Canyon, or our commuter train breaks down, or a museum workman is injured while we are trying to look at a painting, or we suffer from amnesia, then we can see and be in the "lovely ordinary world" (*LR*, 34). The implication is that, without such a disruptive experience, there can be no discovery and thus no access to being.

Percy claims to believe that authentic being and seeing cannot occur through any expected means. They can only be achieved through an awakening like Rip van Winkle's; or a discovery like Robinson Crusoe's seeing the footprint on the beach; or a discovery like that of the passerby who happens to glance through an open studio door and see, unattended on an easel, a nearly finished masterpiece; or, we might add, a discovery like Jean Stafford's when she happened on *The Moviegoer* in a New Orleans bookstore.

Jean Stafford had the rare twentieth-century experience of making a literary find—she discovered Walker Percy. Finding this first novel, she must have felt rather like Percy says Robinson Crusoe felt finding the footprint. That she was also a National Book Award judge that year and along with her fellow judges Herbert Gold and Lewis Gannett awarded *The Movie-goer* the NBA for 1962 was fortuitous. That Alfred A. Knopf had hardly promoted the book and certainly had not nominated it for that award was even better. In Percy's own terms, the novel was unpackaged. Furthermore, the story of *The Moviegoer*'s in-auspicious publication, happenstantial discovery, and subsequent success makes *The Moviegoer* a Cinderella among publishing's wicked step-sisters. And the tale reads like a rotation right out of Walker Percy's own fiction.

That modern day fairy tale cannot but delight Percy fans, but we would be naïve to think that such a discovery circumvents the symbolic complex Percy refers to as "packaging." The discovery experience is unexpected rather than expected, a true antipackage, but it is still a package. As Percy well knows, we cannot think without such complexes. But Percy rather too often hypothesizes as if he believes we should. That is one reason why there is such a curious ambiguity in his work. It is as if he so distrusts the intellect that he disclaims the fruits of his own labors. But so much distrust belies the character of Percy's own fine achievement. Neither art nor theory necessarily deflates experience; both art and theory and their creators can be at once in and of the world around them; thus they need not interfere with our access to being but instead may enhance it.

After all, if we believed Percy on the dangers of packaging, we would not read him any more. Nor would we teach Percy to our students or write essays on Percy or read any Percy criticism. In fact, we would conclude that since Walker Percy's works are now too well known and well respected to be discovered, we had better forget Walker Percy and prowl around artists' studios and out-of-the-way bookstores in hopes of discovering someone else's art that we might see afresh. Walker Percy's fiction itself, however, should caution against such a conclusion, for it suggests that to live life only through moments of discovery or disruption is not to live very completely.

To say that art cannot be seen except through a discovery or reversal of expectation is equivalent to saying that life cannot be lived except through moments of surprise, titillation, or danger.

Percy's novels depict the need for a stratagem that will allow the protagonists to immerse themselves in the world so that there is no distinction between seeing and being. Then the world can open out for them and can be at once known and enjoyed. Each of the protagonists in the first three novels and Percival (Father John) in the fourth seems to find a way home to this world at the end of the novel. Each learns that the ultimate and only stratagem that can integrate seeing with being is to *be* in love and to *see* in faith.

If then Percy's fiction shows us that the contrived stratagems of disruption and discovery do not work but that love and faith do, I believe that the corollary could be said of intellectual and aesthetic experiences. If Percy's protagonists are rescued by love, so may his readers be. I would suggest that an intersubjective relationship, with all that it implies about full knowledge and involvement, has its analogue in art appreciation. Thus, though there is delight in discovering the work of art, there is a fuller joy and deeper satisfaction in returning to it, knowing it well, and deciphering its complications. That of course is the stratagem behind this book.

The contributors of this volume each discovered the work of Walker Percy long ago. Each of us has delighted in his words, his wit, his wisdom. Each of us has returned to his writing again and again with keener vision and renewed appreciation. In studying Percy's work, we do not believe that we have lost the creature or packaged Walker Percy as a specimen to be studied, but trust that we have made more accessible in Percy that which was formerly inaccessible. Thus, though we cannot duplicate Jean Stafford's discovery, we do not need to, for we believe that we have enhanced it.

PANTHEA REID BROUGHTON

THE ART OF WALKER PERCY

Binx Bolling's New Orleans: Moviegoing, Southern Writing, and Father Abraham

1

AS A WAY of suggesting the remarkable achievement of Walker Percy's first novel, *The Moviegoer*, I want to discuss three paradoxes in its hero, Binx Bolling. All three paradoxes arise from speculation about the nature of the relationship between the fictive Binx and the fiction that contains him. My intent, in exploring them, is to cast light on some of the shadowy improbabilities and complexities of both the character Binx and the novel he "writes." The first paradox is that Binx is in his society but not of it. He is at once a typical insider and a classic outsider. As an insider, he lives in his natal city, works in a family business, spends a good deal of time with friends and family connections, and has no enemies. He has, in short, as fixed a position in his society as it seems possible to have. Yet, he feels himself a man almost without identity. Alienated from his culture, he feels that his most fortunate circumstance is that he regains the ability to see his life as a stranger might, freshly and from the outside. How can he be both insider and outsider? An examination of his paradoxical status will clarify the evolution of his character and, in turn, cast light upon the peculiarly tentative opening of Percy's novel.

Second, the narrator Binx is so single-mindedly concerned with himself and his personal response to events that virtually all the other major characters at one time or another accuse him of being selfish or narcissistic. Yet his narrative, Percy's novel, has been widely recognized as the best of this century about New Orleans and as one of the major post–World War II books about the South. How could such a solipsistic narrator write a central fiction about the culture of a city and a region?

The third paradox takes us directly into the heart of the book. Much of the action deals with Binx's "search" for "clues" to the mystery of existence. Whenever he is able, he seeks these clues in the world around him. And he always carries a notebook with him to jot down his thoughts. Yet, except for a brief remark about the relation of science to romanticism, he only uses that notebook once, to record an experience that comes to him at three in the morning. He writes:

REMEMBER TOMORROW

Starting point for search:

It no longer avails to start with creatures and prove God.

Yet it is impossible to rule God out.

The only possible starting point: the strange fact of one's own invincible apathy—that if the proofs were proved and God presented himself, nothing would be changed. Here is the strangest fact of all.

Abraham saw signs of God and believed. Now the only sign is that all the signs in the world make no difference. Is this God's ironic revenge? But I am onto him. (*Mg*, 146)

If "all the signs in the world make no difference," then what is the point of his search for clues?

As these paradoxes suggest, Binx Bolling is a complex, enigmatic figure in a complex work. To make sense of him, it is helpful to examine the evolution of the character in the opening pages; for there Percy deliberately keeps beginning the book over again. Each of the first three paragraphs records a separate narrative: in the first, the opening situation arrives with the Wednesday mail, and it triggers two separate memories for Binx in the next two paragraphs. To complicate matters further, the Binx who gets the mail has just undergone a profound change. He has just become aware of what he calls "the search" that morning. That sudden fresh awareness creates the heightened sensitivity of the opening paragraphs (and the rest of the book) and serves as the true initiating moment of the action. But it is a memory of a still earlier moment of perception that serves to trigger that initiating moment, and the earlier moment thus serves as yet another beginning itself.

Binx, as he reveals himself in the first three paragraphs, is a fiercely introspective, analytical man with an obsessive habit of interpretation. When he receives a note from his aunt asking him to come to lunch, he comments: "I know what this means" (*Mg*, 3). Since he eats regularly with her on Sundays and the note arrives on Wednesday, "it can only mean one thing" (*Mg*, 3). Binx knows that she wants to have a serious talk with him about his future or about her stepdaughter Kate, whose fiancé was killed in a car wreck. Here we see that Binx's sensitivity allows him to interpret events with an almost Jamesian subtlety. And further, his sensitivity includes a frankness and curiosity about his own emotions: he discovers that he is actually looking forward to the forthcoming charged encounter.

This discovery triggers the second narrative, his memory of the death of his brother, Scott, when Binx was eight. His Aunt Emily had taken him for a walk on the street outside the hospital, and she seemed for once entirely willing to walk at Binx's rate and talk about whatever he wanted to talk about. He interpreted her behavior: "Something extraordinary had happened all right" (*Mg*, 4). Finally she told him his brother had died. She told him that she knew he would bear up and act like a soldier. As a child, he wondered: "I could easily act like a soldier. Was that all I had to do?" (*Mg*, 4). This childhood memory triggers a second memory of a movie Binx saw a month before out by Lake Pontchartrain. It was a film about a man with amnesia who was faced with the problem of making a fresh start in life. But it ended happily, Hollywood-style: "In no time he found a very picturesque place to live, a houseboat on the river, and a very handsome girl, the local librarian" (*Mg*, 4–5).

As the reader soon learns, the two memories function as a commentary on Binx's present predicament. The movie exemplifies how it is to live in the world; his aunt's advice suggests how, living in the world, one must face death or loss. Both answers are false because they counsel forms of forgetfulness toward the mystery of human existence, a forgetfulness that Binx knows to be a form of death. But the answers define themselves as the ways to live in the world; thus they are endorsed by that civilization which itself seems organized to deny or suppress any sense of the wonder of life. Hence, Binx, who is acutely aware of that mystery and searches for clues to the significance of his own life, is unable to rest easy with any of the answers conventionally presented by his society.

After the opening paragraphs, Binx sketches in the broad outlines of his present existence. It reveals a man living an ordinary life on the surface, but one deeply alienated from any sense of purpose and painfully conscious of that alienation. He is consciously pursuing what he ironically calls his Little Way. Like Camus' Meursault, he seems intent on getting through his life with deliberately reduced expectations. For the past four years he has been living "uneventfully" in "peaceful" Gentilly, an ordinary, middle-class suburb of New Orleans which he prefers to the gaudy quaintness of the famous French Quarter or the quiet elegance of the Garden District. His job is as banal as his surroundings: he manages a branch office of his uncle's brokerage firm. Like Meursault, Binx has no close friends and likes to spend time in the company of pretty women; he regularly seduces his secretaries, though the practice seems more a hobby than a series of grand love affairs. In the end, each of his secretaries and he "were so sick of each other" that they were delighted to part (*Mg*, 9). His existence, then, may seem everyday, but it is really just empty. That is why Binx goes to movies so frequently and obsessively that he may reasonably be designated "the moviegoer" and this novel named *The Moviegoer*. His obsession betrays his own inadequacy; for all the truly memorable moments of Binx's life seem to have come from movies he has watched. In his portrayal of a man who finds movies more real than his own life, Percy has found the perfect metaphor for the alienated man in our culture; for anyone who feels his own life circumscribed may find it expanded by vicarious participation in the glamour and grandeur of a movie plot, but must also feel that moment of psychic uncertainty and disappointment at the end of a film when he returns to his humdrum self like a rubberband snapping back from the screen.

But it is crucial to remember that Binx did not always live in this fashion. Like Meursault in *The Stranger*, Binx at certain points drops hints of his former life, which was completely at variance with the unambitious, banal behavior of his present existence. It was a life built on longing. Sexual longing seems to have typified a more generalized longing for whatever was beyond his grasp. Binx explains that sex is "longed after and dreamed of the first twenty years of one's life, not practiced but not quite prohibited; simply longed after, longed after as a fruit not really forbidden but mock-forbidden and therefore secretly prized" (*Mg*, 207). Binx is now thirty; but until "Ten years ago I pursued beauty and gave no thought to money" (*Mg*, 196). Also, until ten years ago, Binx was ambitious; he explains, "Once I thought of going into law or medicine or even pure science. I even dreamed of doing something great. But there is much to be said for giving up such grand ambitions and living the most ordinary life imaginable, a life without the old longings" (*Mg*, 9).

Some event in the past was so monumental in its impact on

him that it permanently deflected him from "the old longings," the ambitious attempt to make something of his life in a romantic and conventional way. That event occurred to him ten years before when he was wounded during the Korean War. At that instant, he "woke up"; he began seeing reality as if for the first time as a child might, without the deadening blur of routine that Binx calls everydayness. "I remembered the first time the search occurred to me. I came to myself under a chindolea bush. . . . My shoulder didn't hurt but it was pressed hard against the ground as if somebody sat on me. Six inches from my nose a dung beetle was scratching around under the leaves. As I watched, there awoke in me an immense curiosity. I was onto something. I vowed that if I ever got out of this fix, I would pursue the search" (*Mg*, 10–11).

In a sense, the rest of the novel records his attempts to come to terms with the fact of this experience, to assess the consequences of his sudden full awareness of being alive in a precise, historical moment. This attempt is his search, and it is ultimately religious. Heidegger says in *An Introduction to Metaphysics* that the origin of philosophy lies in experiencing the question, "Why are there essents ["existents" or "things that are"] rather than Nothing?"[1] And Binx's wartime experience raises precisely this question.

His wartime moment of perception led to nothing, at least in Binx's eyes. While on the battlefield he vowed to pursue his search. But as soon as he returned home, he claims, he "forgot all about it " (*Mg*, 11). This claim is not quite true; except during an unsatisfactory hunting trip with war buddies, after the war he gave up all the old, romantic, ambitious, brave, idealized longings and opted for peaceful life in a nondescript suburb where he could "pursue money and on the whole feel better" (*Mg*, 196). He chose everydayness with a vengeance, but at least his existence has not been deluded by a desire for a "meaningful career"; he has not forgotten the search then so much as he has left himself open to it. His is an existence from which he can "wake up" because it is essentially an uncommitted and undirected holding action, while a life spent in pursuit of the old longings would not have been. Precisely because his existence is nonexistence, it does not color or distort the world around him. Instead, it makes it possible for him to see the world and to wonder why it is there. Binx has had such a moment of waking and seeing and wondering on the morning in which his narrative begins. That initiating moment of vision then makes the book possible.

The night before, Binx has dreamed of the Korean War. When he awakens, he remembers "the first time the search occurred" to him ten years before. As a result, "this morning, for the first time in years," he becomes aware of the possibility of the search and thus can begin to "write" his book (*Mg*, 10). He again sees about him as if for the first time. As he puts his belongings back in his pocket from where they rested on the bureau, they appear startlingly different: "They looked both unfamiliar and at the same time full of clues. . . . What was unfamiliar about them was that I could see them. They might have belonged to someone else. A man can look at this little pile on his bureau for thirty years and never once see it. It is as invisible as his own hand. Once I saw it, however, the search became possible" (*Mg*, 11).

Several things are noteworthy about Binx's experience. Most interestingly, Percy insists that it is *not* Binx's first sense of the possibility of the search that leads him to undertake it. Instead, it is the second one, years later, which was triggered by his memory of the first wartime moment of vision. In other words, it is not just his renewed awareness of the *thisness* of his world. (Presumably every child has a similar awareness of this glory of creation but gradually loses it, as Wordsworth says, "into the light of common day.") Rather, Percy emphasizes the importance to Binx of his *memory* of the earlier moment. It is his renewed sense of a self constituted through his own memory, not an identity mediated to him by society (symbolized by his wallet full of "identity cards, library cards, credit cards" [*Mg*, 6]) or one mediated by an awareness of tradition (symbolized by Aunt Emily's speeches about family honor), that makes his quest possible.

Although a sense of self reconstituted through memory is necessary for Binx to begin his quest, his renewed ability to perceive the objects on his bureau as if for the first time is the enabling event. There is, interestingly, a term that precisely names what happens to him. It is *defamiliarization*, a word coined by the Russian Formalist literary critics to describe the recovery of reality that comes from the reading of fiction. Art defamiliarizes the world by permitting the viewer to see it momentarily through another's eyes, the eyes of the artist or writer. By slowing down the process whereby objects are perceived, fiction recovers them from the realm of habit and restores to the reader a sense of the quiddity of his world.

Percy makes an additional use of Binx's defamiliarized reality. It enables Binx to see the minutiae of his own life clearly and, thus, come to understand and ultimately change that life. Moreover Binx reverses the Formalist insight that narrative creates a defamiliarized reality. In his case, the defamiliarized pile of "clues" serves to create a heightened awareness of the implications of things. That awareness was first dramatized in the opening paragraph when Binx tells what Aunt Emily's note "means." It is demonstrated in the continued heightened consciousness that enables Binx to write the book.

The Moviegoer offers itself as a defamiliarized account of Binx's life. As he moves through its pages, he can see himself and his world as he would a stranger's. His consciousness is aware of and able to articulate the world around him much as a playgoer sees a play: he reads the details for significance. But there is one crucial difference. He is not simply watching a play or movie; he is living his life and must become more than a passive interpreter of details. Because he is aware of society's roles as roles, that is, fabrications, he must create his own role from an examination of his personal experience.

In other words, Binx is *in* a culture but not *of* it. For this reason, he is especially drawn to others who, he senses, mirror his situation. Thus he never tires of looking at the photograph sitting on Aunt Emily's mantelpiece which shows three male Bollings on tour in the Black Forest of Germany in the 1920s. Binx explains: "For ten years I have looked at it on this mantelpiece and tried to understand it." He knows that the two elder Bollings, Dr. Wills and Judge Anse, "are serene in their identities. Each one coincides with himself." They are completely defined by their hunting outfits and their public personalities. But the younger Bolling, who is also Binx's father, is different; he "is not one of them." Although he too is wearing an outfit that suggests a successful American hunting abroad, his expression undercuts the pose. "His eyes are alight with an expression I can't identify; it is not far from what his elders might have called smart-alecky. . . . Again I search the eyes, each eye a stipple or two in a blurred oval. Beyond a doubt they are ironical" (*Mg*, 24–25).

His father's eyes fascinate Binx because they suggest that he is aware that he is playing a role. The others are successful Americans on a hunt; they rest completely secure and unquestioning in roles provided for them by their culture. But his father's situation is like Binx's in the dark forest of his life; his culture has not fully integrated him into it. He is going along with the others, but he does so as an outsider, as one consciously acting a part. But, though the father seems, at least in the photograph, to share Binx's outsider status, he could offer Binx no answers about how to act in the world; for he was hardly in the world enough to take food into his own body. In fact, Binx's father carried off "the grandest coup of all: to die" (*Mg*, 157). He even died in Crete in the wine dark sea "with a copy of *The Shropshire Lad* in his pocket" (*Mg*, 25). Like his father, Binx is an outsider. But unlike his father he does not want to die romantically; nor does he want to settle down to everydayness like the amnesiac in the movie or to endure loss stoically like Aunt Emily's ideal soldier. He just wants to live with awareness and wonder. His only tools for doing so are his memory and his ability to see himself as a stranger to the world even while he is very much in the world.

Binx's best model then for being in but not of the world is not his father but those Jews who preserve their Jewishness in the midst of a Christian civilization. From the Wednesday when he becomes freshly aware of the search, Binx notes that he is acutely aware of Jews. Whenever he passes a Jew, the "Geiger counter" in his head "starts rattling away like a machine gun" (*Mg*, 88). He says of Jews, "We share the same exile" but adds that he is more Jewish, that is, more alienated, because he accepts exile. Nevertheless, he insists that "Jews are my first real clue" because they are able to function and to create meaningful lives in spite of not being fully integrated into the society that contains them (*Mg*, 89).

To understand Binx's dilemma is to grasp the dramatic necessity for the book's multiple beginnings. Critics have often remarked on the inconclusive ending of *The Moviegoer* and indeed of all Percy's novels. But what has been much less noticed is the corresponding tentativeness of his beginnings. In *The Moviegoer*, Percy stages an elegant dance of at least five partial beginnings: the opening situation of receiving Aunt Emily's letter, the two memories it triggers, and the two initiating moments when Binx wakes from the everydayness and sees the wonder of life. These fresh starts and false starts comment on each other and finally enact a major theme: the necessity of seeing one's life as a series of fresh beginnings and the corresponding danger of lapses into the everydayness of habit.

2

But it is precisely if paradoxically Binx's alienation from his society that lets Percy make such a major interpretation of that society. To make clear why this is so, I want to consider *The Moviegoer* briefly in a tradition of southern and New Orleanian fiction. It is worth doing so because in his book Percy has solved a continuing problem of writing about New Orleans. The problem grows out of the overabundance of rich, absorbing detail which the city's diverse societies present to its authors. The richness of the surface (and its difference from the rest of the country) tempts the novelist to rest content with merely explaining that surface. Perhaps, for that reason, while the Upper South has produced many major writers, from Edgar Allan Poe to William Faulkner, Eudora Welty, Thomas Wolfe, Allen Tate, Robert Penn Warren, and John Crowe Ransom, the Lower South has produced few. Since the incidence of genius should presumably be the same in both areas or higher in the cultural centers, there must be a reason in the society of the coastal South to explain its relative dearth of major writers. If I may simplify a complex argument, the coastal cities, Charleston, Mobile, and, above all, New Orleans, early developed quite distinctive customs from the rest of the United States. As a result, talented writers in these areas, such as William Gilmore Simms for Charleston and Lafcadio Hearn, George W. Cable, Grace King, and Lyle Saxon for New Orleans felt impelled to interpret the distinctive local cultures to the rest of the country. As a result, the coastal cities have, by and large, served as self-conscious settings for local-color writing. (Something similar could be said, I suspect, about the Los Angeles of the hard-boiled novelists and San Francisco of Herb Caen and the Beat writers.) The sheer differentness of the local scene has tended to block writers from probing very deeply into the human condition and producing major fiction. Whether or not this analysis is always correct, it is certainly true that it has too often seemed the special fate of New Orleans and southern Louisiana writers to be sidetracked into the picturesque bypath of local color.

Even if nineteenth-century writers about New Orleans spent much of their time explaining local customs to the world that lies beyond Lake Pontchartrain, it might still be argued that the increasing homogenization of American society has lessened the temptation toward local color. The extraordinarily high level of the writing in the columns of New Orleans newspapers, much of it local color, especially in the *States-Item*, suggests that the Crescent City's peculiar fascination still compels writers to identify with it and to interpret it to the rest of the world. In *The Moviegoer* something else has happened. Although much blurring has occurred, there are at least two sets of cultural codes operating in the city of Percy's novel. First, there are strong remnants of what is still recognizable as a distinctively southern culture, evident in such details as Aunt Emily's actions and speeches, in Mercer at least when he is acting as a loyal retainer, and in the whole intricate routine associated with Carnival. But this regional culture is in the process of dissolving, blending into the second, national culture. This national culture is revealed in such details as the go-getter spirit of Eddie Lovell, the Mercer who likes to think of himself as "a remarkable sort of fellow, a man who keeps himself well-informed in science and politics" (*Mg*, 24), all the paraphenalia of a modern business society including credit cards, bonds, and stock brokerage houses, and the *Reader's Digest* which Mrs. Schexnaydre gives Binx each month. In addition, Binx is so nearly absorbed into movies, that that particular form of national culture threatens to subsume the New Orleans world he actually lives in. For the movies not only have their quasi-deities like William Holden, but they carry special powers to transform reality by "certifying" it through the heightened sense of place that comes to someone who sees his neighborhood on the screen. In short, though the mix of cultural codes in New Orleans has not remained precisely the same since the nineteenth century, it has remained a mix, offering an enduring temptation to the local-color writer who would save the region from homogenization.

Faced with the intermingling of local and the (then scarcely emergent) national culture, the local colorists of the late nineteenth century, though differing among themselves in many ways, were alike in their fundamental stance toward their subject. They all wrote about local ways and peculiarities with a knowledge of other, more typical patterns of living. In other words, they saw the local patterns of action as picturesque, exotic, and arbitrary. They had a subject because the locals did not behave "normally."

But from the standpoint of Percy's outsider, who sees his own life and all the others around him as a stranger might, *all* the intermingled cultures of New Orleans, local and national, appear equally picturesque, equally exotic, equally arbitrary. He is compelled to interpret them all, not for the interests of a wider audience on the other side of Lake Pontchartrain, but for himself. And, moreover, there is no normative code of behavior available to juxtapose with local ways of perceiving and acting. He must evolve such a way of living for himself out of the raw material of his own life.

The New Orleans of the local colorists was indeed a maze of cultural codes, but a maze in which one could orient himself correctly by reference to relatively easily available ethical systems: Christianity, loyalty to family, belief in human brotherhood, or the ethical standards of northern magazine audiences. Such an orientation limited the local colorist's scope; it did not allow for tolerance or cross-cultural understanding and growth. But neither does the new New Orleans that Percy depicts. In Percy's world it is no longer possible to relate to a single ethical system, but it is also unnecessary; for the city is less a forum than a boutique. Multiple codes of behavior can easily coexist because they have lost their ethical underpinnings. In the banal life of a modern city like New Orleans such underpinnings are outdated. If then such a city, as a characterless agglomerate, can better tolerate variety, so Binx, as an amiable nonentity, can better observe, embrace, and even adopt a variety of patterns for living. Thus because he himself holds no burning commitments or sure affiliations, he can register those that others have.

Binx's solipsistic concern with his own emptiness and alienation then becomes the very quality that enables him to provide a significant portrait of New Orleans and the postmodern world. His vision of the city as a jumble of unrelated sets of behavior quietly conveys an interpretation of Western civilization dying because it has lost its purpose. Percy has transformed that love of exotic details for their own sake which blocked or limited the imagination of earlier writers about New Orleans. *The Moviegoier* shows that those details need not be evaded or ignored. They become significant "clues" if one raises basic enough questions about human identity and purpose. In *The Moviegoer* Percy has reclaimed New Orleans as a valid subject for the imagination.

3

By choosing an epigraph from Kierkegaard for *The Moviegoer* ("the specific character of despair is precisely this: it is unaware of being despair"), Percy suggests that his hero should be viewed in a perspective of other "existential" heroes. Camus' Meursault is one, but an equally strong presence in the novel is that of Kierkegaard's exemplum of faith, the biblical Abraham. The patriarch's story is important to the reader because it is important to Binx. In the one time he comments on his quest in writing, Binx explicitly compares his situation to Abraham's: "Abraham saw signs of God and believed. Now the only sign is that all the signs in the world make no difference" (*Mg*, 146). Binx is not merely saying that he finds conventional signs unconvincing, although that is part of what he is saying. He also writes that "if the proofs were proved and God presented himself, nothing would be changed" (*Mg*, 146).

Binx, it seems, is comparing his lot to Abraham's only to insist that his own situation is more difficult. For that reason, I want to explore what connections he may see between his story and the biblical one. The major dissimilarity between Abraham and Binx is the one Binx points out: immediate access to the Divine Will is not available to modern man. But there are two rough parallels between Binx's actions and Abraham's. Just as Abraham leaves his culture, so Binx rejects the false world view of his Aunt Emily, which imperially seeks to define his life for him. But Abraham's most difficult decision was to follow God's will and sacrifice his son; he is spared from going through with the killing only because God sends a sign and he is adept at reading signs. A bachelor, Binx has no son, but he does have a cousin, Kate, who is drifting toward suicide, and a half-brother who does die of hepatitis at the conclusion of the book. Binx's problem is that he must learn to accept responsibility for Kate's life as well as his own and to accept the death of Lonnie. Instead of remaining a passive moviegoer, content to accept, with private ironies, the world offered him through his culture, he must become a skilled interpreter who creates meaning out of the jumble about him.

In the biblical account, the two parts of Abraham's story relevant here occur sequentially: first the rejection of society, then the demand for sacrifice. In Percy's novel, the parallels are intertwined, but it is possible to untangle them for the purposes of this discussion. It does not require a biblical scholar or a psychologist to realize that Abraham's moving away from the culture that reared him was a difficult action, even though the biblical narrative understates its painfulness. Similarly, Binx makes a difficult, interior journey, away from the world view of Aunt Emily. Although her attitude toward life is one

Binx must reject, Percy takes care to emphasize the seductive appeal of the world view she articulates.

With masterly economy, Percy suggests much of Aunt Emily's character in the first paragraph in the note she sends inviting Binx to lunch. Why a note? Why not a phone call? Obviously, because she sees herself as somewhat deliberately old-fashioned in her manners and, we might expect, her morals. Her final outburst to Binx confirms these hints: she explicitly categorizes herself as an elite member of society, a surviving member of the Old South aristocracy: "I will also plead guilty to another charge. The charge is that people belonging to my class think they're better than other people. You're damn right we're better. We're better because we do not shirk our obligations either to ourselves or to others" (*Mg*, 223).

Coupled with her belief in aristocracy is a historical pessimism. She sees her virtues growing scarcer in the modern world and stoically accepts their defeat: " I am content to be fading out of the picture. Perhaps we are a biological sport. I am not sure. But one thing I am sure of: we live by our lights, we die by our lights, and whoever the high gods may be, we'll look them in the eye without apology" (*Mg*, 224).

At this moment and others, Aunt Emily sounds like a Roman aristocrat watching the barbarians sweep over his world. Her assumed historical identity is a powerful, seductive one, but there is something finally nihilistic in her vision. It rejects too much of reality, and Binx must reject it, but not before he has offered powerful testimony to its appeal. Earlier, during his initial conversation with Aunt Emily, she says of her relatives, "We'll not see their like again. The age of the Catos is gone" (*Mg*, 49). Binx comments in an aside on the power of her nostalgic imagination:

This is absurd of course. Uncle Jules is not Cato. And as for Sam Yerger: Sam is only a Cato on long Sunday afternoons and in the company of my aunt. She transfigures every one. Mercer she still sees as the old retainer. Uncle Jules she sees as the Creole Cato, the last of the heroes—whereas the truth is that Uncle Jules is a canny Cajun straight from Bayou Lafourche, as canny as a Marseilles merchant and a very good fellow, but no Cato. All the stray bits and pieces of the past, all that is feckless and gray about people, she pulls together into an unmistakable visage of the heroic or the craven, the noble or the ignoble. So strong is she that sometimes the person and the past are in fact transfigured by her. They become what she sees them to be. Uncle Jules has come to see himself as the Creole member of the gens, the Beauregard among the Lees. Mercer is on occasions not distinguishable from an old retainer. (*Mg*, 49–50)

Aunt Emily offers Binx a neat if melodramatic historical myth by which he can have access to an identity defined as honorable by the myth. As a child, he can play soldier when his brother dies. As an adult, he can drop his nonsense about opening himself to the wonder, go to medical school, and become a member of the establishment. But Binx can't go along. The adoption of his "Little Way" was a rejection of her attitude toward life, but she only saw it as a "wanderjahr" from which he would mature. But he irreparably destroys her attempt to mold him into a mythic hero by going off to Chicago with Kate without consulting Aunt Emily and then having sexual relations with Kate. These two actions, irresponsible and hence inexcusable in his aunt's eyes, offer even to her transforming imagination proof that he rejects her seductive image of stoic elitism.

But if he must reject her world view, he does so with surprising tenderness. In her final outburst, she asks why he objects to her view. He is unable to explain his objections to her code of honor and the historical myth she lives by. He cannot explain his objections because he does not really replace her code and myth with a rival myth of human purpose. Instead of definitely condemning Aunt Emily's views, he merely finds them irrelevant to his own life. The map she presents does not help with the country of his life: he must do his own exploring.

In politely but firmly rejecting Aunt Emily's notions, Binx is saying *no* to a sense of identity derived from tradition. Through Binx's action, Percy begins his career as a novelist by laying to rest the ghost of historical nostalgia, a spirit whose presence underlies most fiction and poetry of the southern Renaissance. And perhaps Percy is exorcising as well the presence of his cousin, William Alexander Percy (to whom the book is dedicated), whose own *Lanterns on the Levee* contains a potent expression of Aunt Emily's sense of aristocratic ethos.[2] Like Abraham (and Huck Finn), both Percy and his hero head for the uncharted territories of life and fiction, each trusting his own instincts.

But God also asked of Abraham that he sacrifice his son. Abraham was saved from having to go through with this ordeal only after he had demonstrated his willingness to obey God's will in the matter. Even though Binx compares himself to Abraham, there is no single simple parallel to the patriarch's heavy obligation. None could be possible in a world without intimate access to Divine Will. But there are echoes of Abraham's dilemma in two of Binx's relationships, the one with his cousin Kate and the one with his half-brother Lonnie Smith.

Binx recognizes that Kate, unsettled by the death of her fiancé, is seriously disturbed in her mind and drifting toward suicide. A central question he has to face during the course of the novel is deciding his responsibility for her. From being a passive reader of *signs*, a moviegoer, at the start of the novel, he comes gradually to recognize that he must become more involved, that he must create the meaning of his life existentially by his own actions. His starting point, as he writes in his notebook, is his "invincible apathy" to proofs of God's existence. Regardless of the "proofs," he still has to lead his own life, make his own decisions. Out of his apathy and disinterest in anything outside his felt experience comes the need for a leap of faith, a leap more demanding and outrageous than Abraham's since it involves obeisance to a hidden and silent God. Once Binx makes his leap of faith, he begins more actively to invest meaning into his own actions toward others. The night after he compares himself to Abraham in his notebook, he takes Kate on a trip to Chicago. The trip seems inconclusive because Aunt Emily calls them back immediately and because, as Binx knows but Kate doesn't, traveling never changes anything. Nor does the mere act of sexual intercourse, which they perform on the way to Chicago: "flesh poor flesh now at this moment summoned all at once to be all and everything, end all and be all, the last and only hope—quails and fails" (*Mg*, 200). The failure of sex is akin to the failure of signs and solutions outside Binx to provide definitive answers to the problems. But Binx's faith does not fail. Though he does not believe in signs, as Abraham did, his faith like Abraham's is nonetheless strong enough to seek them. And out of that strength of faith itself a "solution" does come: loving commitment to another human being.

The trip is a turning point because Binx accepts responsibility for Kate's life as well as his own. This new commitment occurs in a scene with overtones of a wedding ceremony. Kate tells him that she is a religious person. She explains what she means by a speech recalling Isaac's affirmation of total obedience to Abraham: "What I want is to believe in someone completely and then do what he wants me to do. If God were to tell me: Kate, here is what I want you to do: [leave the train and spend her life speaking kindly to people in Jackson] . . . you think I would not do it? . . . I would" (*Mg*, 197). They each drink ritually from the bottle of liquor; then she asks Binx if he will tell her what to do. He answers, "Sure."

She reiterates her request that he assume godlike responsibility for her life: "You can do it because you are not religious. God is not religious. You are the unmoved mover. You don't need God or anyone else—no credit to you, unless it is a credit to be the most self-centered person alive. I don't know whether I love you, but I believe in you and I will do what you tell me. . . .

Will you?" (*Mg*, 197). Again he answers, "Sure," and they kiss, ending this parodic wedding. Though both momentarily falter from their confidence at this point, they recover and it forms the basis on which they build a new life together. In the face of an absent or silent God, Binx accepts responsibility for Kate's life. In effect, he is an Abraham who is forced to become an imitator of God, not merely a faithful follower. The seeker of signs has himself become one; Binx the searcher allows himself to become the object of Kate's search. The Binx-Kate relationship may have a final parallel to that of Abraham and Isaac. After God produces a sacrificial lamb to avert the killing of Isaac, the angel of the Lord promises Abraham that "because thou hast done this thing, and hast not withheld thy son, thine only son: that in blessing I will bless thee" (Gen. 22: 16–17). Binx acts to save Kate by offering his love and direction, but he never withholds her from the onslaught of reality. He never pretends that her recovery will be easy or steady. In fact, his attempt is to bring her back to reality, not shield her from it. Because he does not withhold truth from her then, he is blessed with her love.

But if the felt presence of a hidden God forces this modern Abraham to become godlike in acting to save Kate, who can be saved, that same presence shapes Binx's acceptance of the death of his half-brother Lonnie, whose death from hepatitis cannot be averted. In the epilogue, Percy lets the death of Lonnie serve to reveal Binx's reaction to human mortality. Significantly, he reveals himself only in actions and speeches; the self-conscious narrator of most of the book disappears after Binx and Kate are married. His replacement by a less confessional Binx dramatizes the notion that, though total absorption in one's reactions may be the beginning of a search for significance, it is not the end. The way for Binx lies not in greater and greater narcissism but in a leap of faith and in acceptance of community with Kate.

In any event, the Binx of the final pages talks less about himself than about events. He becomes a relatively reticent, problematic figure. His two dramatized actions in the epilogue suggest what he has become: we see him compassionately directing Kate's life as he agreed to do and accepting the death of Lonnie. After talking with Lonnie, Binx discusses the fact of his death with Kate and Lonnie's brothers and sisters with a matter-of-fact frankness which provokes Kate to accuse him of being cold-blooded. But he also answers seriously the children's queries about how Lonnie will appear in heaven and offers, for diversion, to take them to an amusement park to ride the train.

The scene mirrors the death of his brother in the second paragraph of the novel, with Binx now in the role of comforter that Aunt Emily had earlier assumed for him. The book has come full circle. If Binx's story begins when he learns of death, not as an abstract idea but as a tragic event that occurs in one's own family, it ends when he transmits that severe knowledge to the next generation. But if he has come to the same situation as Aunt Emily's, then his journey has left him with a different consolation, one which measures the distance between his quest and hers. She told the young Binx to be a soldier; in other words, she urges him to face mortality with a historical myth, deliberately to play a role in a metaphysical drama without asking about a possible author or audience. Binx also counsels acceptance of death but in a way that prevents that acceptance from becoming either callous or a source of pride. When Thérèse asks if her brother is going to die, Binx replies: "Yes. But he wouldn't want you to be sad. He told me to give you a kiss and tell you that he loved you" (*Mg*, 239).

Binx's consolation points at the mystery of human life and death; it does not cover it up with a romantic distorting myth. In its unblinking look at death, it is palpably, painfully honest. This honesty, to summarize, enables Percy through Binx to set down a significant, convincing portrait of a civilization dying because it has lost the ability to convey a sense of purpose to people like Binx and Kate. Furthermore, it is Binx's honesty that causes him to undertake his search and articulate his findings. And it is Binx's unsparing honesty that accounts for the popularity of *The Moviegoer*, a popularity that attests to the convincingness of Binx's character and suggests that both his disaffection and his quest for faith are more widespread than might be suspected.

But that sense of honesty is a function of Walker Percy's skill as a novelist, not the fictional insights of his created hero. Percy's skill creates a Binx who breaks away from false answers not by rejecting the world but by *seeing* it, and this paradox underlies and explains the three paradoxical questions with which I began. Binx is both outsider and insider because he who would lose this world must find it. A self-absorbed writer, he writes a revealing book about New Orleans because he who gets away from the city can have it back. Skeptical of signs, he has the faith to go on looking for them because he who would find himself must lose himself.

Percy's imagination uses paradox not to provide a meretricious journalistic surface for his narrative but to explore the richness and contradictory forces at work in a single human life. His use of paradox enables him to convey in a convincing fashion the paradox of time itself in which each moment in a life is simultaneously the summation of all previous moments and a new start.

He concludes his novel with an emblematic image of Binx watching Kate that brings together many of the book's themes: "I watch her walk toward St. Charles, cape jasmine held against the cheek, until my brothers and sisters call out behind me" (*Mg*, 242). Watching his wife leave on a journey that may be fraught with terror for her and hearing the voices of his surviving brothers and sisters, the figure of Binx symbolizes the permanent human tensions involving life and death, the wide net of human obligations, and the continuing necessity for new beginnings. For all he has learned in the course of the novel, Binx must still improvise, create the rest of his life when the book ends. It is a measure of the power of Percy's novel that we recognize our own situation in Binx's. In writing *The Moviegoer* Walker Percy has become a local colorist of the human condition.

MARTIN LUSCHEI

The Moviegoer as Dissolve

IN HIS FIRST published novel Walker Percy found his voice, and one of the joys of reading *The Moviegoer* emanates from the sound of Percy's laconic tone cutting a crisp swath through the magnolias. More exciting than his voice, though, is the vision, the sense of discovery one feels as Binx Bolling looks about him as if for the first time and *sees*. What Binx sees is molded and tinted by his moviegoing, which Percy astutely plays upon to explore his own existential themes. The film medium of course influences what Percy himself sees, and this particular novel provides an admirable ground for testing whether his moviegoer's world could be rendered in a medium other than verbal, whether film would serve his purpose as well as fiction.

Studying *The Moviegoer*, then, can reveal something about the potentialities and limitations of both film and fiction. Perception is central to both media. D. W. Griffith, the great pioneer of film art, echoed Joseph Conrad almost word for word in describing his supreme intention as being able "to make you see." There is a root difference, however, as George Bluestone notes in citing the coincidence, between the percept of the visual image in film and the concept of the mental image in fiction. Both media use tropes; what distinguishes the literary trope is its "connotative luxuriance," the "packed symbolic thinking" contained in it, as against the "enormously restricted" nature of the film trope.[1]

To speak of packed symbolic thinking in this context is to recall Percy's profound interest in symbol and language, and to work in the literary medium is to be struck by the connotative luxuriance of much of Percy's language. Given his care with words, it can be fascinating to examine the tropes he uses. One of the tropes recurring throughout *The Moviegoer*, by design or by chance, names a stock device of film art—the dissolve. And when we remember how as a medical student Percy marveled over the discovery of *"dis*-order" and *"dis*-ease,"[2] we wonder what meaning the term *"dis*solve" offered up for Walker Percy.

The novel's action, I have demonstrated elsewhere, concludes the antithesis phase of a dialectic in Binx's life as his Little Way, a lifestyle constructed as a refuge—from his aunt's expectations in particular—gradually disintegrates, and Binx finds himself impelled into a synthesis phase.[3] In the telling of the tale Percy adapts various techniques of film art, presenting his fictional world through fades and filters, superimpositions and intercuts, an occasional jump cut or zoom, and focusing effects both sharp and soft, along with tantalizingly nascent dissolves foreshadowing what is to be, or not to be. In this bag of filmic tricks the most important is the dissolve, for virtually the entire novel is structured as a lingering dissolve, a pleasantly painful transition between two phases of Binx Bolling's life. And as we watch one scene slowly fade out while another fades in over it, we realize that the dissolve is theme as well as technique in *The Moviegoer*.

In selecting the dissolve for analysis here, I am not merely toying with a metaphor appropriate to a book entitled *The Moviegoer*, but using the metaphor to yield up meaning. The dissolution of personality is a central theme of the novel. Early in the book we see the phenomenon in Mercer, Aunt Emily's black butler. "Mercer has dissolved somewhat in recent years" (*Mg*, 23), Binx tells us matter-of-factly, stressing the visual meaning of the word. Binx can see him more clearly than usual today, but Mercer is lost somewhere between his former role as Emily's faithful retainer and his new pretensions as an expert on current events. Emily, whose lens on life has an automatic focusing feature that transforms everything into sharp but flat images, sees Mercer as the loyal retainer. But Mercer, like Binx, has a dialectic of his own. Ordinarily what obscures him from view is "the devotion"—what in film might be a sort of rosy filter. But Binx can see through the filter: he and Mercer are not in the least devoted to each other. Binx sees in Mercer a man more sulky than devoted who takes kickbacks from servants and tradespeople, and it is he who waits on Mercer, rather than Mercer on him. Binx is uneasy lest Mercer too, as he threads his way between servility and presumption, catch a glimpse of himself between filters. Binx is more at ease with either of Mercer's self-delusions. He hates it when Mercer's "vision of himself dissolves . . . his eyes get muddy and his face runs together behind his mustache" (*Mg*, 24).

Although the dissolve trope is seldom used so conspicuously as in this arresting vignette of Mercer, the threat of dissolution of individual being pervades the entire novel. Various characters in *The Moviegoer* have dissolved themselves into roles. Eddie Lovell, for instance, projects the image of productive businessman and devoted husband. Binx meets Eddie following the episode in the Quarter with William Holden, whose aura leaves everything in his wake dimly lighted. Binx is vulnerable; the heightened technicolor of the movie star has paled to irony, yellowish and gray-tinged. Eddie appears, and ten minutes of his cogent talk leave Binx with no clue as to what has taken place: "As I listen to Eddie speak plausibly and at length of one thing and another—business, his wife Nell, the old house they are redecorating—the fabric pulls together into one bright texture of investments, family projects, lovely old houses, little theater readings and such" (*Mg*, 18). The connotative luxuriance of the fabric metaphor offers a simple instance of the power of language. Although a montage sequence in a movie might replay the scene's constituent elements, it could not achieve the metaphor's rich layering of associations.

Percy replaces the fabric image with a hard clear shot of Eddie in all his bustling and productive earnestness, suggesting how desperate Eddie is to keep his self-image from dissolving. Binx realizes: "this is how one lives!" (*Mg*, 18). Evidently one lives by using activities as refuge from and cover for despair. Eddie's wife, Nell, does the same. Seeing her plaintive eagerness, Binx wonders why she talks as if she were dead: "Another forty years to go and dead, dead, dead" (*Mg*, 102). We can see this death not because it is filmically attainable but because it is realized through the generalizing and suggestive power of the word.

Nonbeing, then, is like being in that it cannot be *shown*, as Marcel said, but only alluded to.[4] A visual medium, with its constricted figurative power, is less richly able than a literary medium to capture the ether of nonbeing, to see the "thin gas of malaise" (*Mg*, 18). The most imaginative camera work could not convey what Percy filters through Binx's consciousness, or his subtle tonal effects. Mood and tone here will elude the camera just as Camus' intricate concept of alienation, for instance, could not be captured in the film *The Stranger* merely by close-ups of Marcello Mastroianni's stolid and uncomprehending visage.

Nell and Eddie share a malady diagnosed by Percy after Kierkegaard and Marcel.[5] Their individual being dissolves into the fabric they weave by a ceaseless activity they call living, a constant state of motion designed to elude awareness. Unlike people with stimulating hobbies, they are not even "tranquil-

lized in their despair" (*Mg*, 86), but must maintain the neurotic
pace they have set for themselves. That pace so effectively dissolves the potential selves of such characters that they offer apt
instances of what Kierkegaard called the "curtailed I";[6] they
have simply failed to materialize their authentic selves.

The novel provides illustration of many such dissolutions,
and of many dissolutions that, rather than dissolve the self, instead dissolve the world around one. Jules Cutrer easily dissolves his New Orleans into a "friendly easy-going place of old-
world charm and new-world business methods where kind
white folks and carefree darkies have the good sense to behave
pleasantly to one another" (*Mg*, 31). And Jules is oblivious not
only to social injustice in the City of Man, but also to his own
daughter's crisis, assuming conveniently that "nothing can
really go wrong in his household" so long as Emily is mistress
there (*Mg*, 34). Mrs. Smith, Binx's mother, whose lifestyle is
totally different from that of Jules, shares with him a knack as
common as her name for dissolving the world around her. Her
principal accomplishment is "the canny management of the
shocks of life" (*Mg*, 142). She sees life through a "standard comic
exaggeration" (*Mg*,151), as when she tells a "malignant joke on
Lonnie and God" (*Mg*, 142). In the student days of her eldest
son, Binx, she could easily dissolve him into "Dick Rover, the
serious-minded Rover Boy" (*Mg*, 139). And though for years
she "has thrown it out as a kind of proverb that I should marry
Kate Cutrer," Binx acknowledges that in fact his mother has
also "made an emblem out of Kate and does not know her at
all" (*Mg*, 155). Mrs. Smith has managed the death of her first
husband through the same canny ability to emblematize: "My
mother's recollection of my father," Binx explains, "is storied
and of a piece. It is not him she remembers but an old emblem
of him" (*Mg*, 152). She dismisses the elder Bolling's long rumi-
native strolls along the levee, so apt an analogue for his son's
horizontal search, as "his famous walk" (*Mg*, 151). And the

grandest gesture of his life, his enlistment in the RCAF, she has subsumed under a visual image of him in uniform: "And so— cute!" (*Mg*, 157).

Such a dissolve to an animated image is an emotional evasion, but less painful than contemplating the actual import of her husband's gesture. "Sure he was cute," Binx reflects; he had found a way to "do what he wanted to do and save old England doing it. And perhaps even carry off the grandest coup of all: to die" (*Mg*, 157). When Binx attempts to communicate an experience of his own in Korea, his mother emblematizes the moment with a self-protective vagueness that resounds with unconscious irony: "We'll never know what you boys went through" (*Mg*, 158). "No more heart's desire, thank you" (*Mg*, 142) has become her guide. Even her fondness for Binx is a "fondness carefully guarded against the personal" (*Mg*, 158). In this, he reflects, "Strangely, my mother sounds more like my aunt than my aunt herself" (*Mg*, 154). It is hardly coincidental that they both think Binx should go into research.

Aunt Emily is a master at dissolving the world and its inhabitants, and she knows better than to care too deeply. Her withering lecture on the topic of Binx's "intimacy" with Kate reveals that she cannot empathize with stepdaughter or nephew. Emily has withdrawn into a wintry stoic kingdom where she can renounce the vulgar world. There she preserves her constricted self intact; from there she can dissolve others' selves. The novel's opening suggests Binx's fear of his aunt's expectations of him. "I know what this means," he says of her invitation to lunch; it foreshadows a talk, over lunch or on some early occasion, about what he "ought to do" (*Mg*, 3). What he ought to do is so clear and compelling, in Emily's eyes, that all he has to do is remember it. But Emily's "ought" is Binx's annihilation. The Little Way he has ingeniously built for himself in Gentilly is a deliberate holding action against her solution, which is actually a *dis*-solution of Binx, since it would assimilate him into a role that does not suit him. He is not fitted for "research," which he has put behind him along with the vertical search, or for any of those togas with which Emily likes to outfit the Catos of her imagination.

Another kind of dissolution, a familiar Percyan form, is depicted in Binx's trip to Chicago through a repetition. Fleeing from his own repetition of a visit to Chicago twenty-five years earlier with his father, and from the "genie-soul" of the city with its "great thundering-lonesome Midwestern sky" (*Mg*, 206), Binx takes Kate to see Harold Graebner, the old war buddy who saved his life in Korea. Harold is a simple, cheerful fellow who has grown rich. The bleak black and white of Chicago has gone to color by the time Binx and Kate leave the bus in Wilmette. They pass "noble Midwestern girls with their clear eyes and splendid butts" and skip on "like jaybirds in July" (*Mg*, 207). Harold's handsome new house emerges in bright technicolor, filling the screen. There is a slow dissolve to the interior, the dissolve itself depicting the anywhereness of the city and suburb. Percy does not film the actual greeting and entry but bridges it with a recapitulation of the war and some thoughts about the common joy of making money. It is in keeping with Harold's state of being that we cannot tell whether his exclamations and "baby-claw" (*Mg*, 209) gesturing are taking place in general or specifically, here and now.

Once inside, we find the screen reflecting a subtle confusion. No one knows quite what to say or whether to sit. "This is great, Rollo," says Harold, who is glad to see Binx again; but Binx sees too what Harold sees, and we watch with Binx as it comes over Harold powerfully: "what a good thing it is to see a comrade with whom one has suffered much and endured much, but also what a wrenching thing" (*Mg*, 209–10). Harold is overwhelmed by the repetition, the unexpected confrontation of a time past, "a time so terrible and splendid in its arch-reality" (*Mg*, 210), a heroic backdrop against which his present cheery affluence suddenly stands diminished. We get a dissolve to an earlier episode, a brief scene from that stark life-and-death time in Korea, a combat scene filmed in documentary black and white, and the dissolve back to Wilmette is to a pallid technicolor, faded like an old film, in which the hero wants to punish the man whose life he once saved for giving him as repayment a "wrenching in the chest" (*Mg*, 211). The vividness of past crisis has exposed the blurriness of Harold's domesticity.

What happens in this passage is interesting both technically and thematically. The screen clears and Harold's vision of himself dissolves, but in reproducing that sharp clear image from the past, Binx simultaneously drops his ironic posing and speaks in straightforward, candid sentences: "I walked in and brought it with me, the wrenching in the chest. It would be better for him to be rid of it and me" (*Mg*, 211).

Customarily Binx views the world through self-protective irony, a pale yellowish filter. This ironic pose accomplishes his distance and suggests his superiority to whatever he sees. But just as Harold's rosy filter is threatened by a clear sharp focus, so is Binx's yellow filter. And so is Binx's Little Way—"the worst kind of self-deception" (*Mg*, 18)—threatened by the search; for the search first of all is a completely undistorted way of seeing.

Metaphorically, the search may be described as a lens capable of an absolutely clear, sharp focus. The search enables Binx to see the pile of objects on his bureau, the familiar belongings emptied from his pockets. "What was unfamiliar about them," he remarks, "was that I could see them" (*Mg*, 11). And after he has seen him, early in the novel, the search becomes possible for the first time in years. The movies are onto the search, Binx informs us, but they always "screw it up" (*Mg*, 13) and end in despair. The failing comes not from any necessary limitation of the film medium but from the demands of that industrial tyrant the box office. Unlike the movie hero, Binx wants to avoid abandoning the search and ending in despair. But the search would obliterate the Little Way, and Binx also, throughout most of *The Moviegoer*, is reluctant to abandon its consolations. Binx's dialectic then moves between the Little Way and the search. Here the search works in two ways at once. Thematically, it functions as a moral focus for the narrative voice. Aesthetically, it functions as a visual motif which sharpens Binx's and the reader's view of the human dilemma.

Most of the characters in *The Moviegoer* seek to dissolve the individuality of themselves and of those around them; thus, like the romantic on the Scenicruiser bus, they can be moviegoers without going to the movies. Binx, on the other hand, wants to defend himself against dissolution. His Little Way, like the movie roles he plays so self-consciously, is ineffective and inauthentic, but it shows just how precarious his sense of self is. He talks to theater owners and ticket sellers to avoid the danger of "slipping clean out of space and time" (*Mg*, 75). His posturings as Tony or Rory or Gregory, to adapt Frost's view of a poem, are momentary stays against dissolution. Binx resorts to his ironic filter and to a dozen little stratagems to preserve what has yet to become his self. Beauty—his father's romanticism—to him is a whore. Money-making and love-making too are his formula, but his love affairs with Marcia and Linda and now Sharon, all filmed initially in vibrant color, have a way of fading as the long telephone silences begin.

The clear lens of the search surprises the viewer from time to time with nascent dissolves, tonal shifts that foretell the state of being to come, in the synthesis phase of Binx's dialectic. One such shift occurs early in the novel, following the lunch to which Emily invites Binx, where Kate is present, though off camera or on the periphery of a long shot. The lunch is filmed with mild irony, Binx warily fending off both Emily and Walter. When he goes to the basement to talk to Kate the filter is removed and the tone goes conspiratorially direct as Kate tells Binx he is worse than she is; she wonders how he got through a war alive.

The two of them are in league, in some yet undefined way. Kate's voice, when she says she is sick of talking with Emily about Binx, suddenly takes on her "objective" tone, a sort of "droning scientific voice" (*Mg*, 44) that might be represented on film by some telescopic or foreshortening effect distancing her from herself as well as from her subject. That objective tone is a pose, like several that Binx adapts, intended to preserve the self against dissolution. But Binx and Kate do learn by the novel's end that posing as another cannot save the self.

It is noteworthy that of the novel's five sections and the epilogue, all but one close on Kate, reinforcing a theme with variations: Kate's "long nightmare" (*Mg*, 63) turning whatever she touches to horror; Kate moaning and hugging herself; Kate "dry-eyed and abstracted" at the "strange city" (*Mg*, 218) of New Orleans in the soggy aftermath of Mardi Gras; Kate shredding the flesh of her thumb until it bleeds; Kate begging for reassurance that Binx will be thinking about her on the streetcar. Binx's tone with her is always serious, never ironic; for as Kierkegaard wrote, irony and humor are essentially different from the passion of faith, and where Kate is concerned, Binx acts in faith. Irony and humor, said Kierkegaard, belong in the sphere of the infinite resignation, which anyone is capable of attaining.[7] The clear lens in *The Moviegoer*, which can solve rather than dissolve, is put on with faith.

The Knight of Faith is Lonnie. The one section of the novel that does not close on Kate, the section recounting the trip to the Gulf Coast with Sharon, leaves the emphasis on Binx's conversation with Lonnie. Sharon's emblematizing of Binx at the section's end as "a good old boy" (*Mg*, 166) only heightens by contrast the seriousness of his talk with Lonnie. Binx shares many a secret with Lonnie, who has "the gift of believing that he can offer his sufferings in reparation for men's indifference to the pierced heart of Jesus Christ" (*Mg*, 237). In Binx's conversation with Lonnie about Lonnie's habitual disposition, there is no tint of irony; the lens is absolutely clear. Binx and Lonnie are open to each other, with no filters intervening. The quality of their relationship prefigures the inner quality of Binx's life after he makes the great leap of faith in marrying Kate.

Percy suggests the quality of that life through one succinct scene in the epilogue. Binx opens the epilogue on what sounds like a mildly ironic note, talking about his "thirtieth year to heaven, as the poet called it" (*Mg*, 236) and distinguishing "ass-kicking" from edification. He italicizes *religion* as a peculiar word and "something to be suspicious of" (*Mg*, 237), but anyone who is onto Percy should be alert to the possibility that such remarks tend to throw us off. The preceding section has prepared the way for a radical transformation because it has brought Binx face to face with the despair of his life and shattered his Little Way. He has recognized Kate as Rachel and consecrated their relationship in a sort of Eucharist by kissing the blood from the shredded flesh of her thumb. There is only one thing to "do," he reflects: "listen to people, see how they stick themselves into the world, hand them along a ways in their dark journey and be handed along, and for good and selfish reasons" (*Mg*, 233).

At novel's end the fading image of Binx's Little Way dissolves to a new image that is not what it seems. Percy's method is highly elliptical, and readers have often been unable to follow Binx to his new habitation, the nature of which cannot be suggested by any spatial metaphor. The most accurate metaphor for this change may be a chemical one. Marcel once likened experience to a chemical solution's receptivity to varying degrees of saturation and suggested that our "urgent inner need for transcendence might . . . coincide with an aspiration toward a purer and purer mode of experience."[8] In this aspiration we have a good image for the feeling of transcendence Percy captures in his closing pages, a feeling compounded of relief and exultation. The solution has become purer and less saturated.

Although many a perceptive reader has concluded that at the end of *The Moviegoer* Binx dissolves into familiar everydayness, he has instead become a true wayfarer. In the end the novel's substructure surfaces enough to give us definitive clues that Binx is now a man on the road to somewhere who hands people along and is handed along in turn. The change is an inner one. We see it in his patience with the emotionally crippled Kate and in his tenderness with his half-brothers and sisters, who have become brothers and sisters. The new life he is so reticent to speak of has been foreshadowed in the nascent dissolve earlier depicting his relationship with Lonnie, and it is confirmed by the tone, which in the epilogue is never flippant or ironical. Tone and technique establish Binx's state of being as now authentically his own; he is at one with his existence. The lens through which he sees is there too for the reader who elects to use it—the clear lens of faith.

There is really no way to capture in film, it seems to me, the transformation disclosed between the lines of Percy's closing pages as this scene emerges in clear crisp images from the prolonged dissolve that has been the novel. Certainly the prospect of making a good film from *The Moviegoer*[9] will be enormously challenging. It is for film-makers of course to test the possibilities of the film medium and expand them, and my judgments here as to what could and could not be filmed are intended to be provocative rather than presumptuous. My analysis here brings us back to the recognition that the literary medium has its own singular powers. George Bluestone is right: novel and film, "overtly compatible, secretly hostile" by tradition, meet at a point like two intersecting lines and then diverge to points where "what is peculiarly filmic and what is peculiarly novelistic cannot be converted without destroying an integral part of each."[10] A novel whose resources can be exhausted in the filming is not a novel in the fullest sense.

In *The Moviegoer* Walker Percy, a novelist with acute powers of observation, has produced a book rich in film-like visual effects. But as a novelist of consciousness and of ideas, realms in which film works under inherent disadvantages, he has also delivered us a *novel*—that recalcitrant if often lamented creature that ignores its proclaimed dissolution and the arrival of pallbearers and continues among the quick. Once again the ceremony has been delayed.

Binx Bolling and the Stages on Life's Way

SØREN KIERKEGAARD saw human existence as a progression of stages he characterized as aesthetic, ethical, and religious. In each stage man attempts to answer what Kierkegaard saw as the two crucial questions of human existence: how to live and how to die. Each stage offers increasingly more adequate answers to the question of how to live. But only in the religious stage, Kierkegaard believed, does man really learn both how to live and how to die.

The influence of Kierkegaard on Percy need not be reviewed here. What I do want to point out in this essay is the way that Kierkegaard's three stages form a matrix in which Percy conceives character and event; for Percy presents the central conflict of each novel in terms of the protagonist's struggle to rise above the aesthetic to the ethical and to pass through the ethical to the religious mode of existence. Because these stages provide Percy with a basic structural framework in each novel (including the fourth, though Lancelot Lamar himself only moves from the aesthetic to the ethical), I hope by examining the significance of the stages in the first novel, to suggest something of how they function in the others as well.

In Kierkegaard's aesthetic stage man lives only for the outward pleasure of the moment; in other words, he lives in the realm of immediacy. According to Kierkegaard "the immediate man helps himself in a different way: he wishes to be another. . . . For the immediate man does not recognize his self, he recognizes himself only by his dress . . . he recognizes that he has a self only by externals."[1] However, when externals no longer provide fulfillment, the aesthete may experience despair. If the individual is aware of his alienation from his real self and of the invalidity of the aesthetic mode, he may seek more authentic expressions of his identity.

The ethical stage involves an effort on the individual's part to "divest himself of the inward determinants and express them in an outward way."[2] Discerning one's concrete existence is the problem the ethicist attempts to resolve. The ethical stage may encompass responsibility to laws and rules, but Percy is primarily interested in that aspect of the ethical stage which concerns individual reality. He insists with Kierkegaard that "The sole ethical interest is the interest in one's own reality."[3] For Percy's protagonists this frequently involves repetition or recollection, "a backward movement" into the past in order to integrate one's past with the present, and in this to discern concrete actuality. Like the aesthetic stage, the ethical is inadequate, but for different reasons. The ethical view does offer a synthesis of the external and the internal or the universal and the particular. But that synthesis is impermanent; it will not endure through time because it fails to suggest answers to the second of Percy and Kierkegaard's most important questions, how to die.

The difference between the religious and the ethical is that the ethical is based on a relationship between the universal (*i.e.*, the whole) and the particular (*i.e.*, the individual or the part); whereas the religious view is based on a particular (individual) relation between God and man. With the achievement of a religious view, ethical principles are subordinated but not necessarily annihilated. The religious sphere is a paradox involving complete resignation or surrender to God (*i.e.*, forfeiting universal or ethical views) followed by the leap of faith through which the universal is returned not by man but by God. Faith, as defined by Kierkegaard in *Fear and Trembling*, "is the paradox that inwardness is higher than outwardness."[4] It is finally through this life view that Percy's protagonists attain valid alternatives to alienation which enable them to function in a fragmented and empirically oriented society. They discover that the religious existence fuses existence in the finite world with transcendence to the infinite. Consequently the fragmented self exemplified in Binx of *The Moviegoer*, Will of *The Last Gentleman*, Dr. More of *Love in the Ruins*, and Lance in *Lancelot*, is reunified in varying degrees by the conclusions of the novels, enabling each to begin resolving subjectively the problem of how to live and how to die.

In *The Moviegoer* Walker Percy writes of a man, Binx Bolling, whose fragmented existence can only be reunified through a search for authenticity. Binx launches his search for options to alienation because he perceives the ineffectiveness of an everyday existence that stresses such finite entities as material possessions, professional achievement, traditional heritage, and social status. Emphasis on external or secular pleasures fails to alleviate alienation because such options hold him in the finite, so that the infinite remains unacknowledged. Binx recognizes that "the search is what anyone would undertake if he were not sunk in the everydayness of his own life. . . . To become aware of the possibility of the search is to be onto something. Not to be onto something is to be in despair." The search, then, is impossible if one is "sunk in everydayness" (*Mg*, 13).

The movies imply the pattern for the search. They depict individuals seeking consciousness and achieving awareness. But as Binx perceives, "they screw it up. The search always ends in despair. They like to show a fellow coming to himself in a strange place, but what does he do? He takes up with the local librarian, sets about proving to the local children what a nice fellow he is, and settles down with a vengeance. In two weeks time he is so sunk in everydayness that he might as well be dead" (*Mg*, 13). The movies betray their own power to present experience afresh, for they too only reconfirm the everydayness of human existence.

Nevertheless, the movies project a "peculiar reality" (*Mg*, 17). Because of the very size of his screen image, such an actor as William Holden seems larger and therefore more heroic than the rest of us. But that idealized image masks Holden's real identity. His screen image changes in each movie so that the selfhood of William Holden is never revealed. Awareness of Holden's idealized image and his inability to be anonymous attracts Binx to Holden, since in contrast Binx must struggle to prevent his own anonymity and the everydayness afflicting his existence.

The supporting characters with whom Binx comes in contact in the course of the novel provide proof that neither an aesthetic nor an ethical existence will overcome alienation. They also illustrate the fragmentation engulfing modern man and exemplify the odds Binx struggles to surmount. In Mercer, his Aunt Emily's butler, Binx sees one who in Kierkegaardian terms "wishes to be another." Consequently, Mercer "does not recognize his self, he recognizes himself only by his dress . . . he recognizes that he has a self only by externals."[5] In Mercer, Binx sees the total reduction of a man to aesthetic or worldly alternatives.

Walter, Kate's fiancé when the narrative begins, reaffirms the insufficiency of the aesthetic view by measuring self-worth in terms of outward success. Walter's success requires certification through others rather than through himself. A houseboat adventure, undertaken with Binx after the Korean War, illustrates Walter's need of approval: "Goddam, this is all right, isn't it? Isn't this a terrific set up, Binx?" (*Mg*, 40). In "The Loss of the Creature" Percy states that such questions ask whether or not a person is "having the acceptable experience" (*MB*, 53). They indicate that for people like Walter an experience is validated only through others' confirmation.

As Binx wades through more encounters with relatives and friends, he begins to see, as Percy intended, the need for a continued search. He sees in Jules, Emily's husband and Kate's father, modern man's perception of the ideal Christian. "He [Jules] has made a great deal of money . . . he gives freely of himself and his money. He is an exemplary Catholic." Outwardly, then, his life seems ideal, but as Binx adds with an element of satire, "it is hard to know why he takes the trouble. For the world he lives in, The city of Man, is so pleasant that The City of God must hold little in store for him" (*Mg*, 31).

Binx recognizes that these individuals have chosen to impersonate others rather than exist as themselves. The result of inauthentic transformations is despair, but as Kierkegaard suggests, "In spite of the fact that a man is in despair he can perfectly well live in the temporal . . . life. What is called worldliness is made up of just such men, who . . . pawn themselves to the world. . . . spiritually understood, they have no self, no self for whose sake they could venture everything."[6]

Through a romance with Sharon Kincaid, his secretary, Binx, however, attempts to achieve such worldliness. Yet his relationship with Sharon never seems quite real to Binx except when it realizes itself as a rotation, or "the experiencing of the new beyond the expectation of the experiencing of the new" (*Mg*, 144). Thus Binx deludes himself into thinking that a rotation will suppress his alienation. Doing so, he indeed "pawns" himself to the world.

The gradual demise of his relationship with Sharon, however, modifies Binx's aesthetic delusions. Aesthetically satisfied following a rotation, Binx nevertheless remarks: "I do not love her so wildly as I loved her last night" (*Mg*, 135). Once gratified, the aesthetic challenge ends and their relationship becomes routine, an everyday affair, wherein communication becomes increasingly difficult and the "malaise settles on [them] like a fall-out" (*Mg*, 166). Their car accident creates a crisis which momentarily disperses the malaise. And by its nature it intensifies reality; they become "a thing to look at and witnesses gaze at us with heavy-lidded almost seductive expressions. But almost at once they are past and those who follow see nothing untoward. . . . We are restored to the anonymity of our little car space" (*Mg*, 125). Through experience Binx perceives that ordeal and "rotation" are only temporary alternatives to alienation, since the despair increases as the newness of the rotation diminishes.

Juxtaposed to his sensuous relationship with Sharon is Binx's more profound relationship with Kate. Partially because Kate herself is aware of the ineffectiveness of aesthetic choices, Binx feels no need to buoy up their friendship by transforming it into a series of rotations. And, because he recognizes and appreciates Kate's authentic rejection of everydayness, Binx does not try to deceive her. Unlike her step-mother, Emily, and her psychiatrist, Merle, who try to appease her to prevent despair, Binx is truthful and honest: "I tell her the truth because I have not the wit to tell her anything else" (*Mg*, 176). The honesty Kate promotes in Binx helps him eventually to expect less of aesthetic choices and to renew the search instead. Yet, though Kate will not live in the aesthetic stage, she cannot seem to move easily into the ethical stage. Her consequent despair results from her inability to develop inwardly. Perhaps Kierkegaard's analysis of such a problem as a "failure to appreciate that man is spirit"[7] explains Kate's dilemma; for she can neither pawn herself to this world nor believe in another.

Percy juxtaposes Sharon and Kate to establish Binx's dilemma, to show how much he vacillates between aesthetic and ethical choices. He also juxtaposes Binx's mother, Mrs. Smith, with Aunt Emily to illustrate the various, encumbering aspects of the aesthetic and ethical spheres. Binx sees how his mother's "election of the ordinary" devalues existence. For "after Duval's death she wanted everything colloquial and easy, even God" (*Mg*, 142). Her adherence to the ordinary makes living easy, but in actuality it diminishes life and diminishes her; for, as Kierkegaard asserts, "only that man's life is wasted who lives on, so deceived by the joys of life or by its sorrows that he never became eternally and decisively conscious of himself as spirit."[8]

Instead of deflating the value of existence, Binx's Aunt Emily, on the other hand, inflates its value. Yet she too remains in the aesthetic sphere because ideas for her are roles she puts on. When Binx says, "My aunt likes to say she is an Episcopalian by emotion a Greek by nature and a Buddhist by choice" (*Mg*, 23), the artificiality of the phrasing alone establishes that Aunt Emily specializes in inauthentic transformations. In her "Lorenzo posture" (*Mg*, 32), she can hardly be herself. Nevertheless, she is mistress of a household whose master thinks his daughter's nervous breakdown just "the sort of normal mishap which befalls sensitive girls" (*Mg*, 34). Myopically Jules cannot acknowledge Kate's flirtation with suicide because suicide has no place in his world. He can shift the entire responsibility for Kate's well-being onto Emily because Emily's sense of duty does have reality status in his world. Duty, for Emily, is a way of integrating the ideas of the past with the actualities of the present. When she achieves that integration, Emily Cutrer probably does pass beyond aesthetic posing and into ethical responsibility.

Binx makes that same passage but for him the ethical stage is a transitional one; there he, in Kierkegaard's terms, "sees that he himself is meanwhile in the process of becoming."[9] That process is temporarily exemplified in the "deliverances from

alienation" (*MB*, 86) known as rotation and repetition.[10] Binx's
visit to Mrs. Smith's with Sharon and his trip to Chicago with
Kate—both combined repetitions and rotations—are catalytic
elements in reviving the search and achieving Kierkegaard's
religious stage. Through them Binx perceives the fallacies and
the ineffectiveness of the aesthetic sphere, and he recognizes
the impermanence of the ethical options offered through repetition and rotation.

Binx's visit with his mother becomes a repetition, as Richard
Lehan phrases it, a "return to the past in search of self—a coming to terms with a haunted and guilt-laden world, a theme
that abounds in southern fiction."[11] Included within this repetition though is a rotation. Binx takes Sharon with his half-
brother Lonnie and two half-sisters Thérèse and Mathilda to
the drive-in movie to see *Fort Dobbs*. Conscious of the "Southern night" around them, Binx and Lonnie share unexpected delight on hearing Clint Walker in a "Western Desert" say to a
saddle tramp "in the softiest easiest old Virginian voice: 'Mis-
ter, I don't believe I'd do that if I was you'" (*Mg*, 143). The improbable mix of being in the South and hearing a westerner on
film speak as if he were in the South is, to Binx and Lonnie, a
"good rotation" (*Mg*, 144).

The visit with the Smiths is itself a repetition, of course, for
Binx. He awakens at three in the morning "amid the smell of
dreams and of the years come back and peopled and blown
away again like smoke" (*Mg*, 144). Binx, however, finds that
"good as it is, my old place is used up (places get used up by
rotatory and repetitive use) and when I awake, I awake in the
grip of everydayness. Everydayness is the enemy. No search is
possible." Binx has learned better than to trust rotation and
repetition to defend him against the everydayness which is
"everywhere now"; nevertheless, he vows "I'm a son of a bitch
if I'll be defeated by the everydayness" (*Mg*, 145). Clearly, if the
means he has used to fend off everydayness no longer work, he

must find other weapons. He seems to reason that if everydayness can destroy the search, perhaps the search can vanquish
everydayness. Thus Binx writes in his notebook:

REMEMBER TOMORROW
Starting point for search:
It no longer avails to start with creatures and prove God.
Yet is is impossible to rule God out. (*Mg*, 146)

Binx knows that the objective empirical method, that is, starting "with creatures to prove God" (*Mg*, 146), only reduces God
to the realm of the everyday. And yet it is necessary to search
even while knowing that there can be no concrete verification
of God's being. Binx is constitutionally prepared to do so; for
his "unbelief" has been "invincible from the beginning." Even
as a child, he explains, "I could never make head or tail of God.
The proofs of God's existence may have been true for all I know,
but it didn't make the slightest difference. If God himself had
appeared to me, it would have changed nothing." To Binx,
"proofs of God's existence" is an oxymoron; Divine Essence is
by definition beyond mortal proof (*Mg*, 145). Having intuitively
understood that all his life, Binx is prepared to make what
Kierkegaard calls "the leap of faith."

But the later trip to Chicago with Kate is a joint testing not
of religious but of aesthetic and ethical choices. The train ride
itself is a repetition for both of them. Kate remembers train
rides to Baton Rouge to see football games, and when Binx
first gets on the train he feels "the last ten years of my life take
on the shadowy aspect of a sojourn between train rides" (*Mg*,
184). On the way to Chicago Binx and Kate try to experience a
rotation within a repetition by making love for the first time.
Kate's reasons for inviting Binx to make love to her, however,
seem to have less to do with passion than with her theory that
sex, "a little fling" (*Mg*, 198), is "the real thing" (*Mg*, 199). But
her theorish bold "carrying on" so frightens Binx that "The

burden was too great and flesh poor flesh, neither hallowed by sacrament nor despised by spirit (for despising is not the worst fate to overtake the flesh), but until this moment seen through and canceled, rendered null by the cold and fishy eye of the malaise—flesh poor flesh now at this moment summoned all at once to be all and everything, end all and be all, the last and only hope—quails and fails" (*Mg*, 200). At "plain old monkey business" (*Mg*, 198) the pair "did very badly and almost did not do at all" (*Mg*, 200). The flesh fails (or almost fails) them because they have asked too much of it—that it be the real thing and make them real too. They discover, or rediscover, that sex alone, like rotation and repetition, cannot save them from everydayness.

Binx's uneasiness when he realizes how much Kate is expecting of their love-making is a repetition of a childhood reaction to his father's expectation that they be "very special father and son" (*Mg*, 204). Dr. Bolling took both Binx and Scott to Chicago twice; then after Scott's death he took Binx once. But, Binx remembers "seeing in his [Binx's father's] eyes the terrible request, requiring from me his very life; I through a child's cool perversity or some atavistic recoil from an intimacy too intimate, turned him down, turned away, refused him what I knew I could not give" (*Mg*, 204). As a child with his father in Chicago and years later with Kate on a train to Chicago, Binx's instincts fight against intimacy when it is called upon to provide more than a human relationship can.

But Binx's problem is that something must provide him an escape from everydayness. In Chicago he rediscovers that mere rotation and repetition will not suffice. The rotation of haphazardly charting a path across Chicago to Harold Graebner's house in Wilmette, and the repetitions of seeing Harold and of going to "the mother and Urwomb of all moviehouses" (*Mg*, 211) do not imbue his life with being. The trip fails Binx and Kate, not because Aunt Emily calls them home, but because they have expected it to do more for them than any mere journey could.

Later when Binx and Kate marry, their relationship is founded upon intersubjectivity which Percy defined in the essay "Symbol, Consciousness, and Intersubjectivity" as "that meeting of minds by which two selves take each other's meaning with reference to the same object beheld in common" (*MB*, 264). Intersubjectivity is a unification which allows each person to transcend his own separateness through sharing with and caring for the other. Bringing joy and meaning and completeness to two lives, such a relationship combines aesthetic enjoyment with ethical responsibility. In the epilogue to *The Moviegoer* Kate and Binx share an intimacy that Binx need not recoil from, as he did previously with his father after Scott's death and with Kate on the train. For his relationship with Kate, though demanding, asks of him nothing that he cannot give.

Binx's decision to attend medical school, though it may appear to be capitulation to Emily's aspirations, instead demonstrates a harmonious balance, a synthesis which establishes his authenticity and eternal validity. Having achieved the religious stage, finite concerns no longer confuse him. Kierkegaard explains, "one can discover nothing of that aloof and superior nature whereby one recognizes the knight of the infinite. He takes delight in everything, and whenever one sees him taking part in a particular pleasure, he does it with the persistence which is the mark of the earthly man whose soul is absorbed in such things. He tends to his work. So when one looks at him one might suppose that he was a clerk who had lost his soul in an initricate system of book-keeping, so precise is he."[12]

Kate does not fully understand Binx, but she realizes that he offers her stability. Part of what Binx deems as the job of a castaway like himself is to "listen to people, see how they stick themselves in the world, hand them along a ways in their dark journey and be handed along" (*Mg*, 233). The final scene shows Binx trying to hand Kate along on her journey, for he feels the necessity to help those along who may never attain the same passion, realizing that "for the man who does not so much as reach faith life has tasks enough, and if one loves them sincerely, life will by no means be wasted, even though it never is comparable to the life of those who sensed and grasped the highest." [13] Also Binx is now honest with his brothers and sisters about their brother Lonnie's impending death. He refuses to hide the truth from the Smiths or to prescribe how they are to act after Lonnie's death. Clearly, Binx has learned how to live well in this world.

In the epilogue Binx has no inclination to speak of the search, but he seems to know now that the search for one sphere cannot be satisfied with answers from another. Binx does not speak, he says, because, "For one thing, I have not the authority, as the great Danish philosopher declared, to speak of such matters in any other than the edifying" (*Mg*, 237). Their religious significance is an individual matter beyond explanation or communication. Such an ultimate search into the religious sphere, Kierkegaard says, "I make by myself, and what I gain is myself in my eternal consciousness, in blissful agreement with my love for the Eternal Being." [14] At the end of *The Moviegoer* Binx seems silently to have renewed his search. Thus he has become one of Kierkegaard's men of faith. Because he is such a believer, Binx can see Lonnie die and not be wrenched apart by grief. At the close of *The Moviegoer* Binx has learned both how to live and how to die.

Each Kierkegaardian mode of existence has its analogue in Percy's metaphor from "The Message in the Bottle" of man as castaway on this island earth. The first includes people who have "made do" on the island and are unaware that they are castaways. Most of the minor characters in Percy's novels are people who, in their adjustment to this world, remain in the aesthetic sphere. But the individual who knows he is a cast-away, is dissatisfied with his island predicament, and searches for another way to live passes to the ethical stage. Most of the secondary characters in the novels exemplify this category. Percy's final category is reserved for the individual who knows he is a stranger, yet who waits, and searches, and lives in hope that a message from beyond the seas will come. Percy's protagonists are such individuals. To see Binx Bolling's progression in Kierkegaardian terms is to illumine the modal design of the three novels that may be described as Walker Percy's Kierkegaardian trilogy. It is also to suggest something of how, though Percy's fourth novel is radically different from his first three, *Lancelot* does make use of this same Kierkegaardian frame.

RICHARD PINDELL

Toward Home: Place, Language, and Death in *The Last Gentleman*

IN A SCENE in Hawthorne's *The Blithedale Romance* the novel's excessively romantic hero, Miles Coverdale, stands meditatively before a window when a dove flies directly toward him, swerves, and then vanishes, as does also "the slight, fantastic pathos with which he had invested her."[1] Coverdale readily invests the dove with portent because, after millennia of symbolic associations, both he and Hawthorne's reader agree on the dove's specialness. A dove flies on extended wings in whatever stately mansions of the soul. But now suppose, the postmodern reader is tempted to ask, we were to change before Coverdale's very eyes that dove into a pigeon. The embarrassing predicament that would ensue finds its artist in Walker Percy.

Entropy (the pigeon) and news (the dove) are the generating poles of *The Last Gentleman*. The novel dramatizes a contest for the attention of Will Barrett, the title character; he is torn between a stagnant mentality of entropy and an imaginative expectancy of news. Two rival arts of being-here, one essentially entropic or reductive, the other essentially news-making or creative, converge on the prime world-making *materia* of place, language, and death. Out of these three phenomena Percy bodies forth Will's inwardness and tracks his possibilities, and failures, of progress toward receptivity to news. Finally it is within an imagination of home that Percy advances and unifies the dialectic relationships within place, language, and death. By so doing, he seeks to restate man in such a way as to possess him of his potential.

I shall center this essay in a discussion mainly of three emblematic scenes which exemplify the workings of the imagination of home: Will and Kitty's failed love-making in the Central Park "sniper's den"; Will's visit to Valentine Vaught's piney-woods mission school; and Will's attendance at the deathbed baptism of Jamie Vaught.

Percy begins Will's journey in Central Park at "ground zero" (*LG*, 48). The term is well calculated to record the terrifically emptying impact of a historical climax, when the dove of epiphany turns into the pigeon of entropy. The climate of loss is total. Entropy defines itself here as the measure of disorder consequent to postmodern leveling. "Nothing is *really* real for mankind," says a commentator on Romano Guardini's *The End of the Modern World*, "until it can be located, until man can find it in some given place."[2] The statement is an apt journey text for Will, who is, perhaps, the most explicitly place-conscious character in Western literature. But in the detritus of vanished landmarks and forgotten unities at ground zero, how can anybody or anything be located and thereby realized?

Such a crisis of orientation informs Will's occupation with Kitty one night in a rocky hideaway in Central Park: "The place was down a ravine choked with dogbane and whortleberry and over a tumble of rocks into a tiny amphitheater, a covert so densely shaded that its floor was as bare as cave's dirt. By day it looked very like the sniper's den on Little Round Top which Mathew Brady photographed six weeks after the battle: the sniper was still there! a skeleton in butternut, his rifle propped peaceably against the rocks" (*LG*, 107).[3] The redundancy of place-notation—"amphitheater," "covert," "cave," "den"—is neither idle nor mistaken. In this parcel of delocalized acreage Will, whose chronic amnesia symbolizes among other things contemporary self-absence, needs to memorize where he is! The accumulating rhetoric of dwelling resounds his effort to persuade himself he is a somebody somewhere rather than a nobody nowhere. In the end he only feigns inhabitation. The impossible transmigration of locale through Brady's camera and Will's memory dramatically exposes Will's substituting a preoccupation with place for any real occupation of space.

Significantly, in the sentence immediately following the above description of the place, Will seems to take his cue from the dead sniper. Preparing to embrace Kitty, he acts out the sniper's relinquishment of his rifle: "He set the police special in the dust beside him" (*LG*, 107). At this point in Will's journey the sniper is his ironic occupational model. Like a sniper, Will stands outside the space, both inner and outer, that he is meant to control or, at the very least, contest. Unoccupied by himself and well-nigh, like Central Park itself, a public space, he is up for claim by whatever aggressive local, past, or fantasy presence. (The same holds true for Kitty. While Will orients himself toward a historic impossibly transplanted spirit of place, Kitty is a mouthpiece of the *Zeitgeist*, whose leveling presence solicits from her the forms of behavior preached by its myriad quack ontologists and faddish lifestylists.) At ground zero Will is the nothingness through which we see, as through a ghost, the landscape.

The *sniper* is one of a cluster of space-control designations— *janitor, engineer, proprietor, Adam, genius loci*—which throughout Will's journey function in a choric role, vis-à-vis his sources and methods of self-orientation. The repetition of these designations suggests Will's desperate but unfulfilled need to place himself. The term *proprietor*, as Will is sometimes called in reference to his ownership of the two-hundred-acre remnant of

the old family plantation in Mississippi, is particularly sum-
mational, as is *planter*, a variant form of *proprietor*. Will is "the
strangest of planters, proprietor of two hundred acres of black-
berries and canebrakes," and Percy puns on Will's strenuous
efforts to "plant" himself in the root-resistant debris of leveled
landscapes (*LG*, 74). Taken socially, *proprietor* betokens Will's
last gentlemanship—his honorable upholding of old-fashioned
proprieties. As such, *proprietor* achieves succinct biographical
descriptiveness: Will is character in search of personality. Turning its traditional connotation of territorial suzerainty completely inward, *proprietor* at once comments ironically on Will's
vacancy—he is both literally and psychospatially an absen-
tee landlord—and underlines the necessity of self-sovereignty
incumbent upon him.

One cannot be a proprietor without language; for to name
something is to claim sovereignty over it and to be unable to
name it is to fail to establish sovereignty. Farther along in his
journey, during his brief visit to Valentine Vaught's pineywoods
mission school in Alabama, Will learns as much. For it is at
Val's that language is introduced as the peculiarly human mode
of sovereignty over inner and outer space.[4] With Val in south
Alabama, he sees how, as existential model, *proprietor* intersects
with and yields to *Adam*, who was first landlord of the creatures
in the Garden because he was their namer.

Val's mission settlement in the pines is likened to a "place
of crude and makeshift beginnings on some blasted planet"
(*LG*, 302). This landscape, a vision of the world after the Bomb,
logically succeeding ground zero, stages a confrontation between the word and pure space, which asserts language's first
and immemorial task: the provision of an order within and a
shelter from space. Scene and event at Val's, conversation and
underconversation, all espouse the spatio-temporal lordship of
language.[5] Language is presented in its highest power: naming.
"When they do suddenly break into the world of language,"

Val tells Will of her backward pupils, "it is something to see. They are like Adam on the First Day. What's that? they ask me. That's a hawk, I tell them and they believe me. . . . They were not alive and then they are and so they'll believe you" (*LG*, 301). Naming particularizes language's power of placement. A name gives the named thing "form and habitation," that is, a negotiable shape and a conjured setting, wherein it is let free to declare itself (*LG*, 11). Through naming the namer gains admittance to the going agreements about what is real that we call the truth, and the world begins to assume for him the recognizable features of a place. Naming confers reality not only on the thing named but on the namer; it is both a giving and a receiving of news. Naming is the Eureka bond between a person and the other: that which was lost is found.

As a mode of placement, naming is not only a celebrative act, one, that is, which occasions a reciprocal greeting between namer and named, but a competitive act as well. By his words man competes with the given for room to live. Through language he endeavors to wrest himself free from what around him conduces to inertia. This rivalry between language and thingness, the verbal and the reific, is dramatized early in the novel in a flashback to the summer when Will worked in his father's law firm. There he would overhear his father "speak with his clients, a murmurous sound compounded of grievance and redress. As the summer wore on, it became more and more difficult to distinguish the words from the sound, until finally they merged with the quarrels of the sparrows under the windowsill and the towering sound of the cicadas that swelled up from the vacant lots and filled the white sky" (*LG*, 16). The surrounding space breaks down the words spoken in it, converting them into its own mindless din, an ironic Babel of "towering sound." Language is naturalized, leaving Will ludicrously adream and speechless among the beasts, tending his allergy-swollen "great baboon's nose" (*LG*, 16). The tone is light enough. But behind the mocking squib of Darwin upside down is a monitory truth: the leveling of language—the disintegration of news into noise —risks the loss of man.

Because of the crucially sensitive political relationship between language and space, Barrett could not establish sovereignty in the "sniper's den" scene. The trial-and-error naming of the Central Park hideaway—"amphitheater," "covert," "cave" and finally "sniper's den," as it is thereafter designated—is in its very tentativeness and redundancy a travesty of the Adamic function (*LG*, 111). Language serves a mnemonic rather than a nominative purpose. The name settled upon, in that it is borrowed from another time and place, approaches the height of namelessness—interchangeability. (For a name, like a place, is a concentration of energy, felt as a presence, within *inimitable* bounds.) Unnamed, the place arrogates to itself decisive powers. "Setting" overturns its meaning, moving from complement to whole, stage to stage-manager. The place not only lends Will and Kitty a separate audience, but also, one senses, dictates what they say. Kitty, for whom the hideaway acts as a test space for her sexually liberated consciousness, speaks of her love for the dance; Will, for whom the place acts as a sensorium for his nostalgic and topophiliac fantasies, speaks of an ancestor who fell at the siege of Petersburg. But concomitant with the weakening of language's spatial authority has come a decline in its exchange value. Neither party hears the other. Speech degenerates into speeches, dialogue into monologue. In the darkness they have difficulty "placing" each other even by touch (*LG*, 111). Will fully clothed, Kitty naked, they lie beside each other full of words and incommunicado. Their failed love-making is appropriate because their language carries no spatio-temporal lordship. Unable to possess the place, they are unable to possess themselves or each other. Utterance is reduced to a form of existential absence. Despoiled of their sovereignty, the two remain vacancies in a void.

As a paradigm of postmodern man's increasing inability to take place, the "sniper's den" scene includes as well the two principal shapers of the entropic landscape: history and science. Under the aegis of these two forces, which converge in Brady's camera, Will and Kitty perform their emptiness. Will labors under the burden of historical superfluousness. With the major exception of Val's place, most of the places in his journey, until he reaches the desert, are already occupied by the dead. The environs of a Bear Mountain ski lodge are dominated by a "shadowy knoll associated by tradition with Mad Anthony Wayne" (*LG*, 22), and the golf course adjacent to the Vaughts' in Alabama is "haunted by the goddess Juno and the spirit of the great Bobby Jones" (*LG*, 241). In the "sniper's den" scene the dead sniper's solid reality and serene repose contrast markedly with Will's and Kitty's somewhat laborious compilation of evidence that they exist. An apt gloss on the scene is this reflection of Frederick Brown's: "Like Beckett's anti-heroes, we inhabit nowhere; only the dead, happily immured, enjoy place."[6] Also like Beckett's antiheroes, we are upstaged by these unriddable corpses. Their stubborn vitality, their continuing displacement of our space—"the sniper was still there!"—consigns us to the ghostly realm of the vicarious. In places predominated by another presence one's gestures easily become histrionic, mimetic. (As we have noted, Will's putting down his police special involuntarily mimicks the sniper's relinquishment of his rifle; the historically rich corpse momentarily serves Will as a stand-in self.) The "cave" of man's beginnings has become the "amphitheater" of the end game, in which the obscurely exhausted players pile parody upon parody, as if trying to sustain the illusion of having something to parody.

Where history preempts individual living space by the sheer redundancy of its overkept accumulations, science usurps it by its attractive methods of acquisition. "The price of the beauty and the elegance of the method of science = the dispossession of [the] layman" (*LG*, 280).[7] By ordaining the analytic faculty as the only credible, or sufficiently beautiful, locus of event, science disinherits its users of the world it opens to them. People are specialized out of existence. "It suited them [Will and Jamie] to lie abed, in the Trav-L-Aire yet also in old Carolina, listening to baseball in Cleveland and reading about set theory and an Englishman holed up in Somerset" (*LG*, 163). Place, baffled through a trunk line of exotic transmissions, reduces to nonplace: Old Carolina, "a region immersed in place and time," to a site of "abstract activity which could take place anywhere else, a map coordinate" (*LG*, 280). Characteristic of the false art of being-here, the law of change at work is not creative but cooptative. In this scene in the camper, results parody needs by substituting their opposites: mediation is taken over by media, participation by consumption. The place is, in effect, bracketed by history, presuming to be the record of the past, and by science, presuming to be the record of the future, but the occupants are not present. Indeed, the meticulous placing of the two travelers merely begs the question, where are they? Often such reality-loss, in an intolerable intensification of emptiness, can lead to panic. Periodically Will is beset by swarms of unlocalized fears called "ravenous particles" (*LG*, 26). At such times he is desolately terrorized by a cessation of being without the release of death. But this scene, which so well demonstrates Max Frisch's shrewd observation, "technology . . . the knack of so arranging the world that we don't have to experience it," is as cozy as it is precisionistic.[8] Plainly Will is lost in admiration for what separates him from experience.

If postmodern man remains enthralled in the idolatry of his own creations or, more precisely, in the *idolatry of his omissions*, can he hear news? In the deathbed baptism scene the dying Jamie Vaught, who has sent for a book on entropy, receives, instead, news of his salvation. But Will hears only words. "Here," says Percy of this scene, "Barrett has eliminated Christianity. That is gone. That is no longer even to be considered. . . . He *misses* it!"[9] Will fails to make the discovery of his fundamental identity upon which the hearing of news depends. He misses what he is. "Man," says Percy, "is alienated by the nature of his being here. He is here as a stranger and as a pilgrim, which is the way alienation is conceived in my books."[10] In *The Last Gentleman* alienation is rehabilitated from its emotional unrecognizability as a literary theme and established not as the agon of a particular age but as the universal human condition.

The second fall of man, then, is not to recognize his first one. Man perpetuates his forgetfulness of his fundamental identity as a pilgrim stranger—Will's amnesia is representative—by supposing himself an organism adapting to an environment. Postulating for himself the latter's pure ecological connectedness, he, in effect, dissembles his alienation and lives in bad faith. Will is scandalized in the deathbed baptism scene by the homely, makeshift performance of the rite and the overpowering stench of death. His aroused rote defense of his Episcopalian raising, in order to invoke right appearances and exempt him from the Catholic priest's proceedings, is but the ceremony of his innocence. Even as he involuntarily uses religion to evade religion, so his social embarrassment completely conceals his ontological embarrassment. For, as a pilgrim stranger, Will is born embarrassed, born at a loss.

Suppression of real human identity with a parody of it is the ironic point of another scene, which the deathbed baptism forcefully recalls. There in a New York hospital the occasion is Jamie's temporal rather than eternal birthday. By way of celebration, "the interns made a drink of laboratory alcohol and frozen grapefruit juice, as if they were all castaways and had to make do with what they had" (*LG*, 76). With their peculiarly adaptive drink (in the hospital surroundings the "laboratory alcohol" crudely suggests sterilization and preservation) the celebrants secure themselves as organisms in an environment. Then in a prodigy of imposture they pretend to be what they are —"castaways"! The festivities take on the astonishing obliviousness, the self-perpetuating unreality, of the dancing on the *Titanic*.

Later Will's identity is presented to him, albeit unapprehended by him, in a parody of the Fall. Regaining consciousness, but not memory, on the camper seat after falling and striking his head on a monument during a campus uprising, Will asks, "'Oh, where is this place? . . . Where am I bound and what is my name?'" (*LG*, 293). For all the novel's marvelously sensed catalogue of places, this nowhere (echoing God's question to Adam after the Fall, "Where art thou?") is *The Last Gentleman's* symbolic center. For the three questions Will asks after his fall evoke, respectively, place, death and home, and language; thus they couch in the riddling manner of oracular utterances, clues to their answers. Man is a die-er and a home-goer, that is, a pilgrim stranger—a wanderer to a fixed and unknown point. He is also, it follows from his homelessness on this earth, a placer and a namer; the latter two corollary identities refer to his ways of taking charge of time and space. Man, in sum, is potentially a *sovereign* pilgrim stranger.

The sovereignty of man, the efficacy of his placing and naming, the most felicitous possible fulfillment of his being here, roots directly in his lived nomination of himself as a pilgrim stranger. Will misplaces himself because he misnames himself. In the "sniper's den" scene his self-locating gesture is an elaborate falsification of his fundamental identity. In a superimposition of the Gettysburg sniper's den he seeks to convert area into place by installing in the Central Park hideaway a place-presence—the aura of the dead sniper. But a place, we remember, is a concentration of energy, felt as a presence, within inimitable bounds. Like a name, a place is not interchangeable. Indeed, traditionally, a *genius loci* exists coterminous and consubstantial with its place in guarantee of that place's incalculable individuality and absolute immovability. Ostensibly a placer, Will here is really an antiplacer. He contributes to the pervasive leveling of place occurring today, when the sound of the bulldozer is heard even, and especially, in the place-rich South; there the novel's "loess" and "moraine"—soils transported from elsewhere—characterize a landscape accumulating toward the extinction of places (*LG*, 169, 303, 79). Will's promotion of delocalization in his apparent resistance to it exposes his in-trained environmental view of things. Ultimately the sniper, whom, as we have seen, he briefly mimicks, is established as the external stimulus that conditions his behavior. Overlooking his pilgrim strangerhood, Will construes himself as an organism adapting to an environment. Therefore he is hard put in the pitch darkness of the "sniper's den" literally to "place" Kitty or, symbolically, himself (*LG*, 111). Brady's camera symbolizes the encroaching invisibility of himself and his world. "People in the modern age," says Percy, "took photographs by the million: to prove despite their deepest suspicions to the contrary that they were not invisible" (*MB*, 26).

Postmodern man's mistaken identity is both source and consequence of the contemporary denaturing of language. Will's failure of sovereignty, it is true, follows his misnaming of the "sniper's den" but such misnaming creates a condition in which naming can hardly be true. Instead, we have false naming—the naming that kills—when the name comes to obscure the thing. Such a fundamental slippage between names and their referents further vitiates language itself. We see how such a double-speaking process works in the language used by Lamar Thigpen. Contemplating with self-consciously heroic complacency the Vaughts' three black servants waving a picturesque farewell from the back steps, Lamar says, "'There's nothing like the old-timey ways! . . .' even though the purple castle didn't look much like an antebellum mansion and the golf links even less like a cotton plantation" (*LG*, 272). Despite the radical change of the picture its caption is read the same. Language is reduced to a parody of its nominative and presentational function. Increasingly, phenomena drift about unnamed. The age itself, the frequent "nowadays" of the novel, lacks a name; "postmodern" is a stopgap no-name, which, like the expression, "the hereafter," admits only the expectation of chronological sequence and the complete ignorance of our fate. Detached from the things they are meant to articulate, words increasingly appear, in effect, in quotation marks. The word *intimate*, for example, is relegated to precisely this status as a possible adjective for Will and Kitty's contact without communication in the "sniper's den."

But identity and sovereignty can be positively interrelated; for man's discovery of his pilgrim strangerhood is the dislocation that makes things visible. With Will, journeying under the post-postlapsarian curse of mediateness, which divides him from his every activity, things are either so far away they are merely picturesque or so close they block themselves out. Minus a countering identity to focus things, Will is fixated or engulfed by them. But the recognition of the otherness of things and persons makes mediation possible, as opposed to mediateness; and with mediation, reciprocity; with reciprocity, love. When Jamie Vaught, confronted by his own death, in a sovereign act of self-choosing, in effect, christens himself a pilgrim stranger, he becomes, in Flannery O'Connor's phrase, "a realist of distances." That is why he hears news and Will only words.

Will's journey with terminally ill Jamie Vaught is also a death vigil, a postmodern installment on the theme of "as I lay dying." The deathbed baptism scene powerfully enacts the novel's major explicit premise, its working creative principle: "The certain availability of death is the very condition of recovering oneself" (*LG*, 372). Thus the intensification in the novel of the memento mori establishes as man's last hope his last extremity. Man is a die-er. Death is a going, a progress. *Homo moriens* is *homo viator*. Implicit in the recognition of the personal reality of death is the demand to be oneself—a pilgrim stranger, a placer, and a namer. For death, the distance between man and home, is the distance between man and the other. While false naming kills, true naming, then, gives life. "What's that? they ask me. That's a hawk, I tell them, and they believe me. . . . They were not alive and then they are and so they'll believe you" (*LG*, 301). Hence Valentine Vaught, when in this way she presents language as naming and naming as news, is portrayed as a death figure: "a woman dressed in black, feeding entrails to a hawk in a chicken coop. She looked familiar. He eyed her, wondering whether he knew her" (*LG*, 296). The far-away model here is Orpheus, who, presiding over the giving of life to things in the form of names, sojourned in the realms of both the dead and the living. The topic at Val's, in short, is incarnation. As Val hand-feeds the chicken hawk chicken "gut[s]" (*LG*, 301), she refers to her bishop as "chicken-hearted" (*LG*, 297); and later Val, whose lovelessness keeps her more a symbol than a fulfillment of mediational and affective powers, admits to hating certain people's "guts" (*LG*, 303). "Mind, in order to bear its witness," says Gide, "cannot do without matter. Hence the mystery of the incarnation."[11] The wit of the primitive punning is wit-ness to that mystery. If the word is man's ever materializing, ever vanishing bond with things, death is the bond between the man-made word and the thing it names. It engenders the numen, the presence, that makes the name represent the thing. Death is the transfiguring factor. It is the defamiliarizing familiar, which brings things forth in their forgotten strangeness. As the deathbed baptism scene shows, the possibility of news depends upon the credibility of death.

But death has, like place and language, borne the brunt of postmodern leveling. It is suppressed by the new prudery which reduces death the ineffable to death the unspeakable. "Death is as outlawed now as sin used to be" (*LG*, 372), remarks Sutter

Vaught in his journal"[12] Percy's task in the course of the novel
is to resurrect the personal reality of death. To this end, in the
deathbed baptism scene, as opposed to the "sniper's den" scene,
not the dead but death itself is present. "There arose to the engineer's [Will's] nostrils first an intimation, like a new presence
in the room, a somebody, then a foulness beyond the compass
of smell" (*LG*, 401). The fallen sniper is but one of a number of
historic personages evoked in Will's journey that, together with
historic events and scientific products and method, are deployed
by Will to ornament his vacancy. There death is picturesque.
Here death is grotesque. There death serves to lend Will a semblance, however false, of place. Here, working as the modern
avatar of the sublime, which Thomas Mann accredits to the
grotesque, death is essentially displacing. It becomes, in Heidegger's words, that "strange and unhomely thing that banishes
us once and for all from everything in which we are at home."[13]
Astonishingly, in fact, death, the "presence," the "somebody,"
in the room, merges with the "*genius loci* of [the] Western desert," described as a "free-floating sense of geographical transcendence" (*LG*, 349). Death and home, scene and change of
scene, coexist in one unified potentiality. A stereotypical nonplace—the hospital room—becomes in its numenization a
place, and place itself is now finally defined as *anywhere one
hears news of home*.

Here, squarely under the Δ sign, a kind of transvestiture occurs: the dying man puts on life, the living one puts on, unwittingly, death. Making placelessness radiant, death repeats the
ontological imperative of ground zero: out of nothing Will must
make something; he must fabricate a plot for his life. But the
materia at hand, in the form of the makeshift baptismal vessel,
the "clouded plastic" hospital glass, offends Will's well-bred
sensibilities: "But surely it was to be expected that the priest
have a kit of some sort" (*LG*, 405). In a parody of Christ's agony
in the garden—"let this cup pass from me"—the glass remains

unincarnate, untransfigured by the leap of faith which endows something other with symbolic value. Will sees in the "clouded plastic glass" only the gratuitous insufficiency of materials which embarrasses his environmentalist expectations. The stubborn extraness of the item, its ungreetability by imagination and its immunity to synthesis, witnesses to Will's deafness to the summons to pilgrimage. He is unable to begin his life. In that deficiency he assumes the likeness of death, and in a most appropriate specific form. Reducing the mystery of death to a problem in manners, turning news, as ever, into knowledge, astonishment into inertia, Will, not death, appears at the last as the great leveler.

The gravitational pull of home is felt in *The Last Gentleman* in several ways. The word tolls throughout the book. "Take me home," says Kitty at the end of the "sniper's den" scene (*LG*, 117). I'm taking Jamie *home*," declares Mr. Vaught in New York (*LG*, 79). On his deathbed Jamie speaks "seriously of going home, no, not home but to the Gulf Coast" (*LG*, 372). Will's continual expulsion from places, even in mid-occupation, as a consequent of his mediateness, begins too in the course of the book to suggest its contrary: a rehearsal for ultimate inhabitation. His very flight, that is, begins in a kind of palimpsest effect, characteristic of the novel's most important mode of disclosure, to reveal the possibility of pilgrimage. Finally, the increasing aerialization and celestialization of imagery in the novel— the sky in the desert is "empty map space" (*LG*, 356)—suggest the belief that, in Mircea Eliade's words, "man desires to have his abode in a space opening upward." [14] For the home Will ultimately seeks is not in his hometown of Ithaca, Mississippi, but in heaven, and the father he ultimately seeks is no earthly one but the Father of Souls. Man's only home on earth is *the road home*. It is not a state, some plugged-in *locus amoenus*, but a status—that of a sovereign pilgrim stranger. The finally relevant question is never, where is man? but, what is man? And the finally relevant answer is not an ecology of life but a theology of being.

To this end, Will's blind, unwitting search for home is at once bound up in and set off by Percy's own quest in the novel for authority. As a Christian existentialist, Percy has communication problems that extend beyond the deadening of responses consequent to stimulus flooding and psychic overloads. His outreach as a religious writer is peculiarly crippled by contemporary exhaustion of charismatic and prophetic properties, which are reflected, as we have seen, in the leveling of place, language, and death. In addition, Christian notions of "sin" and "grace" are as remote today as alchemy or the four humors. Orthodox religious counters are simply dead issue–nonnegotiable. Will, the title character, upon whom the novel is lost—he "misses it!"—is the putative reader. Percy's altogether formidable task, as it was Flannery O'Connor's, is to make God real in His absence. God must be invoked without being named. Necessarily eschewing appeal to vestiges of man's old religious consciousness, which would reinforce spiritual indifference and make dismissal irresistible, Percy endeavors to become postmodern man's new, lost memory. To keep the religious vision in a time of trouble, to echo William Blake, Percy works with the "religious" in "its root sense as signifying a radical *bond* . . . which connects man with reality—or the failure of such a bond —and so confers meaning to his life—or the absence of meaning" (*MB*, 102–103). Will's repeatedly missed appointments with his fundamental identity at once express directly the accelerating contemporary appetite for instant, disposable creation and obliquely an objectless, irreligious dream of God. Percy's authorial role is as decreative as it is re-creative. If man realizes his loss, perhaps he will recognize it. If he forgets being, perhaps he will discover it firsthand. Like O'Connor with her sacred blasphemies, Percy works through indirection. Harboring perhaps equal malice toward man's organized ignorance of his own nature, Percy seeks his authority in scandal.

But how to make scandalous the scandal of contemporary loss? The scarcity of scandal—any scandal—is one of the embarrassments of present-day dearth. In his nostalgia for sin and longing for apocalypse, Sutter Vaught, the novel's surrogate author, embodies Percy's need to create scandal. To this end, Percy, like Sutter, woos death. Death in the novel, as demonstrated by its progress out of the picturesque into the grotesque, is a symbol always being overtaken by reality. Death is concieved as at once the symbol and the scandal—that is, the scandalization—of man's existential absence, his missing of himself. The chaos without freedom; the end without revelation, consequent to postmodern leveling; man's outliving of himself by confusing the Bomb and the Second Coming, the survival of a body and the salvation of a soul; the reduction of love to an impersonal narcissistic attraction of emptiness for emptiness: these states Percy scandalizes by experiencing them through the novel's recollective consciousness as the sensations of a dead world body.

Intensifying its presidium over the novel's successive precincts, until it emerges in the deathbed baptism scene as a "presence," a "somebody," in the room, death is not only a scandalmonger, it is also the most visible manifestation of the author's Muse. "The consciousness requires a presence," says Percy, "in order that a literature be conceived between them."[15] Like Yeats's antiself, death is the necessary adversary that forces the conceiving self to exceed itself. In this excess, of which scandal is but one specific form, Percy finally bases his claim to authority. His intimacy with death is the exhibited necessity of his freedom. In the character-action of the novel his artist-Muse relationship with death is subsumed in a host-guest relationship, which is all-important to the novel's shaping intentions.

The politics of this relationship impose a need for ritual, and not (as Will thinks in his concern over the seemliness of the baptismal utensil) for technique. The ritual base requisite for alluding to being—our only way of expressing it—and for the reinstatement of spiritual quest is wrought in *The Last Gentleman* under the tutelary genius of death.

In his choice of a home for Will, where, presumably, he and Kitty will live after they are married, Percy passes on to Will his own exacting problem of rehabilitating leveled materials. There the trinity of resources—place, language, and death—exist challengingly in a bathetically reduced condition. The home features a "ferny dell" and a "plashy brook" (place), a "'bridge'" (language), as its former seafaring owner, Cap'n Andy, has nicknamed the ridge overlooking a plain, and, circling above, "buzzards and crows" (death) (*LG*, 285). Cap'n Andy, we learn, "bored himself to death" (*LG*, 382). He succumbed, that is, in Saul Bellow's definition of boredom, to the "pain caused by unused powers, the pain of wasted possibilities or talents . . . accompanied by expectations of the optimum utilization of capacities."[16] Like Will, by and large, especially in the deathbed baptism scene, Cap'n Andy embodies the definition of entropy as energy unavailable for work during a natural process. Cap'n Andy's is a museum exhibit of leveled human resources. We are back at ground zero.

But the carefully wrought underwork of the novel, articulating the opposed imagination of news, prepares us to find latent in ground zero a possibility of the sacred center (hence the location of the former in Central Park). There Will might successfully return place, language, and death to their wonted inexhaustibility. He might successfully hold them in regenerative unity (acting out the novel's most teasing phrase—"a perfect pyramid, shedding itself" *LG*, 166). If so, then the pigeon of entropy turns before our eyes into the dove of epiphany. With its "best view on the ridge" (*LG*, 367), its open upward accesses, the place is built for the reception of news. The "'bridge'" bespeaks language's mediational powers and the bonding strength of the namer's faith. The circling "buzzards and crows" picture Will's gyration outward in search of his center, his true home, and symbolize the companioning ministry of death that instructs him in his alienation. This, together with the analogue of the place as a ship (it has a "'fo'c's'le'" too) and with Cap'n Andy's rank of command, suggests the continuous activation of Will's status as a sovereign pilgrim stranger. Seen thus, the place is the road home: a portable capability of self-renewal, a dynamic repose in the insufficiency of the given.

In this way the place sums up the two dominant sensations of the novel: danger and hope. The leveling of the world may become a demonic end in itself. Perversity will be felt as originality, problems as solutions, and loss, intensified, as gain. On the other hand, leveling may proceed finally to de-create man's falsified identity as a tourist and a consumer and to reveal his true identity as a pilgrim and a participant. The astonishing failure of the things in which man has misplaced himself may lead to his self-recovery. The immaculate solitudes of the desert, where we leave Will, are either the verge of extinction or the preliminary to communion. The novel is a network of uncompleted arrangements, a series of transformations held firmly, almost intolerably, in reserve. Yet the novel's very open-endedness is, in contrast to the closed system of an end game, a gesture of hope. And Will, we note, is at the conclusion of the novel less the fugitive of history (he no longer tries to avert Confederate defeats) (*LG*, 358) and less the prisoner of science (he has set aside his telescope) (*LG*, 358). His last word in the novel, "Wait," is the watchword of the author himself.[17] It betokens, we can hope, an orientation at once chastened, almost suppliant, and alert, toward news. Does it suggest a nascent vulnerability to the grace to continue? Perhaps the novel is, at the end, best described as a "balance of stone—with gestures to grow."[18]

SIMONE VAUTHIER

Narrative Triangulation in
The Last Gentleman

IN "THE MAN ON THE TRAIN," Walker Percy
has evoked "the triple alliance" that fiction can establish between reader, character, and author. The experiential "triple
alliance" mirrors, on a different scale, the triadic nature of language which Walker Percy has investigated in several of his
linguistic essays. But it is also reflected within the text in the
trinity of narrator, narration, and narratee.[1] Since this trinity
is the basic structure of narrative, as it is of discourse, obviously
only wide ranging variations of the relations among the three
elements distinguish different kinds of narrative. In a given
story the fundamental set of relations undergoes changes as
the narrator's distance to his subject and/or to his narratee increases or diminishes. The narrative triangle is never a static
form, though it may be more or less dynamic. Examination of
the shifts in narrational relations is therefore as important to
the understanding of a novel as content analysis. Walker Percy's
nonfictional work provides a special incentive to study his fiction in this light. I have analysed elsewhere the situation of discourse in *The Moviegoer*.[2] Here I propose to explore *The Last
Gentleman*. Within the limited scope of this essay, however, it
is impossible to chart all the shifts in the narrational structure,

and I shall merely take a few soundings to establish some of the narrator's positions in that structure.

A comparison of the beginning and ending of *The Last Gentleman* throws light on the narrator's journey on the narrational map. Although Kierkegaard and Guardini stand double guard at the gates, the epigraphs of *The Last Gentleman* need not scare away the reader: the domain within, as one enters it, seems reassuring: "One fine day in early summer a young man lay thinking in Central Park" (*LG*, 3). However wary modern fiction may have made us, we feel reasonably confident that the story will tell us who the young man is, what he is doing in Central Park, and why the fine summer day is of special importance. Is not all this promised us in the familiar phrasing and tone, the very shibboleth of the storyteller? Nor do the following paragraphs, although they modify the almost legendary lilt of the first sentence with more matter-of-fact descriptions, disappoint our expectations: they provide and withhold information about the young man in the most satisfying manner, while showing that the knowledgeable narrator is firmly in control: "In the course of the next five minutes the young man was to witness by chance an insignificant, though rather curious happening. It was the telescope that became the instrument of a bit of accidental eavesdropping. As a consequence of a chance event the rest of his life was to be changed" (*LG*, 3). Yes . . . chance, change, and destiny . . . all the ingredients of a good traditional narrative.

However, the expectations aroused by the first chapter do not simply concern the content of the story but its narrational configuration as well. Clearly, the vague chronological specification, which sets the subject at some undefined and indefinable temporal remove from the narrator and the narratee, would have been in keeping with the novel's two alternative titles, *The Fallout* and *Ground Zero*. Moreover "one day" presupposes an indeterminate series of other days and the indefinite article "a young man" a background of human beings from which a selection has been made, presumably because of its significance. The beginning of *The Last Gentleman*, unlike those of *The Moviegoer* and *Love in the Ruins*, implies that the narrative discourse is a segment of an infinite narration. It suggests the remote, abstractive attitude of the narrator and the exemplarity of the particular story which is about to be told.

But who is going to tell this story? With the first sentence, some hesitation is still possible since a first-person narrator might yet make his appearance as a witness to the scene. But the rest of the page confirms the impression suggested in the opening line that we are reading a third-person narration. If the narrator is undramatized he is by no means absent. He first intervenes to evince previous knowledge of the "next five minutes" and "the rest of [the character's] life" (*LG*, 3). He stresses the articulation between the near and the far future by explaining that the telescope is to be the instrument of the change. The mention of the telescope, the function of which is to transform the insignificant into the fateful, can be heard as a statement of fact. But it can also be heard metaphorically, since an optical instrument turns into a means of eavesdropping.

The narrator turns to the subject of the announced transformation: "He was an unusual young man. But perhaps nowadays it is not so unusual. What distinguished him anyhow was this: he had to know everything before he could do anything. For example, he had to know what other people's infirmities were before he could get on a footing with them" (*LG*, 3–4). The comment, "he was an unusual young man," at once endows the character with his first explicit psychological feature, and gives the extraordinary events about to be told a semblance of realistic motivation, the common-sense assumption being that unusual things happen to unusual people. But at this point the narrator pauses. Can he really depend on such a norm? The idea that the allocutor may differ from his notion of the usual clearly impels the narrator to add an oddly concessive clause ("What distinguished him anyhow was this . . .") and to produce an "example," reasserting his right to define the young man. Phrases like *anyhow* and *for example* also show a narrator didactically presenting his information for maximum discursive effect, while the present tenses and a number of deictics call attention to the act of narration. Despite the lack of a grammatical *I* the situation created is that of discourse, or what Benveniste calls *récit*, an utterance assuming a speaker and a hearer and in the speaker the intention of influencing the other in some way.[3] From the first page of the novel it is clear that the set of relations established designates rather than effaces its triangularity. However unspecified the locus of the narration, the locutor outlines a subject for the benefit of an allocutor. The three elements are held in balance. One might diagram the narrative configuration as an equilateral triangle.

To turn to the last section of the book is to face a narrative situation which, although basically no different, is significantly changed. Of the three terms of the narrative triangle, the subject has now come to the foreground. Apparently unaware of the narratee, the narrator, no longer accenting his act of narration, reports a conversation between Will Barrett and Sutter Vaught, limiting himself to a few stage directions and introducing only six out of forty-eight of the characters' replies. On half a dozen occasions, he tells about sensations or thoughts of the protagonist's (*e.g.*, "His heart began to thud" [*LG*, 408], and "a style of driving which the engineer faintly recalled from the 1940's" [*LG*, 408]). The narrator has moved away from the narratee whom he no longer instructs and guides, closer to the hero, with whom he even seems to identify. Almost transparent, he leaves us to face the characters' words, their few gestures, or the car's shuddering to a stop, and to decipher the meaning of the scene. (Hence the impression that the ending, as many critics and the author himself have noted, is ambiguous.) Change therefore not only occurs at the level of the diegesis but also takes place at the level of the narration, affecting the locutor-subject-allocutor triad. As the narratee's apex has receded into the background and narrator and subject have come closer, the shape of the initial narrative triangle has considerably altered.

The final narrative unit fixes the figures of discourse in one ultimate position, but the narrational balance has all along been shifting. The shifts in triangulation appear most clearly when one looks at those aspects of the narrator's function that distinguish him from more traditional narrators.

One activity sharply differentiates the narrator of *The Last Gentleman* and is instrumental in defining his standpoint—I mean his nomenclature. Take the naming of the hero. Let us grant that he was originally christened by the author. Williston Bibb Barrett is provided with a full-sounding name, including not only first name and surname but also a middle name, all of which are, in common southern fashion, patronyms. The whole name functions in the way in which proper names do in fiction—that is to say independently from the impersonal narrator but not from the narration which dictates certain kinds of names and assigns to each individual instance a place in its own onomastic system. For his part "the novelist typically indicates his intention of presenting a character as a particular individual by naming him in exactly the same way as particular individuals are named in ordinary life";[4] furthermore since the proper name is, as Roland Barthes has noted, "the prince of signifiers," it is rich in connotations, whether social or symbolic.[5] The symbolic code can only be tentatively apprehended as one first hears the name: not until the end of the story can one evaluate to what extent *nomen est omen*. But the socioeconomic code is more immediately decipherable. With its three patronymic signifiers, "Williston Bibb Barrett" connotes good old "Anglo-Saxon" stock, as against such Irish names as Gallagher or Sheehan, or such continental European names as Gamow or Fava, and southern origins against the

midwestern suggestions of Carol (Kerrel) Schwartz or the metropolitan sound of Morton Prince, which seems to belong to a
character in a *New Yorker* story; it connotes upper-class and
aristocratic breeding in comparison with such plebeian names
as Bugs Flieger, Beans Ross, or Myra Thigpen. Fittingly what is
recorded of the past in the hero's name is conflicting, Bibb suggesting slavery, while Barrett recalls the efforts of Lysander
Barrett to have slavery abolished in the District of Columbia,
and Williston a famous Harvard Law School professor.[6]

Usually the proper name is a commodity to the author-
narrator insofar as it conveniently gathers and identifies a
number of semantic traits, themselves making up that word-
construct, the fictional character. But, strange to say, the narrator of *The Last Gentleman* is very reluctant to avail himself of
the triple handle to the character with which he has been fur-
nished. He names the hero only twice and contents himself with
designating him. This feature of the narration has not gone un-
noticed, but Martin Luschei, to my knowledge, is the only critic
to have attempted to explain it:

> It is instructive to watch how the author refers to him through the first
> chapter. Here in this homeless place he is presented as "a young man."
> More frequently the designation is simply "he," but in this first chap-
> ter Will's specific designations alternate between "the young man" and
> "the Southerner." In the office of Dr. Gamow, his analyst, he becomes
> "the patient" or "the other. . . ." The changing designations reflect the
> reality because here in New York he is a chameleon, indentified[sic]
> by successive functions, changing color protectively to conform to his
> surroundings: these are his roles. Percy weaves "the engineer" in un-
> obtrusively a dozen times by way of preparation and actually names
> him Williston Bibb Barrett just before he identifies him permanently
> as "the engineer."[7]

Interesting as it is, the analysis falls a little short. For one thing
Martin Luschei seems to refer to the narrator's *second* act of
naming. The first occurs before the visit to Gamow and deserves
more attention: "For another month or so the young man, whose

name was Williston Bibb Barrett or Will Barrett or Billy Barrett, sat rocking on the gallery with six women." (*LG*, 17). The information—which in the third-person novel is usually conveyed much earlier—is here yielded incidentally, sandwiched in the relation of an iterative scene and by way of introduction to a list of *unnamed* but vividly depicted women, as though the young man's name dubiously guaranteed his difference. And, in truth, is the narrator really naming the hero? The willingness with which he rattles two other cognomens, the interchangeability of which is underlined by the repetition of *or*, is in fact evidence of his reluctance to fix the identity of the character, all the more so since nicknames, being situational, have not the same general validity. The surplus of names seems to point to some lack, some failure of the proper name to denote. With the exception of the one time he is again called Williston Bibb Barrett, the character will henceforth be simply designated, though the process of designation is not as straightforward as Martin Luschei indicates.

Undoubtedly *the engineer* is, after the first chapter, the most constant appellation. But others are occasionally introduced, the most frequent being *the boy, the young man, the youth*—not to mention *he*. The hero also variously appears as *the patient, the hitchhiker, the passenger, the tutor, the interpreter, the visitor, the other*, and even *the Englishman*. (The last denomination is not literal but metaphoric in the context of the novel—for the Englishman repeatedly stands for a certain fictional and cinematographic type gifted with a capacity for both eavesdropping and survival.) Moreover the narrator keeps playing with the basic designation by qualifying it with an impressive number of epithets—*sentient, courteous, poor, bemused, attentive, puzzled, sweating, canny, mystified, shivering, prudent, forgetful, gentlemanly, flabbergasted, interested, sleepy, frowning, tactful,* etc. Now he doubles the epithets: "the poor addled engineer," "the pleasant forward-facing engineer"; now he doubles and

opposes them, "the chivalrous but wry engineer," "the courteous but terrified engineer"; now he triples them, "the poor bemused shivering engineer" or he triples and opposes them "the
hard-pressed but courteous and puisant engineer." These adjectives may be referential either when they define a quality of
the engineer (like *sentient, courteous*, respectively referring to
the aesthetic and the ethical sides of Will, and *bemused* which
indicates a frequent state of mind) or else when they describe
a particular response to a particular stimulus ("the frowning
engineer" or "the reeling engineer," etc.). Again they may be oriented no longer toward the referent but toward the speaker,
revealing the narrator's attitude ("the poor engineer"). Some
may be used "straight" in one context and ironically in another.

Whatever their meaning, the epithets perturb the smooth
flow of the narration. Without them the signifier "the engineer"
would soon become emptier than it already is and function
much in the way of a third-person pronoun, as a shifter. The
adjectives, however, keep reestablishing the threatened status
of the signifier and they create a subtle interplay of tensions.
Since some of the qualifiers are also recurrent, some syntagms
(notably "the sentient engineer" and "the courteous engineer")
tend to become clichés of the narration and as such to be now
obtrusive, now transparent. Roughly speaking—and leaving
aside the problem of ironical use—the relation of the narrator
to his subject when he employs an identical phrase seems to be
the same but his relation to the narratee is paradoxical: he invites the narratee to recognize the syntagm as familiar, *i.e.*, to
accept it as both adequate, and as somehow insufficient since
it needs to be repeated so often; on the other hand, repetition of
the proper name, which supposedly expresses a particular
identity, can have no such implications. Further, the relation
of the reader to the cliché-loving narrator and his narration is
slightly changed with every recurrence. Either the repetition is
not perceived—the phrase *has* become a shifter—or it is per-

ceived and then felt as redundant or meaningful, destructive or constructive.[8] The fact that so many of the repetitions in the story included significant variations, of course, incites the reader to look for meaning in recurrence, just as the epithets modulate the use of the fixed syntagms. The designation "the engineer" therefore is like a coin the exchange value of which keeps altering as it circulates from context to context, from narrator to narratee, and from author to reader.

Such convertibility, however, is not merely the effect of what is repeated and/or added: it is a property of the token itself which the modifiers enhance. Face-up or face-down, it is not the same figure of speech. The designation can be seen as a *metonymy*: Will Barrett has a job as a "humidification engineer" (*LG*, 18), that is, as "a kind of janitor" (*LG*, 18). The word itself is therefore a euphemism which the narrator, together with Macy's and society at large, prefers over the more homely and humble "janitor." But if the stakes of modern technological society are clear—while it reduces the man to his function in the system of production, it nominally aggrandizes the function by blurring the outlines of its designation—the stakes of the narrator in this mystification are less obvious. Probably he is poking sly fun at our grand use of language. In any case, he is distancing himself from the hero. More important, the appellation also works in his discourse as a *metaphor* and this metaphor no longer embodies a sociolinguistic code, but echoes the very thoughts of the protagonist: "I am indeed an engineer, he thought, if only a humidification engineer, which is no great shakes of a profession. But I am also an engineer in a deeper sense: I shall engineer the future of my life according to the scientific principles and the self-knowledge I have so arduously gained from five years of analysis" (*LG*, 41). Employing the word metaphorically, the narrator would seem to accept the character's self-image. And perhaps he does on occasion. But things are in fact more complex. What with his lapses of memory, *déjà vu*'s, and "little fits," the poor engineer is in reality not able to engineer much.

That inability is precisely his possibility of salvation; for life can be managed empirically and scientifically only at the expense of authenticity, of being. Thus the narrator's use of the appellation functions as a point of irony or as a pointer to a blank: "the engineer" opens a series of empty spaces—between the word and the referential occupation, between the function and the person, between the person and his self—until they seem to riddle the narration and light a fuse chain of questions. Beyond the self—what? To sum up, "the engineer" is not a permanent identification, both because the frequent label designates no viable durable role but a void, and because the narrator occasionally changes the label. Two of his alternatives deserve consideration. "The boy" (or "the youth") occurs in those moments when the past surfaces again in the narration and a different Will Barrett is resurrected. This disjunctive device underlines the fragmentation of the agent into different actors, but the phrase "the young man" can also make the junction between the remembered and the remembering selves. "The other" is interesting because of its collocations: it appears mostly in the conversatons with Sutter Vaught, when Will has become able to speak in his own name and to establish an intersubjective relation. "The other" is not the narrator's casual way to solve the narrative problem of referring to the hero; else its occurrences would be more evenly distributed. It marks the fluctuating relation of the narrator to the object of his narration who is then seen as part of a locutory situation; Will Barrett can only be "the other" in reference to someone and when looked at from the angle of an observer. The narrator momentarily ceases to use Barrett's focus of vision as he can (and often does) even when calling him "the engineer." Moreover, since Sutter is Will's Significant Other, the narrator in those final conversations seems to turn the tables and to show that both diegetic locutors have become equals from his viewpoint.

"The engineer" also resounds as an unexpected echo to a phrase which, after it is introduced in the novel, we keep looking for in vain through the text. There is a tension between the connotations of "the engineer" and those of "the last gentleman": the former connotes modernity, pragmatism, empiricism, possibility (significantly a crash course turns Will Barrett into a maintenance engineer); the latter connotes the past, a vanishing social and moral code, gentility, caste—one must be to the manner born—the end of the line, impossibility. If we take it that "the last gentleman" is Will Barrett, then the two designations define the old and the new existential postures open to him, neither of which can really help him out of his problems. But curiously, rather than between significations, the resonance is between the ever-present signifier and the *absent* one. And also between an unambiguous designation and an ambiguous one—for which of the Barretts, Ed or Will, is the last gentleman? The title also creates an empty space which the text never quite saturates, the reading process never satisfactorily fills out, since even if we choose to call *Will* the last gentleman the indeterminacy of the reference still remains. What is more, the very recurrence of the identification tag goes on widening the gap between the two designations, in symbolic reflection, perhaps, of our riven world, and in textual reflection of the nonidentity of narrator and author.

The narrator's reluctance to name the protagonist, which, I insist, is personal to him and not to be mistaken for the author's, his fondness for generic names (the actor, the pseudo-Negro, and the Handsome Woman, etc.) are part of the novel's general onomastic system. In particular, they must be evaluated against the carefulness with which he reports all the appellative courtesies used by the characters. Apart from such common terms

as *man, baby, honey, son,* and Rita's esoteric *lance corporal*—
the hero is variously addressed or introduced as Mr. Barrett,
Barrett, Will Barrett, Billy Barrett, Williston, Will, Bill, Mist'
Billy, Billy Boy, Ed Barrett's boy, Mr. Ed's boy. He is even given
pseudo names which manifest joviality or playfulness: "another
five minutes and they'd call him Rocky" (*LG*, 148); "They called
him Bombo, the son of Tarzan and Mr. Clean. The engineer had
to laugh. They were good fellows and funny" (*LG*, 192). But
when the supercilious actor persists in calling Will Barrett
Merle, he betrays his own arrogant rudeness. We can say of
pseudo names what Levi-Strauss says of the use of proper
names: *On signifie toujours que ce soit l'autre ou soi-même*.[9] The
multiplicity of names is undoubtedly correlative of the various,
conflicting images of Will which the characters have and perhaps need. In this context both the playful nicknaming and the
actor's willful confusion are grace notes which draw attention
to the importance of naming and its relation to roles. For similarly, in the speech of others, Jamison becomes Jamie, Jimmy,
Jimbo, Tiger; Valentine is Val, Sister Johnette, Mary Vianney,
Sister Val, Sister Viney.

What's in a name? *The Last Gentleman* asks: Something of
you for me? Something of me for you? But it also asks, "Under what circumstances does naming really name?" All the
names conferred upon Williston Bibb Barrett fail to name him
fully. In his fugue states, the hero himself cannot remember his
identity. Will Barrett, whose nervous condition seems related
to his father's suicide, blots out the patronym that links him to
all the short-lived Barrett males. At the beginning of the story,
even when remembering it, he has to have it confirmed by a
card: "My name is Williston Bibb Barrett, he said aloud, consulting his wallet to make sure." (*LG*, 151). His name is what it
is to a child, "the name that we are told is ours."[10] The novel is
partly the story of his acceptance of himself as a subject through
the free use of his name. As late as the Ithaca episode, there oc-

curs an incident when he has to remind someone of who he is; and he says: "'This is Will Barrett, Beans . . . Mr. Ed's boy'" (*LG*, 324). The giving of his name, being mere identification for the other, ends in depersonalization: the *I* is reduced to a mirroring third person doubly reflected in the deictic *this*, which registers the gap between the speaker and what is pointed at, and in the referral to himself as his father's son. Only at the end will he be able to appropriate his name and even turn its utterance into self-affirmation: "'Dr. Vaught, I need you. I, Will Barrett'—and he actually pointed to himself lest there be a mistake, '—need you and want you to come back'" (*LG*, 409). The odd gesture translates in body language, but, being centripetal and no longer centrifugal, it *reverts* the verbal "this" of the earlier incident. "For," in the words of Lewis A. Lawson, "by exercising will he becomes a self. . . and in willing one thing, Will, according to Kierkegaard, is showing purity of heart."[11] What must be stressed, however, is that the act of will is a speech act requiring the assumption of the name of Will—a diegetic event which is highlighted by the narrational practice of designation; for now the designation "the engineer" disappears.

Avoided by a narrator who constantly privileges designation, hesitantly worn by a protagonist unprepared to endow his name with meaning, *Williston Bibb Barrett* becomes an ambiguous signifier to be decoded diversely as the story unfolds. Since the narrator has refrained from providing the narratee with clues, the deciphering becomes the reader's entire responsibility. As we first play with the name, negative suggestions come to mind: Will-is-not, will-is-not. Will a man provided with a Bib(b) be able to feed himself, to go beyond dependence on a sustaining parental figure? (Both Val and Vaught, let it be noted, suggest value.) And what a strange *bar* in the patronym! What does it obstruct?—what forbid?—what cross? But then we realize that Will-Bear-it is perhaps programmed in the name.[12] And why not I-will-bar-it? Now that I assume my name

I can lay down the law in my turn. So perhaps Will (will)-is-not-barred. Yet even at the last we feel the tug in the name, *Will* pulling against *Bar*rett. An emblem of the riven self? A symbol of the tension between will, the subjective self, and a higher law that demands from man that he relinquish his personal will? An onomastic inscription of the predicament of man faced with possibility / impossibility? As it can no longer be taken for granted, the name becomes a matrix of significations, hidden yet active, which are left to the reader to name.

The functioning of names must therefore be seen in a global perspective. It is not enough to say that the changing designations reflect the reality of the protagonist's role-playing. The substitutions of all kinds also point to the drift and displacement of subject and object through the text. When he calls the hero "the engineer," or "the Englishman" or "the other," the narrator stands in a different relation to him or to his narration. By the same token, it is not enough to say that "the *novelist* distances his hero with patronizing names" (emphasis mine),[13] since the distance must be constantly reassessed and is not really condescending; at most the narrator is mildly amused at the vagaries of the poor engineer but he remains sympathetic to his foibles and to his plight. The distance furthermore is an aesthetic effect that shapes the reader's response as much as it reveals the narrator's attitude. When it subverts the fictional convention that makes the patronym the sign for a person, *The Last Gentleman* undermines the mimetic illusion. The repetition of *the engineer*, however diversified, is like a blinking light, issuing the warning: this is a *character*, you are reading a tale.[14] Thus it diminishes our blind dependence on the text, our willingness to accept it as representation.

To this extent, *The Last Gentleman* comes closer to avant-garde fiction than *The Moviegoer*. However, the narration here only undercuts the representational value of the novel in order to enhance its poetic truth. The dysfunctioning of names does not work toward a dissolving of the concept of person or toward what Walker Percy would call a "loss of the creature." It rather throws into relief their potential functioning. Proper names appear to be not only signs but symbols of being; they have the power of all names freshly used to "bring about a new orientation toward the world."[15] Not that names can symbolize me or you; but they symbolize that I am and you are, and on this basis we can establish an intersubjective relation—and perhaps a relation to being. In the extended naming process that is the novel, a dynamic movement orients Will Barrett away from engineering and reliance on cards in his wallet toward self-autonomy and true dialogue, and similarly directs the reader away from unthinking identification with the protagonist, or absorption in a "reflection of life," toward an active role in the exchanges that are taking place.

Another activity of the narrator leads to greater or lesser modifications of his angle in the narrative figure: when he (re)-produces a character's discourse, whether oral or mental, the narrator is obviously closer to him than when he describes him or narrates his actions.[16] (Indeed the very bulk of conversations in the fictional web of *The Last Gentleman* is in itself significant, all the more so since this emphasis is not a necessary development of the initial narrative situation. Of course it powerfully contributes to the elaboration of the themes—the theme of the quest, which is a quest for the Word, and the theme of the increasing difficulty to act meaningfully.) Whether the narrator conspicuously asserts his control over the reproduced discourse or surreptitiously effaces himself behind the characters' words depends on his choice and handling of relays of speech. If we take even the simplest case, what we may call the conventionally reported dialogues, *i.e.*, those in which the inverted commas duly allocate ownership of utterance,[17] we see that the narrator runs the gamut of possibilities. At one end of the spectrum, there are the long stretches of verbal intercourse in which

the various utterances are left unassigned without as much as
a *he* or *she said*. In such passages, the mediation of the narrator
is almost invisible, although the inverted commas are, in a
sense, his guarantee of literality.

In other passages, such as the conversation at the end of the
eighth section of Chapter 4, narrative mediation obtrudes heav-
ily. Often the narrator intervenes in an effort to reproduce more
than the verbal content of the conversation. He may translate
in his comments the unspoken intentions of the speaker: " 'No,
it's not the game,' said Rita, gazing steadfastly away but pat-
ting Jamie's arm with hard steady pats. Kitty's gambit didn't
work, she was saying" (*LG*, 232). He also may make a consistent attempt to render the tone and quality of voice of some of
the locutors. One or another speaks in a "loud voice, all squeaks
and horns," "in a low voice," "through his teeth," "in anguish
again," "sternly," "earnestly." He records the bodily gestures
or facial expressions accompanying the utterance: "still pat-
ting," "Rita ran a hand through Jamie's hair," "twirling his
keys glumly," "actually holding his head." He registers the
pauses and silences: "he could not bring himself to say anything," "Sutter sighed," "Jamie groaned," "asked Rita after a
moment." Or he stresses the speed of answers: "said Jamie instantly and soberly." He carefully notes the orientation of the
locutor: "Rita, speaking for some reason to the engineer," "looking around for the adversary," "he glared at Rita angrily," "looking behind him as if he was expecting someone."

Thus the situation of interlocution can often become as important as the utterances themselves.[18] The care with which the
narrator specifies the global situation renders us as sentient as
the protagonist who, listening to Rita, "took her import not
from the words she said but from the signals" (*LG*, 274). While
the narrator uses the whole spectrum of possibilities for reporting direct speech, he often locates himself at either end, instead of either mixing the two techniques or privileging one, as

is more usual. Now with the omission of all tags, he tiptoes into the wings, taking the narratee with him and leaving the characters onstage in splendid isolation. Now with great consideration for the narratee he specifies the situational context of each speech act through a wealth of details; and playing stage manager, author, and director, he upstages the characters. The sharp contrast of the two methods emphasizes his flexibility and above all the nature of the narrative structure, the changeability of the narrative triangle.

The narrator can further perfect his vanishing trick when the conversations are not conventionally reported. For instance, section 12 of Chapter 2, after starting abruptly with "Kitty said" —a mention which is recalled only once a few lines later— transcribes a lengthy dialogue between the girl and Will Barrett without the benefit of single quotation marks and without any connective comment; thus one may wonder whether speech attribution must be ascribed to the subject or to the narrator. In any case the use of free direct discourse which reaches the reader without any apparent mediation, syntactical or typographical, is common practice throughout the novel. While it always makes the narration more transparent and brings the subject to the foreground, it may have diverse effects depending on the contexts.

When it is employed within ordinary direct discourse, it may give the impression of a close-up:

"But seriously now, here's the proposition," she said. And he found that when she gave him ordinary directions he could hear her. *As of this moment you are working for me as well as for Poppy. Perhaps for both of us but at least for me. Keep Jamie up here long enough for Larry to give him a course of huamuratl. . . . Now when you get through with Larry, take Ulysses and take off. Go home. Go to Alaska. In any event, Ulysses is yours. . . . Here is the certificate of ownership, which I've signed over to you and Jamie. It will cost you one dollar. Jamie has coughed up.* She held out her hand. "I'll take my money, please." (emphasis added, *LG*, 96).

The italicized sentences in free direct discourse stand out from the rest of Rita's utterance as though seen under a magnifying glass. Yet paradoxically because their literality is not certified in the usual way they somehow have less authority than the opening and closing statements; they seem to be filtered through the subject's consciousness. Fairly often, the nonliteral free direct discourse is employed to distinguish spoken from nonspoken thoughts: "'Who? No.' *If he needed a good shaking, Sister, you should have given it to him*. But he said: 'Do you like your work here?'" (*LG*, 298). Here the emphasis is authorial; and the free direct discourse seems to reproduce the more authentic thoughts of the speaker. Similarly it can also underline the intent behind the words: "'Do you know what that joker told me last night?' (This is the way we speak.) 'I always horse around with him'" (*LG*, 396). Or free direct discourse can be employed to stress the meaning of silence itself: "Jamie dispensed himself and paid no attention: I'm sick and I don't have to oblige anybody" (*LG*, 231). One might call this the stereoscopic effect because it discriminates between the two kinds of reported discourse, inner and outer, or two levels of narration, certified and uncertified. In all such cases the narrator provisionally disappears yet ends in making us aware of his knowledgeability, perhaps his omniscience.

   If sometimes free direct discourse renders a character's inner speech with more immediacy and greater idiosyncracy, sometimes on the contrary it generalizes the inner speech in a soft-focus effect: "The engineer looked at the other as the half second wore on. You may be in a fix and I know that but what you don't know and won't believe and must find out for yourself is that I'm in a fix too and you got to get where I am before you even know what I'm talking about and I know that and that's why there is nothing to say now. Meanwhile I wish you well" (*LG*, 333). Will Barrett has just met on the street a Negro, "a young man his own age" whom he presumably used to know but to whom he has nothing to say. The incident describes the new quality of race relations. Free direct discourse here makes the reflection both concrete yet impersonal and the *I* is the generalized *I* of philosophical discussion.

Finally one might speak of a dissolve effect when the use of free direct discourse permits the superimposition of one person's utterance over another's:

As he got change from the cashier . . . [Will] began to grieve. It was the shame of it; the bare-faced embarrassment of getting worse and dying which took him by surprise and caught his breath in his throat. *How is this matter to be set right?* Were there no officials to deal with the shame of dying, to make suitable recompense? It was like getting badly beaten in a fight. To *lose*. Oh, to lose so badly. *Oh, you bastards living so well and me dying,* and where is the right of that? Oh, for the bitter shame of it (*lose*, the author's italics; other emphases added). (*LG*, 390)

Through the flexible weaving of free indirect discourse and free direct discourse—emphasized in my quotation—a voice is heard which at first is clearly Will Barrett's. But then another voice—Jamie's voice—comes through. Because of the unobtrusive shift of pronouns made possible by this method of rendering inner speech, Will's monody becomes Jamie's lament, and modulates into a lyrical cry whose subject is mortal man, rather than a particular individual.

Unmarked free direct discourse occasionally tends to blur the contours between the character's and the narrator's discourses sending ripples through our image of the narrative triangle: "It *was* like home here, but different too. At home *we have* J. C. Penney's and old ugly houses and vacant lots and new ugly houses. Here *were* pretty wooden things" (emphasis added; *LG*, 164). The blurring is all the more important in the case of questions because then the addressee changes: "The puzzle is: where does love pitch its tent? In the fine fervor of a summer night, in a jolly dark wood wherein one has a bit o' fun as the English say? Or in this dread tenderness of hers?" (*LG*,

107–108). This is probably a rendering of Will's thoughts and the question therefore is self-addressed, but some hesitation is made possible by the tense of the introductory verb, "the puzzle *is*," so that the narratee (and thus the reader) is also invited to ponder about the nature of love.

Needless to say, a similar blurring is often obtained through the reproducing of thoughts or utterances in free indirect discourse. Since for long stretches at a time the focus is internalized and the viewpoint is that of Will Barrett, it is at times difficult to ascertain whether the narrator immediately records what the hero sees or mediately reports his consciousness of what is being seen. Hence the mistaken idea of one reviewer that Barrett is the narrator, or the more percipient remark of Benjamin DeMott that the narrator is an alter ego of the protagonist.[19] These views however discount all the passages in which the narrative agency relays the *thoughts* of other characters, as illustrated in some of the examples above, or renders *collective thoughts*. (One of the best of many possible illustrations is the description of the Vaught servants in the third section of Chapter 4, which mixes commentary, free indirect discourse, and free direct discourse in a prose as subtle as its subject.) In short our brief study has proved the narrator's interest in *situations of language*, his resourcefulness in reproducing them, his pliancy in selecting the parameters to be excluded or included, the wide range of degrees of his interposition. Even through his role as relay of speech, therefore, the narrator is able to modify the angles of the narrative triangle.

Examination of the shifts in viewpoint also emphasizes the narrator's mobility on a larger narrational scale. All possible narrative stances are represented in the text in varying proportions. The narrative instance is now within the character's consciousness, now behind him but close by and lacking superior knowledge, now outside him and in a position of knowledge. In the last instance, he is not averse to passing judgments on the hero: "He had, of course, got everything twisted around. Though he took pride in his 'objectivity' and his 'evidence,' what evidence there was, was evidence of his own deteriorating condition" (*LG*, 28–29). Faced with such assessments, however, we may feel inclined, possibly urged by the narrator, to qualify his own assertions. (The above quotation goes on: "If there were any 'noxious particles' around, they were, as every psychologist knows, more likely to be found inside his head than in the sky" (*LG*, 29). The generalizing explanation, "as every psychologist knows," is suspicious especially to anyone familiar with Walker Percy's thinking; the statement about the noxious particles being "in his head" is scientifically dubious in its present formulation.) But commentaries crop up throughout, for instance in the recurrent tag "the engineer who always told the truth." The narrator will even briefly map out the protagonist's future near the end of his story, thus providing the reader with a major clue: "Perhaps this moment more than any other, the moment of his first astonishment, marked the beginning for the engineer of what is called a normal life. From that time forward it was possible to meet him and after a few minutes form a clear notion of what sort of fellow he was and how he would spend the rest of his life" (*LG*, 389).

In a sense, of course, the vagaries of the narrator correspond to those of the hero. Since Walker Percy wanted to present Barrett's "symptoms" "equivocally" he needed a narrator who would not be wholly consistent.[20] That these contractions and expansions of the field of vision alter the rapport of the narrator to his subject needs hardly to be stressed—except to suggest that the alteration powerfully contributes to the more realistic tone of Jamie's death scene. That they modify the terms of the triple alliance established between author, reader, and narration deserves more attention. Even a third-person narrator can prove unreliable. How are we to trust one who diversely identifies himself with the lost protagonist—and with great success too as in the episode in Chapter 5 with the nurse when "all at once time fell in"? (*LG*, 394)—yet who is also careful to mark his distance from the protagonist? (The narrator even feigns ignorance in Chapter 3 of where the protagonist spent the night.) The legitimacy of the narrator's role seems to be impugned, and the authority of the narration called into question. The variableness of the narrative agency opens a series of gaps between the text and the reader which accounts for some of the early reviewers' uneasy response to the book.

Yet while he shares in the duplicity inherent in all narrative instances, the narrator of *The Last Gentleman* is about serious business. Witness his constant irony—the mask of a commitment to values. Witness the considerable space he devotes to Sutter's thought-provoking, indeed provocative, notebook. His own didactic penchant is manifested in the numerous phrases that articulate his narration, serving as guide-posts to his narratee: "no doubt," "anyhow," "to be specific," "strange to say," "if the truth be told," "strangest of all," "no wonder," etc. Also his didacticism appears in many evaluating commentaries and generalizations: "In hospitals we expect strangers to love us" (*LG*, 50).

The story is obviously directed toward a narratee who is crucial in determining the balance of the narration. Of necessity his figure is not entirely clear-cut, either. At times it seems to become double, as in one of those old badly printed color pictures, when a sentence can be ascribed either to the narrator or to the character: "He had of course got into the Yankee way of not speaking to anyone at all. In New York it is gradually borne in upon one that you do not speak to strangers and that if you do, you are fairly taken for a homosexual" (*LG*, 202). A study of the pronoun *you* in the novel would show how its extension can vary. The *you* can be a generalizing *you*: a familiar equivalent of *one* it embraces both the character and the extradiegetic narratee who could have, or has had, a similar experience, as

in the above example. Or the *you* is generalizing but intradiegetic as in the description of Lugurtha the cook who "spoke to
you only of such things as juvenile delinquency" (*LG*, 198); it
makes of the narratee one of the fictional people since they alone
can converse with Lugurtha. In the following example things
are more complex: "Yet it fell out, strange to say, that when he
did find himself in a phone booth, he discovered he had spent
all but nine cents! Oh damnable stupidity and fiendish bad
luck, but what are you going to do?" (*LG*, 306). Is the narrator
assuming his commentator's role, as "strange to say" suggests,
and is he then addressing the hero—an intradiegetic narratee
—in mock pity, or is he taking an extradiegetic narratee to witness? Is the narrator rather reporting the character's inner
monologue, in which case Will is talking to himself alone, and
the narratee is metadiegetic? Or is he thinking of himself and
anyone in the same circumstances, which makes the narratee
both meta- and intradiegetic? The very indeterminacy of the
allocutor is a textual effect which we must respond to.[21]

Although I cannot draw here a full portrait of the extradiegetic narratee, let us note that like his partner in the act of
narration he is a man of wide knowledge. The very numerous
comparisons which are supposed to help him picture or imagine things more vividly imply that his own "radar" is finely attuned to Western culture in general (*e.g.*, Mort Prince in Levit-
town is "like Descartes among the Burghers of Amsterdam"
[*LG*, 140]; a housewife is a "regular La Pasionaria of the suburbs" [*LG*, 141]). The radar is also attuned to American culture, past and present, middle brow and high brow, and to
southern life and mores in particular. Indeed the narratee must
be as familiar as Will Barrett with the Civil War to pick up the
allusion to the ancestor who died in The Crater or to the con-
troversy about General Kirby Smith, or the ravine in Central
Park which is like a sniper's den, that "Brady photographed six
weeks after the battle" (*LG*, 107). Phrases like "they were Sewa-

nee episcopal types" (*LG*, 265), "an equable lower-South episcopal face" (*LG*, 151), "the peculiar reflected style of the deep
Delta," an Alabama voice as "ancient and visible and unbut-
toned" as Tallulah Bankhead's (*LG*, 110)—all assume that
the narratee knows about southern types, voices, nuances. He
equally remembers enough of the life of the saints to appreciate the simile that has Barrett plunge "into a brierpatch like
a saint of old" or turn to money as saints to contemplation.
Moreover what narrator and narratee share is not simply a
body of knowledge but a language. In this regard the numerous
clichés serve not only as subject-oriented word pictures that
describe the character through mimicking his particular cant,
but also as addressee-oriented meeting-points where narrator
and narratee (or reader) can communicate and commune in
derisive dissociation from stereotyped speech and stultified life.

This encyclopedic shared knowledge ranging from Abou Ben
Adhem to Wittgenstein and Woody Woodpecker is of course
counterbalanced by the narratee's total ignorance of the hero's
adventures—wherein he differs from the narrator. Although an
effort of imagination is sometimes enjoined upon him ("Take an
ordinary day in New York. The sun is shining." "Imagine their
feeling"), native curiosity is more usually attributed to him. So
the narrator relays and answers his questions: "What happens
to a man to whom all things seem possible and every course of
action open? Nothing of course" (*LG*, 10). Should he wonder,
"And Kitty?" the next paragraph will supply the information.
Sometimes the narrator queries the narratee in his turn: "he'd
have struck out for St. Louis (the question is, how many people
nowadays would not?)" (*LG*, 6), "Has not this been the case
with all 'religious' people?" (*LG*, 355). Thus the likeness between the narratee's fundamental situation and that of the
character is hinted at while his distance and difference are recognized. More curious still are the questions which could be
the narratee's and which are answered seemingly by the char-

acter: "There is the painting which has been bought at great expense and exhibited in the museum so that millions can see it. What is wrong with that? Something, said the engineer" (*LG*, 27). In this way an internal dialogue is set up within the text, between the figures of the narrative triangle.

Briefly, the narratee is expected both to recognize the truth of what he is being told and to take a critical attitude toward it. He must evaluate possibilities, existential attitudes, draw analogies between the familiar—the assumptions and information he shares with the narrator—and the unknown, the lostness and dislocation of this particular hero who only becomes predictable at the end of the story. But of course the comparisons end in throwing as much light on the "happiness" of the South (or the "homelessness" of the North) or the modern post-Christian world as on the protagonist's "symptons." Thus the presence of the narratee does not annul the vacillation created by the narrative agency, but it counterpoises it in two ways: first, insofar as it underscores the link between the fictional universe and the outside world, it precludes any interpretation of the story as merely a tale or a game played with and against narrative rules. Second, it outlines for the reader a possible perspective. If there is one figure of the narration with whom we are invited provisionally to identify, it is that of the narratee. We have to test the familiar against the unfamiliar, the unfamiliar against the familiar until, it is to be hoped, we grow in wisdom or at least become aware of our ignorance. To the reader, the slight estrangement of the whole fictional universe is a further heuristic challenge which I leave to the thematic critics to meet. It seems to me that the tale is told not in exchange for our immersion in the fictional world, our willing suspension of disbelief but rather for our *questions*, our engagement / disengagement, in exchange for our *desire*. Desire to know (but to know what?—the face of Death?—the face of God?). Desire at any rate to be.

In any case to insist on the credibility of the narrator is finally to ask for realistic representation whereas the function of the narrator in *The Last Gentleman* is eminently poetic. Far from being discredited by his changeability, he appears as the unnamed Namer who constructs a world like ours and unlike ours, sets his action in a time that may be ours or "an as yet unnamed era," who makes us cohearers of a polyphonic universe of language.[22] The narration counterpoints a number of voices; they echo, contradict, or answer one another in an incessant dialogue that goes on, as we have seen, even within the narrative triangle. Walker Percy is close here to the "dialogism" of Dostoevsky.[23] An ironic but not unkindly ventriloquist, the narrator weaves an incredible number of fashionable cants into a highly idiosyncratic triumph of mixed styles, cultural clichés, social vacuities, and intellectual absurdities until they recover a lambent pregnancy, and we become convinced that we have been hearing a unique, prophetic voice. A mythic creator, the narrator points to his own begetter, the occulted author. Just as the designation "the engineer" served as a pointer to the narrator, the narrative chain reduplicates both the alienation of origins and the permanence of the Other in the act of speech. In addition, the narrator's shifts from presence to copresence to seeming absence become significant, perhaps symbolic. They generate the sense of another absence, the desire of another presence.

In this light, rather than the telescope image, the most pregnant structural metaphor for *The Last Gentleman* is the baptism scene to which the novel leads up as its harrowing climax and effulgent core. With the priest bearing God's news to Jamie, and Will interpreting Jamie to Father Boomer, the episode dramatizes a double process of mediation. Through the two overlapping triads a circulation of meaning and being is established between the diegetic participants.[24] Similarly in the extradiegetic triple alliance that unites author, character, and reader, the reader is made to share in an exchange which may link him to "the silent Word" beyond the novelist's words. Just as the action leaves the hero groping toward a new orientation, free to accept or not "the message in the bottle" that has thus indirectly reached him, so the narration leaves the reader wondering about "what happened," free to resonate or not to "the unspoken word, the Word unheard / The Word without a word, the Word within / The world and for the world."[25]

Whatever our personal interpretation of the novel, *The Last Gentleman* impels us not only to participate in the construction of its meaning but to do some thinking of our own about language, about the relationship between words and things and people and being. In *The Moviegoer* the narrator-protagonist was absorbed in the wonder of naming. In *The Last Gentleman* this activity is one which the narration, largely through the manipulation of the narrative triangle, demands from the implied audience. Walker Percy's concern with "Naming and Being" may therefore be less evident in his second novel; but it is no less profound.

PANTHEA REID BROUGHTON

Gentlemen and Fornicators:
The Last Gentleman and a
Bisected Reality

IN EVERYTHING he writes Walker Percy protests against doubleness. In "A Theory of Language," for example, Percy criticizes the linguists for perpetuating a "somewhat decrepit mind-body dualism" (*MB*, 300); in "Culture: The Antinomy of the Scientific Method" he insists that scientists must instead "forgo the luxury of a bisected reality" (*MB*, 242). And yet that very dualism for which he chides linguists and scientists seems to be a habit of mind with Walker Percy. That is, even as Percy protests against dualism, he presents in his fiction alternatives which tend to be either / or choices: either body or mind, bestialism or angelism, immanence or transcendence.

Fiction of course depicts the human experience; it cannot be faulted for being amoral or violent or dualistic if the world it grows out of is so. Nevertheless, I wonder if the doubleness Walker Percy presents and protests may not to some extent be a projection from within himself. If so, Percy's dualistic conceptualizing may buttress the ideational structure, but it also undermines the imaginative fullness of his fiction.

Percy's conception of a bisected reality informs *The Last Gentleman*. Structuring the book around a series of foils, Percy exemplifies the split between the body and the mind in the way he juxtaposes the South and the North; in Will Barrett's books of "great particularity"—as opposed to Jamie Vaught's books "great abstractness" (*LG*, 161); in Barrett's two guides for finding Sutter and Jamie—the reassuring Esso map "with its intersecting lines and tiny airplanes and crossed daggers marking battlefields" (*LG*, 283) and Sutter's difficult and disturbingly abstruse casebook; in Barrett's memories of a black man's "working" Mr. Ed Barrett for money, while Mr. Barrett spoke abstractly of the "cheapness of good intentions and the rarity of good character" (*LG*, 329); and in the way Percy foils such minor characters as the resident and the priest who preside at Jamie's deathbed and such major characters as Val and Sutter.

Characterization as a whole is structured in terms of the mind / body split; thus the minor characters tend to exemplify bestialism, while the major characters are afflicted with angelism. In *The Last Gentleman* the minor characters are remarkably alike in their self-satisfaction, adjustment, insensitivity, and blindness. Mr. Vaught who confronts death by side-stepping, joking, and buying presents exemplifies this type; for Poppy Vaught "did not know what he did not know" (*LG*, 195). The students at the university too, who seem to Will remarkably "at-one with themselves," are living life in its lowest common denominator (*LG*, 202). The fraternity brothers that Son Thigpen brings to the Vaught's house are, for example, completely set "for the next fifty years in the actuality of themselves and their own good names. They knew what they were, how things were and how things should be" (*LG*, 265). They are comfortable in themselves, well-adjusted, because they have no other idea of what else life should hold; thus they coincide with an entirely finite mold.

Of the fraternity brothers, Will Barrett asks, "why ain't I like them, easy and actual?" (*LG*, 265). He is not because he is tortured by ideals and mental constructs which intervene between himself and his world. Suffering from angelism or excessive abstraction, Will is better at abstract games and systems than at living. He has to "know everything" before he can "do anything." Thus an education only "made matters worse" for him because it had "nothing whatever to do with life" (*LG*, 201). It guaranteed his existence in a condition colloquially but aptly described as "out of it." The minor characters tend to be "in it" and adjusted while the protagonist is "out of it" and alienated; the absolute dichotomy between them indicates how much Percy characterizes, structures, and conceptualizes in terms of that very decrepit and shop-worn split he deplores.

But Percy's dependence upon that split is most explicitly exemplified in *The Last Gentleman* in matters sexual. One day Will Barrett longs for "carnal knowledge, the next for perfect angelic knowledge"; one day he is "American and horny"—the next he is "English and eavesdropper"(*LG*, 170). Kitty Vaught offers to be either whore or lady for Will, and Will begs Sutter to tell him to be unchaste or chaste, to fornicate or not to fornicate, but to tell him one or the other.

To Barrett, the Cartesian split is exemplified in one overwhelming question: to be a gentleman or a fornicator. For Will the matter is not simple. With his great-grandfather, being a gentleman was not a matter of breeding but of willingness to act on principle; that ancestor "knew what was what and said so and acted accordingly and did not care what anyone thought" (*LG*, 9). But successive generations of Barretts have become less and less sure of what is right. Mr. Ed Barrett was actually "killed by his own irony and sadness and by the strain of living out an ordinary day in a perfect dance of honor" (*LG*, 10). For Mr. Ed, honor had become a dance, an artificial pattern, an obligatory reenactment of the code of *gentillesse* which was woefully anachronistic for his times. In Will's age, moreover, that code is not only anachronistic, it is ludicrous. It provokes Will to challenge another Princeton student for failing to exchange "hellos" or polite "what says"; and it compels him to blow up a Union Army plaque—a perfect ineffective gesture since "no one ever knew what had been blown up" (*LG*, 267).

Clearly the causes which demand that a gentleman act with honor are not so plentiful or clear-cut anymore. There are no more noble wars; Will is drafted for an apparently meaningless and purposeless two-year hitch in the army. The one question Will can answer affirmatively about his father is that he was a gentleman, for in Mr. Ed's day at least honor meant something. But in Will's own time, being a gentleman has been reduced to maintaining the proprieties around women. Will considers himself "bound south as a gentleman" and therefore chastizes himself for behaving like "white trash" with Forney Aiken's daughter (*LG*, 135–36).

Will makes a stilted apology, but "what saved him in the end was not only [his] southern chivalry but [her] Yankee good sense" (*LG*, 137). The word *saved* there is a peculiar one. We are reminded of the *conversation* (I use the word loosely) that Will has with Kitty about dances. Kitty asks Will to take her to a dance, tells him that her grandmother composed the official ATO waltz, and says she loves to dance. Will, all the while, is telling how the Confederate officers continued to go to dances even during the worst of the fighting. But to Will the really curious aspect of the tale is that during the Civil War his ancestor "did not feel himself under the necessity, almost moral, of making love" (*LG*, 112).

Will sees love-making as obligatory in a permissive society; thus he is fascinated by a time when honor "saved" a man from a sexual encounter with a lady before marriage. That fascination may indicate sexual insecurity; more probably, however, it is a manifestation of moral insecurity. Will's ancestors knew right from wrong and could act accordingly. Morality was not necessarily and exclusively sexual, but nevertheless their sexual code serves as an apt analogue for the rigidity of their moral code. And similarly, twentieth-century sexual ambiguity is a fitting emblem for contemporary moral ambiguity. Because sexual and moral absolutes have been submerged in a flood of relativism, Will Barrett feels cast adrift. Thus he wishes to find a mooring somehow with someone who will tell him unequivocally what to do.

He cannot coerce Sutter into doing so, and so he takes recourse in the dictates of a code from simpler times. Will determines "I shall court [Kitty] henceforth in the old style" (*LG*, 166). Thus he "aimed to take Kitty to a proper dance, pay her court, not mess around" (*LG*, 174). But during the entire course of the novel Will neither takes Kitty dancing as a gentleman might nor messes around as a fornicator would. He feels frustrated and wonders if being a gentleman in this day and age causes his terrible sense of uneasiness and dislocation. He asks Sutter " 'whether a nervous condition could be caused by not having sexual intercourse' "(*LG*, 224). Sutter knows of course that Will is asking permission to break the gentleman's code for reasons of health, and Sutter refuses to play that game. Instead he says "Fornicate if you want to and enjoy yourself but don't come looking to me for a merit badge certifying you as a Christian or a gentleman or whatever it is you cleave by' " (*LG*, 225).

Will wishes to cleave to a concept of himself as a gentleman. Yet being the last gentleman (Percy did intend that the title refer to Will)[1] makes Will miserable because it necessitates his being chaste in an age when chastity seems to be a dead issue. Thus though all Percy's protagonists find their experiences "evacuated," Will is more "out of it" than the others. Percy's other protagonists try out a variety of methods for putting themselves back in touch with the physical world. But because he sees the malaise chiefly in terms of sexual deprivation, Will imagines that he may regain the world only by losing his virginity; yet remaining a gentleman is necessary to his self-esteem.

So Will is in a double-bind, for to him *gentleman* and *fornicator* are mutually exclusive terms.

Curiously, Will blushes over "the word 'fornicate.' In Sutter's mouth it seemed somehow more shameful than the four-letter word" (*LG*, 225). The word is shameful to Will because it conjures up memories of his father whose epithet for all lower class whites was *fornicators*. Mr. Ed Barrett in fact felt that because modern-day sons of gentlemen were now fornicators, all principles were dead. Just before committing suicide, Mr. Barrett said to his son: "'Once they were the fornicators and the bribers and the takers of bribes and we were not and that was why they hated us. Now we are like them, so why should they stay [and confront me]? They know they don't have to kill me'" (*LG*, 330). In other words, the southern aristocracy has betrayed its own principles so that there is no longer any need for confrontation between lower- and upper-class whites.

For a man whose own father took him to a whorehouse at the age of sixteen, this logic is rather peculiar. It seems, in fact, that to Mr. Ed whoring was not fornicating. He could condone open sexuality among blacks; he told Will that "'They [blacks] fornicate and the one who fornicates best is the preacher'"; but he was shocked by white people who "'fornicate too and in public and expect *them* back yonder [the blacks] somehow not to notice. Then they expect their women to be respected.'" Mr. Barrett's fear was that the black man and the white man were each going to "'pick up the worst of the other and lose the best of himself.'" He went on to instruct Will to be like neither group—neither like a black—"'a fornicator and not caring'" nor like a middle class white—a "'fornicator and hypocrite'" (*LG*, 100–101). Thus Mr. Barrett seems to have told Will that sex should not be abused by either promiscuity or hypocrisy.

Yet Mr. Ed's instructions to Will on sexual matters were not so well reasoned. He spoke neither of commitment nor of intimacy. What he did tell Will was only, "'Go to whores if you have to, but always remember the difference. Don't treat a lady like a whore or a whore like a lady'" (*LG*, 100). The whole question of human sexuality and morality was distilled for Mr. Ed into a matter of social distinction. The gentleman could "take his pleasure" (*LG*, 118) (an old-fashioned phrase Will uses when he realizes that he almost seduced or was seduced by Kitty in Central Park) with a whore, but his women were to be respected. Mr. Ed was a great believer in character, but his message to his son, as Will recalls it, seemed to define morality in terms of propriety, and propriety in terms of distinguishing between a lady and a whore.

No wonder Will sees his choices in either / or terms: gentleman or white trash, chivalry or fornication. Sutter cannot figure out what Will wants of him, but he says, "'I suspect it is one of two things. You either want me to tell you to fornicate or not to fornicate, but for the life of me I can't tell which it is.'" Will replies by begging Sutter "'Tell me to be chaste and I will do it. Yes! I will do it easily! . . . All you have to do is tell me.'" But Sutter will not tell him, and Will instead implores "'Then tell me not to be chaste'" (*LG*, 381). Will would adopt either of the two absolutely opposed courses of action if only a parent figure would dictate the course for him. Certainly his desire to be told what to do stems from personal insecurity and the insecurities of the age; yet his Manichean opposition is clearly the special legacy of his father.

Will's father was an idealist. He liked to listen to the sad old Brahms records and walk under the live oaks at night and speak to strangers "of the good life and the loneliness of the galaxies" (*LG*, 330). For him whoring was apparently an acceptable means for reclaiming the lost world, but not an especially important one. Instead Mr. Ed Barrett felt that action as an application of high principles was the way to reenter the world. Thus he told Will of the Klu Kluxers "'I'm going to run them out of town, son, every last miserable son of a bitch'" (*LG*, 238). But when he discovered that the Klan was not interested in a showdown with him, that the issues were obsolete, Mr. Barrett took a double-barrel twelve-gauge shotgun and fitted its muzzle "into the notch of his breastbone" and pulled both triggers (*LG*, 331).

Mr. Ed Barrett assumed that putting principles into action was the means for reclaiming a lost world. He committed suicide because his life could be redeemed only by a set of principles which, he discovered, were no longer in the world. The suicide then was for him a logical extension of the recognition that he and all he lived for were "out of it."

Sutter Vaught too attempted suicide—and for much the same reason, though as a scientist Sutter's problem was not idealism but objectivity. Nevertheless, both the idealist and the objectivist suffer what Percy in *The Moviegoer* calls "the pain of loss" (*Mg*, 120). The price modern man pays, according to Sutter, for "the beauty and elegance of the method of science" is dispossession (*LG*, 280). Man has lost touch with the world he lives in, and Sutter can see no means for reclaiming that world except lewdness. Sutter considers lewdness to be the "sole portal of reentry into [a] world demoted to immanence; reentry into immanence [can occur only] via orgasm" (*LG*, 345). Thus Sutter insists that "lewdness itself is a kind of sacrament" (*LG*, 281) because through sex the transcendent becomes immanent. But of course the union of transcendence and immanence through orgasm does not last and "post-orgasmic transcendence [is] 7 devils worse than" (*LG*, 345) the original abstracted state. Thus pre-orgasmic suicide is considered "as consequence of the spirit of abstraction and of transcendence" (*LG*, 345). Sutter Vaught has written up these theories in a scientific article on post-orgasmic suicides which result from "The Failure of Coitus as a Mode of Reentry into the Sphere of Immanence from the Sphere of Transcendence" (*LG*, 65).

Sutter seems to have lived his own life under the assumption that "fornication is the sole channel to the real" (*LG*, 372). Thus his method for overcoming depression and abstraction has been to pick up a strange woman and take her to bed with him. That method has been singularly ineffective. Thus, finding himself even more depressed after one such affair, Sutter concluded that *"There is no reentry from the orbit of transcendence"* (*LG*, 345), and made an abortive suicide attempt. Perhaps sex fails to salvage Sutter not only because it is short-lived but also because for Sutter it is unlived. That is, Sutter never fully participates in the life of the body. Instead he isolates genital sexuality from the entire complex of human relations and expects it to be sufficient to ground his abstracted state. He too then, like other characters in *The Last Gentleman*, treats sex as an abstraction.

The way sex can become an abstraction is most clearly exemplified by a book by Mort Prince which Will Barrett vaguely remembers reading. As he recalls it, Prince's *The Farther Journey* was "a novel about a writer who lives in Connecticut and enters into a sexual relationship with a housewife next door, not as a conventional adultery, for he was not even attracted to her, but rather as the exercise of that last and inalienable possession of the individual in a sick society, freedom" (*LG*, 140). Clearly for that writer, sex was an idea; it was not even physical. It may only have been authorial wishfulfillment, for Mort Prince clearly is not the "mighty fornicator" his heroes are.

Kitty too is an inveterate abstractionist. She has to aim to be herself, and Barrett does not know how to tell her just to be herself. In Central Park, she takes off all her clothes and throws herself into Barrett's arms not because she loves him or desires him but to conduct "'a little experiment by Kitty for the benefit of Kitty.'" She wants to prove that there is "nothing wrong" with her (*LG*, 109). That episode is aborted ostensibly because Kitty gets sick from hikuli-tea; but Barrett is disconcerted enough to vow to "court her henceforth in the old style" (*LG*,

166). When she kisses him, he figures out what is wrong: "is this right, she as good as asked." She takes "every care to do the right wrong thing. There were even echoes of a third person: what, you worry about the boys as good a figure as you have, etc. So he was the boy and she was doing her best to do what a girl does. He sighed" (*LG*, 167). Kitty cannot show her own feelings, whatever they are, because she is busy impersonating, trying to do the "right wrong thing." She has abstracted both the method of love-making and the substance: "Love, she like him, was obliged to see as a naked garden of stamens and pistils" (*LG*, 167). As a modern woman, she feels obliged to see love as a matter of sex alone. Sex then for Kitty is an abstraction, as it is for Rita. According to Sutter, Rita made sex an exercise in technique. They became "geniuses of the orgasm" (*LG* 246) and she was fond of publicly declaring that the two of them were "'good in bed'" (*LG*, 350). For Rita, sex seems unrelated to privacy or intimacy—as we see when she suggests that Will and Jamie find themselves a "couple of chicks" (*LG*, 159).

Rita's methodological and therapeutic approach to sex scandalizes Sutter who wants science and sex utterly dissociated. But Sutter, though he is "overtly heterosexual and overtly lewd," is also an abstractionist about sex. Sutter is an abstractionist in two ways. First he makes sex into theory—describing himself as a "sincere, humble, and even moral pornographer" (*LG*, 281); and second, he abstracts from complex and involved human relations. And so sexuality in his terms cannot possibly satisfy all that he demands. Sutter tries to compensate by attempting to intensify the touch of flesh—through the use of games, an extra woman, or pornographic pictures. Sutter speculates that "genital sexuality=twice 'real'" because it is "touch, therefore physical, therefore 'real,'" and again because scientific theory certifies it as the "substrata of all other relations" (*LG*, 280). But apparently it is not real enough for Sutter.

Mr. Ed Barrett and Dr. Sutter Vaught are juxtaposed against each other, yet beneath their obvious dissimilarities they are very much alike. Both suffer from the malaise of abstraction, though Mr. Barrett's problem is transcendent idealism while Sutter's is transcendent objectivity. Mr. Barrett proposes principled action; Sutter proposes genital sexuality as a means of reentering the world. Both means fail. And both men attempt suicide. Mr. Barrett's southern version of the stoic Greco-Roman heritage (indicated by the name Ithaca) and Sutter's desacralizing science offer neither men any continuingly viable ways to live their lives.

The ending of *The Last Gentleman* suggests that the church offers human beings a viable way to live in this world without being consumed by it. Because the pain of dying prevents abstraction, Jamie can *experience* the truths of religion for the first time. Conversion for his sister Valentine Vaught was likewise an experiential breakthrough. Since she was raised in a perfunctory sort of Alabama Protestantism, Roman Catholicism came to Val like news from across the seas and she "Believed it all, the whole business" (*LG*, 301). Yet she did not become spiritual. Her mission in south Alabama may look like a lunar installation, but it is very much a part of this ordinary dull world, as are both representatives of the church in this novel. Father Boomer, with his thick muscular body, healthy skin, and "big ruddy American league paws" (*LG*, 405), looks "more like a baseball umpire" (*LG*, 398) than a priest. And Val, who does not wear a "proper habit but a black skirt and blouse and a little cap-and-veil business," "remains a somewhat plumpish bad-complexioned potato-fed Vaught" (*LG*, 208). Will's encounter at the mission with the rather fleshy Val feeding entrails to a hawk is calculated to be totally physical, even repugnantly so.

Paradoxically, in Walker Percy's world, the representatives of science are emaciated and other-worldly while the spokesmen for religion are fully-fleshed and this-worldly. That is because they know the secret of living in this world while the abstracted scientist does not. Among the religious, accepting this world is made possible by the knowledge that man is a wayfarer whose real home is elsewhere. Knowing that this life is not his only life gives man the option of savoring experience—just as a castaway temporarily marooned on an island would delight in the serendipitous experience of life there. Thus religion, with its news that man is a wayfarer, puts human beings in touch with the earth and the body.

That perspective of course is not Sutter Vaught's. In his notebook Sutter replies to Val: "Let us say that you were right: that man is a wayfarer (*i.e.*, not a transcending being nor immanent being but a wayfarer) who therefore stands in the way of hearing a piece of news which is of the utmost importance to him (*i.e.*, his salvation) and which he had better attend to" (*LG*, 353). Then Sutter continues to reason that even knowing that he is a wayfarer and that news of ultimate importance is offered to him, a man like Will Barrett will not be affected. According to Sutter, he would "receive the news from his high seat of transcendence as one more item of psychology, throw it into his immanent meat-grinder, and wait to see if he feels better" (*LG*, 354). In other words, Will is so hopelessly abstracted that he could not experience the immediacy even of news of his own salvation.

Nevertheless, being a wayfarer is Walker Percy's metaphor for man's condition on this earth. That image should mend the existential rupture and make enjoyment of the immediacy of time and place possible. For when human beings see the world afresh, as the castaway does when he finds himself washed ashore and as Will Barrett does when he recovers from a siege of amnesia, they can delight in it.

For Walker Percy the special charm of being a wayfarer, though, seems to be a matter of being neither one nor the other. For that situation the best analogue in the book is the Trav-L-

Aire which is "in the world yet not of the world, sampling the particularities of place yet cabined off from the sadness of place" (*LG*, 152). Like the camper, the wayfarer is in yet not of the world. He has sovereignty because he can experience the world afresh, yet he can listen to news of his salvation because he knows that there is another world beyond this one.

But the image of man as wayfarer, minus the religious trappings, partakes of the same polarized reality that obsessed Sutter Vaught. Sutter in fact writes to Val that there are no differences between the two of them except that she believes that life can come from the Eucharist, and he does not know where it comes from. Val's ideal image of man is the wayfarer; Sutter's is the fornicating scientist. He asks "what is better then than the beauty and exaltation of the practice of transcendence (science and art) and of the delectation of immanence, the beauty and exaltation of lewd love?" (*LG*, 354). The fornicating scientist can live both outside and inside the actual world, be both transcendent and immanent. Like the wayfarer he is both out of and in the world. In the essay "The Delta Factor" Walker Percy pictures one such scientist; he is an astronomer who works on Mount Palomar during the night and during the day comes down into town to live like other humans. Percy calls him "one of the lucky ones" and explains "His is the best of both worlds: He theorizes and satisfies his need. He is like one of the old gods who lived above the earth but took their pleasure from the maids of the earth" (*MB*, 21).

That image of a "lucky" man is yet another example of dualistic conceptualizing. For there again, as with Mr. Barrett's gentleman of action, Sutter's fornicating scientist, and Val's wayfarer, a split between the mind and the body is presupposed. That split for Will is the choice between being either a gentleman or a fornicator. But Will must somehow himself "forgo the luxury of a bisected reality" (*MB*, 242) and get the mind and the body, logos and eros into harmony with each other. In *The Last Gentleman* there are two instances when that split is transcended. Each instance is noetic and ineffable. Each is a hierophany, what Mircea Eliade defines as an "irruption of the sacred."[2] One of course is the baptismal scene at the end of the novel. Apparently Jamie is ready to accept the truths of religion because he is no longer an abstracted theoretician. Instead, he is gripped by the "dread ultimate rot" (*LG*, 401) of his own body. Then amidst the scandalous stench from his own bowels, while a Holsum bread truck (suggesting the life-giving body of Christ) passes outside, something transcendent occurs. Will and Jamie communicate without words and so, apparently, do Jamie and God. Though he may seem like a "storekeeper over his counter" (*LG*, 396), Father Boomer serves as a messenger of Truth. And Will Barrett, though he believes nothing himself, becomes an agent of Jamie's belief. Apparently the tap water in the clouded plastic glass mysteriously receives the blessing of the Baptismal Water. Performed during the Easter Vigil, the prayer consecrating the water begins: "May He by a secret mixture of His divine power render this water fruitful for the regeneration of men."[3] Will does not understand the "secret mixture" in the mundane glass, nor does he know exactly what happened in the hospital room, but he does know that something mysterious occurred. Even Sutter makes some sort of tacit acknowledgment of mystery, But neither of them has directly experienced the hierophany. That they felt it happening to Jamie is, however, acknowledgment that the mystery was actual.

For Will himself, however, the first-hand experience of mystery occurs only once in the book. It is when he returns home and touches "the sibilant corky bark of the water oak" (*LG*, 329) and relives for apparently the first time the events just preceding his father's suicide. Here is how Percy juxtaposes the touch of the tree and Will's recognition:

Again his hand went forth, knowing where it was, though he could not see, and touched the tiny iron horsehead of the hitching post, traced the cold metal down to the place where the oak had grown round it in an elephant lip. His fingertips touched the warm finny whispering bark.

Wait. While his fingers explored the juncture of iron and bark, his eyes narrowed as if he caught a glimmer of light on the cold iron skull. *Wait.* I think he was wrong and that he was looking in the wrong place. No, not he but the times. The times were wrong and one looked in the wrong place. It wasn't even his fault because that was the way he was and the way the times were, and there was no other place a man could look. It was the worst of times, a time of fake beauty and fake victory. *Wait.* He had missed it! It was not in the Brahms that one looked and not in solitariness and not in the old sad poetry but—he wrung out his ear—but here, under your nose, here in the very curiousness and drollness and extraness of the iron and the bark that—he shook his head—that—(*LG*, 332)

Years before, Will had implored his father: "*Wait,*" but Mr. Barrett only paused before going in to get the shotgun. Years later, as Will touches the interface between the bark and the iron, he says *wait* again to himself. For he seems to have discovered something that his father had missed.

The image is highly ambiguous, but it seems to me that in touching the iron and bark Will experiences a union of transcendence and immanence which his father did not see as a possibility. Mr. Barrett missed the gratuity of the ordinary world and looked for meaning only above and beyond this world. He lived for abstract ideals whose associations with the commonplace had been severed. But Will feels how the old iron hitching post, redolent of the old days of southern gentlemen, is half covered over by warm bark and *knows* without words that the two need not be dissociated. Percy designed the passage as an answer to the epiphany of matter Sartre presents in *La Nausée*.[4] For Will, as for Roquentin, the experience serves to ground him in the world of matter. And it further reinforces his distrust of his father's abstractions. That distrust manifests itself most explicitly, just after Will touches the tree and says *wait*, when a young black man passes along the sidewalk. His father would doubtless have theorized to the black man about character or the galaxies, but Will does not presume to speak, for he knows that there is nothing he can say that can mean anything to this young man.

Elsewhere, Val's "lip-curling bold-eyed expression" reminds Will that Val is Kitty's sister (*LG*, 213). And a similar repetition of phrase establishes for us the kinship of the two hierophanies. In the first such experience Will "traced the cold metal down to the place where the oak had grown round it in an elephant lip. His fingertips touched the warm finny whispering bark" (*LG*, 332). And later after Will "who did not know how he knew" explains to the priest what Jamie wants, the priest promises not to let Jamie go. Then "as he waited he curled his lips absently against his teeth" (*LG*, 406). The lip of the bark and the lip of the priest serve to associate these two scenes. But the scenes are essentially alike because each presents an ineffable experience in which the categories of transcendence and immanence are overcome. Under the tree Will Barrett did not presume to speak to the Negro, knowing that both of them were "in a fix" and could not understand each other's separate dilemma. And "that's why there is nothing to say now" (*LG*, 330). After Jamie's death, Barrett realizes that he does not have to know what Sutter thinks before he knows what he (Barrett) thinks, and yet he still asks Sutter to wait. He tells Sutter that he will do as he has planned, that is, he will marry Kitty, and that he nevertheless wants Sutter to come back with him. He says: " 'I, Will Barrett . . . need you and want you to come back. I need you more than Jamie needed you. Jamie had Val too' " (*LG*, 409).

Clearly, Will is terrified lest another father figure walk away from him and commit suicide. But it also seems that Will needs Sutter as a representative of transcendence, lest he be submerged by immanence or sunk in the everydayness that life with Kitty promises to be. Will has experienced two hierophanies; yet there is no indication that any such ineffable experience will be a part of his life with Kitty. Will speaks of his future life with Kitty in terms as abstract as any his father might have used and as inauthentic as any Nell Lovell in *The Moviegoer* might have used. We readers probably find our own necks prickling when we read of Will's future plans and hear from the narrator that henceforth Will entered "what is called a normal life" (*LG*, 389). Like Sutter, we cannot imagine talking to Kitty about anything other than The Big Game. And so we cannot imagine how marriage to Kitty can be anything other than a betrayal of the understanding Will achieved under the live oak in Ithaca, Mississippi.

Walker Percy assumes that marriage in itself is an accomodation to the ways of the world. For Will Barrett marriage offers a sort of both / and possibility: an option both to remain a gentleman and to satisfy his "coarse" desires. For Percy it exemplifies Kierkegaard's ethical stage as an acceptance of responsibility in the human community. And a normal married life may also offer the religious man a sort of "cover" so that he may pass incognito through the world. But marriage in itself, to Percy, cannot be transcendent. And that is why Will Barrett still needs Sutter Vaught. Jamie had both Val and Sutter to remind him that this world is not sufficient unto itself. Will must at least have Sutter. Thus he asks Sutter five times to "wait." And when "a final question does occur to him" he runs after Sutter in the "spavined and sprung" Edsel (*LG*, 409). The last sentence of the book tells us that finally the Edsel waited for him (*LG*, 409).

That uncared for Edsel seems a sort of secular sanctuary— at least another reminder that one can live in the world and yet be out of it. Like the Curlee suit which Percy tells us is "double breasted!" (*LG*,389) and the Thom McAn shoes, Sutter's Edsel is intended to exemplify his dissociation from middle-class values (while indicating something of Percy's dependence on those values). Nevertheless, being in the world means distinguishing between a Curlee and a Saville Row suit. Being out of the world means not giving a damn. Percy defines it as transcendence.

Percy is committed to the idea that transcendence is mental; thus he aligns the spirit with the mind not the body. His concept of transcendence is totally Apollonian, but his version of immanence is not Dionysian. His characters traffic in immanence; but, except in the two hierophanies discussed above, they do not transcend in and through it. Immanence to Percy is bestial—a matter of need satisfaction. It is merely the body, merely sex, merely fornication.

Percy uses sexual matters as convenient illustrations of Cartesian dualism. But he fails to see in them a means for overcoming that split, since sex, even for a married gentleman, is still fornication. In the biblical sense, fornication means idolary or mistaking the profane for the sacred; thus the term supposes a dualism. The Dionysian life should, however, transcend dualism. Eros should conjoin the secular and the sacred, the flesh and the spirit, in a union which is ineffable and transcendent.

Will experiences transcendence once because he feels the physical presence of the iron and the bark. Jamie transcends because the decay of his own body destroys his abstracted stance. But no character transcends through love. Will can feel the presence of Spirit as he touches that tree; he can feel it in his final communion with Jamie; perhaps he will feel it someday in an intersubjective relationship with Sutter. But we doubt he will ever feel it with Kitty. Although he knows that the abstract must not be divorced from the actual, he does not seem able to let that awareness infuse his life with a woman. Indeed, Will is doomed to be either a gentleman or a fornicator—for the book suggests no other choices; it describes heterosexual relations only in terms of either inflated Old South rhetoric or reductionist scientific jargon. And so Will seems fated to see love between a man and a woman in either idealistic or coarse terms and, either way, to miss Dionysus.

Thus the problem with the book's ending is that Percy is conceptualizing in terms of that very mind / body split he and his characters deplore. He gives Will both Kitty (sex, responsibility, immanence) and Sutter (theory, knowledge, transcendence), as if having both of them will enable Will to complete his own personality. Percy's vision of the integrated self is then not whole but split. Walker Percy places his faith in triads, but speaks in twosomes. This double vision is I believe rather like a rock fault beneath a city: it threatens the coherence and solidity of his otherwise very beautiful and sound work. And so perhaps Walker Percy's fiction needs a new image: not opposing poles or equilateral triangles but a mandala which, as an emblem of integration and wholeness, cannot be bisected.

J. GERALD KENNEDY

The Sundered Self and the Riven World: *Love in the Ruins*

WALKER PERCY likes to compare his role as a novelist with that of the physician or diagnostician: he probes to discover "what went wrong" and tries to identify the illness. In Percy's first two novels, the illness belongs to a young, disaffected southerner, searching for clues to his past and for access to the spiritual order of existence. But his third novel, *Love in the Ruins*, broadens considerably the scope of his investigation. While the narrator-hero, Dr. Thomas More, suffers from a variety of illnesses, his chief disorder—"More's syndrome, or: chronic angelism-bestialism" (*LR*, 383)—typifies the ailment ravaging "our beloved old U.S.A." (*LR*, 17) and the entire "death dealing Western world." Even as More finds himself victimized by a schism between mind and body, he portrays a society riven by diametrically opposed forces: "race against race, right against left, believer against heathen" (*LR*, 17). Curiously, the political dichotomy mirrors the narrator's mind-body problem: "Conservatives have begun to fall victim to unseasonable rages, delusions of conspiracies, high blood pressure, and large-bowel complaints. Liberals are more apt to contract sexual impotence, morning terror, and a feeling of abstraction of the self from itself" (*LR*, 20). Thus Percy depicts the "Troubles" in American society essentially as a manifestation of the subject-object split which has been central to Western experience since the philosophy of Descartes and the beginning of the modern age. As this essay will suggest, the phenomenon that Percy calls the "Cartesian split" constitutes the philosphical crux of *Love in the Ruins* and forms the controlling metaphor of Tom More's vision of experience.

1

The problem of the divided self has long occupied a vital place in Western thought. According to the Judaeo-Christian tradition, the split between spirit and flesh occurred when man lost his innocence and wholeness of being in the Garden of Eden. The fall made man suddenly aware of a distance between himself and the created universe and of a distinction between the mind (the perceiving self) and the body (the perceived self). With characteristic simplicity the writer of Genesis describes the latter discovery: "Then the eyes of both [Adam and Eve] were opened and they knew that they were naked." At this moment, apparently, the two experienced their bodies as objects (sex objects, as it were) for the first time. Their coming-to-consciousness revealed their own nature and fostered at the same time a sense of homelessness and alienation, which Percy in "The Delta Factor" has called "the enduring symptom of man's estrangement from God" (*MB*, 23).

The Greeks also came upon a distinction between mind or spirit (as in the Latin *animus*) and body when they discovered the faculty of reason. In *Irrational Man*, William Barrett notes that "in Plato, the rational consciousness as such becomes, for the first time in human history, a differentiated psychic function." However, Barrett notes, Plato's realization marked a change in man's concept of the self: "The Greeks' discovery represents an immense and necessary step forward by mankind, but also a loss, for the pristine wholeness of man's being is thereby sundered or at least pushed into the background." Plato's myth of the soul in *Phaedrus* graphically illustrates the perceived disjunction of the self, since (in Barrett's words) "reason, as the divine part of man, is separated, is indeed of another nature from the animal within him." [1] In both the Greek and the Judaeo-Christian traditions, we may conclude, the acquisition of rational consciousness implied a literal fragmentation of being; thought and feeling became distinguishable phenomena as the self discovered itself.

With the philosophy of René Descartes, however, the mind-body duality became a virtual dissociation. Identifying the act of thinking as the central proof of one's existence, Descartes argued in his *Meditations*: "It is certain that I [that is, my mind, by which I am what I am] is entirely and truly distinct from my body, and may exist without it." [2] He thus reduced physical man to an automaton whose various functions (such as the circulation of the blood) might be readily distinguished from the operations of the soul (thought). Ironically, while Descartes intended to reaffirm the Christian doctrine of the soul's immortality, his work had the effect of diminishing traditional reverence for the "temple" of the soul, human flesh. The corporeal frame became a fascinating mechanism, and man became, in Gilbert Ryle's memorable phrase, "the ghost in the machine." Acknowledging the obvious impact of Cartesian thought, Walker Percy dates the devaluation of modern existence from that fateful moment when "the famous philosopher Descartes ripped body loose from mind and turned the very soul into a ghost that haunts its own house" (*LR*, 191).

Nearly all of Percy's writing, fictional and nonfictional, in some sense seeks to answer the rhetorical questions that introduce "The Delta Factor": "Why does man feel so sad in the twentieth century? Why does man feel so bad in the very age when, more than in any other age, he has succeeded in satisfying his needs and making over the world for his own use?"

(*MB*, 3). Although Percy offers a variety of explanations for this predicament—from secularism to the loss of individual sovereignty—his diagnosis of the contemporary malaise frequently hinges on the problem of the divided self. According to Percy, modern man has been victimized by his willingness to accept the Cartesian view of man as an object to be understood and explained empirically. Repeatedly the author attempts to break through the rigid Cartesian distinctions between subject and object by reminding us of man's peculiar nature: of his susceptibility to alienation, of his queer habits of naming and symbol-mongering, of his refusal to behave like "an organism in an environment." A scientific thinker conscious of the limits of science, Percy contends that an objective-empirical theory of man inevitably ignores the mystery of being. Such an objectification must ultimately produce a schism between one's theoretical understanding of human nature and one's immediate, inscrutable, creaturely feelings. As *Love in the Ruins* illustrates, this alienation of mind from body sunders the individual into a "mythical monster, half angel, half beast, but no man" (*LR*, 383).

Popular faith in scientific theory has spawned a variety of other maladies, according to Percy. He observes in "The Delta Factor" that contemporary discussion of man as "a sociological unit, an uncultured creature, a psychological organism" makes no provision for the individual being: "Science cannot utter a single word about an individual molecule, thing, or creature insofar as it is an individual but only insofar as it is like other individuals" (*MB*, 22). Immersed in a scientific culture, modern man therefore risks a loss of self, an erosion of his inherent sense of individuality, which results in a feeling of anonymity. About this situation Percy remarks, "That is why people in the modern age took photographs by the million: to prove despite their deepest suspicions to the contrary that they were not invisible" (*MB*, 26).

Since a scientific culture orients itself primarily toward the normative needs of mass man in its products, advertising, and institutions, a further consequence of the objective-empirical perspective is the impoverishment of daily human experience; preoccupation with the external conditions of being finally produces a superficiality in the order of modern life. Whether this problem manifests itself as the "everydayness" encountered by Binx Bolling or the "ravening particles" of drabness glimpsed by Will Barrett and Tom More, Percy reminds us that if a person is to recover a fresh perception of the world, he must be prepared to circumvent established Cartesian modes of experiencing and understanding reality. Only then can he recover what Emerson called "an original relation with the universe." Only then can he redeem his existence from the patterns contrived by the engineers of human happiness. But until the denizen of the modern world discovers the spiritual bankruptcy of the objective-empirical world view, he cannot begin to guess the sources of his own unhappiness. He must continue to suffer from such maladies as alienation, anonymity, inauthenticity, and despair.

In several respects Percy's third novel, *Love in the Ruins*, brings to a focus his thinking about the Cartesian split and the consequences of living in a scientific culture dedicated to need-satisfaction. The "transcendence-immanence" conflict of Sutter Vaught in *The Last Gentleman* has become "chronic angelism-bestialism" for Tom More, but the issue remains the same: how to reconcile mind and body and recapture a sense of authenticity and wholeness about one's individual existence. In portraying More's quest for harmony of being, Percy offers his most complex and extensive diagnosis of the sundered self; his investigation in *Love in the Ruins* carries him into the diverse areas of science, religion, and history, in pursuit of a solution to the malaise of modern man.

2

The most zany aspect of More's quest is his effort to perfect a scientific instrument capable of healing "the secret ills of the spirit." Using the "More Quantitative—Qualitative Ontological Lapsometer," a device which can identify—in the manner of nineteenth-century phrenology—one's dominant cerebral center, the narrator hopes to treat "a person's innermost self." He describes the lapsometer as "the first caliper of the soul" by which he can measure "the length and breadth and motions of the very self" (*LR*, 106–107); with the right modifications, More believes that he can convert his diagnostic device into a therapeutic instrument. Through a dosage of "Heavy Sodium" or "Heavy Chloride" radiation, he hopes to treat the prevailing brain center and alleviate those excesses of the spirit which produce "angelism" and "bestialism." He openly aspires to correct the damage done by Descartes, exclaiming, "Suppose I could hit on the right dosage and weld the broken self whole!" (*LR*, 36).

No little irony attaches to More's grand design. A good portion of the novel, after all, satirizes the scientific community in general, and behaviorists of the B. F. Skinner stripe in particular, for blind allegiance to empirical methods at the expense of human sovereignty and dignity. Among the research facilities at Fedville, More singles out the Love Clinic (inspired by Masters and Johnson) and the Geriatrics Rehabilitation Center as dehumanizing operations. The narrator makes an impassioned stand against scientific impersonality when he defends the right of a geriatric patient to live out his life rather than be sent to the Happy Isles Separation Center. Yet his crusade against the brave new world of the social scientists rings hollow, for his own solution to the "deep perturbations of the soul"—lapsometer therapy—also involves a violation of the inner man. Even as he depicts a plastic, gadget-oriented world created by modern technology and a research complex dedicated to the behavioral conditioning of our most human responses, More unwittingly adopts an objective-empirical procedure to heal the Cartesian split.

The narrator's ironic position is never resolved in *Love in the Ruins*. Even after Art Immelmann, the Mephistophelian "liaison man" from Washington, has demonstrated the diabolical potential of the lapsometer, More retains a dauntless faith in his hardware. He announces in the epilogue: "Despite the setbacks of the past, particularly the fiasco five years ago, I still believe my lapsometer can save the world—if I can get it right" (*LR*, 382). But More will never get the lapsometer "right," for he has not yet recognized that its fearful power to reshape the human spirit rests in the hands of fallible men. As Hawthorne illustrated in "The Birthmark," no scientist, however wise, can conduct research on the human soul without destroying it. To violate the sanctity of the heart was for Hawthorne the most reprehensible sin; More seems bent on the same transgression, despite his consciousness of the ethical questions raised by modern scientific methods.

More's contradictory attitude apparently mirrors Percy's own ambivalence toward scientific technology. While he criticizes the "objective-empirical" mentality and shows how the "experts" have made the concrete existence almost inaccessible to the modern wayfarer, Percy deprecates the common man for his gullibility. In *Love in the Ruins* More claims that the problem "is not so much the fault of the scientist as it is the layman's canonization of the scientists" (*LR*, 7). In effect, Percy absolves the scientist (the seducer) from moral responsibility for his endeavors—a surprising position for a writer of Percy's theological inclinations. That position seemingly reflects a deep-seated scientific bias; Percy freely admits "My first enthusiasm was science, the scientific method, and I think it was a valuable experience . . . I am convinced of the value of the scientific vocation, of the practice of the scientific method."[3] But Percy is also painfully conscious of the various pitfalls of the scientific method; thus in "Culture: The Antinomy of the Scientific Method," he insists that the "scientists of man" must forego the luxury of a bisected reality, a world split between observers and data" (*MB*, 242). Such ambivalence leads to a certain evasiveness about the ultimate worth of the scientific method; whether mankind will be saved or destroyed by the continued domination of the scientific-technological establishment remains a clouded issue in his work.

Not surprisingly, then, More's continuing pursuit of a scientific solution to the Cartesian split raises several interpretive questions. Are we to perceive his dedication to the lapsometer as an ironic indication of his own limited vision or as a serious endorsement of the scientific vocation? Will the perfection of the lapsometer permit man to "reenter paradise" as a "whole and intact man-spirit," as More hopes, or will it deprive him of that which makes him truly human—the odd mixture of angel and beast? As Percy has suggested in several essays, scientific progress involves both gain and loss: the more of the world the scientist conquers in the name of knowledge, and the more he surrounds that conquered territory with cognitive theory, the less possible it becomes for the scientist to feel a part of that world, since his endeavors have widened the gap between subject and object. As More's satire of the Love Clinic and Geriatrics Rehabilitation suggests, scientific research to eliminate human unhappiness often has the reverse effect of intensifying boredom and discontent. Given the paradox inherent in Cartesian epistemology, it may well be that More retains his essential humanity at the end of the novel by virtue of the fact that he has not yet got his invention "right."

3

The very name of More's invention implies the second dimension of his quest, for the etymology of the word *lapsometer* demonstrates Percy's interest in theological problems. The author makes plain the religious implication in a conversation between More and the director of the Fedville hospital.

"What do you call this thing, Doctor?" the Director asks, exploring the device with his pencil.

"Lapsometer." I am unable to tear my eyes from his strong brown farmer's hands.

"The name interests me."

"Yes sir?"

"It implies, I take it, a lapse or fall."

"Yes," I say tonelessly.

"A fall perhaps from a state of innocence?"

"Perhaps." My foot begins to wag briskly. I stop it.

"Does this measure the uh depth of the fall?" (*LR*, 205)

While the director's reference to a "lapse or fall" here confirms the connection between More's device and man's first transgression in Eden, the narrator elsewhere offers a different explanation of the name: "Only in man does the self miss itself, *fall* from itself (hence lapsometer!)" (*LR*, 36). From these separate explications, we can infer that in measuring the dissociation between the two sides of the self, More in a sense empirically verifies man's fallen condition; his invention demonstrates that the split recognized by Descartes derives ultimately from Adam's mythic misdeed and that the problem of the sundered self is more properly a spiritual than a psychophysical phenomenon.

Percy also signals the theological aspect of More's quest through his constant verbal play on the name of the narrator's subdivision—Paradise Estates. Standing between the town, peopled by "all manner of conservative folk," and the swamp, crawling with "dropouts from and castoffs of and rebels against our society," Paradise Estates constitutes a middle ground: "a paradise indeed, an oasis of concord in a troubled land" (*LR*, 17). Insulated (until the Bantu revolt) from the political and social realities of the rest of the world, the subdivision approximates a modern conception of heaven: "Everything is lovely and peaceful here. Towhees whistle in the azaleas. Golfers hum up and down the fairways in their quaint surrey-like carts.

Householders mow their lawns, bestriding tiny burro-size trac-
tors" (*LR*, 174). But when More diagnoses the "frigidity and
morning terror" of a female resident, he finds her "terrified by
her well-nigh perfect life, really death in life, in Paradise, where
all her needs were satisfied and all she had to do was play golf
and bridge and sit around the clubhouse watching swim-meets
and the Christian baton twirlers" (*LR*, 199). Through such reve-
lations, More exposes Paradise Estates as a technological parody
of Eden, an ironic symbol of human longing for prelapsarian
happiness. The conveniences and comforts of modern suburbia
have led only to a numbing existence, the more deadly because
its inhabitants live with the myth that paradise can be regained
in "the good life."

As most readers readily perceive, *Love in the Ruins* is rife
with Edenic themes and allusions. Percy clearly casts More as
an American Adam (in the tradition described by R. W. B.
Lewis), who in the course of the novel succumbs to the tempta-
tions of a satanic figure, sees a vision of hell in an amphitheater
called The Pit, and ultimately loses his home in Paradise. But
if we accept the seriousness of Percy's allegorical design, *Love
in the Ruins* amounts to a substantiation of the "fortunate fall"
theory. Delivered from the deadening confines of Paradise, More
ironically recovers health, happiness, and religion in the old
slave quarters near the bayou.

The narrator's recovery from waywardness and spiritual
confusion evolves through a series of overtly symbolic scenes.
As the novel opens, More describes himself as a "bad Catholic"
who has "stopped eating Christ in Communion, stopped going
to mass, and . . . fallen into a disorderly life" (*LR*, 6). En route
to the Center with news of the impending Bantu revolution,
however, More has a religious experience of sorts in the Little
Napoleon bar: "In the dark mirror there is a dim hollow-eyed
Spanish Christ. The pox is spreading on his face. Vacuoles are
opening in his chest. It is the new Christ, the spotted Christ, the

maculate Christ, the sinful Christ. The old Christ died for our sins and it didn't work, we were not reconciled. The new Christ shall reconcile man with his sins" (*LR*, 153). The image, of course, is More's own. Infused with the hope of healing "the soul of Western man," the narrator lapses into a reverie that discloses both the angelism of the abstracted scientist and the spiritual predicament of the layman in the post-Christian epoch. The concept of goodness has become so problematical that only a "maculate Christ" can be understood by the present age. More's fantasy becomes an expression of the need for and the desire to become the new messiah; but it is also a recognition of the illness of modern man, a spiritual malaise objectified by the "pox" and "vacuoles." As physician and "new Christ," More apparently intends at this point to heal himself, and mankind as well.

More's figurative death and rebirth, perhaps the most blatant symbolism in all of Percy's fiction, occurs when Uru, the black militant, locks the narrator in an abandoned Catholic church. More escapes from this mausoleum of lost faith through an air-conditioning duct which in Freudian terms he compares to the uterus and to paradise. In darkness "black as the womb," he muses that "refrigeration must be one of the attributes of heaven" (*LR*, 310). However, the fate of Adam, reenacted biologically in the trauma of birth, necessitates expulsion from the womb-paradise. Pushing through a loose panel, More delivers himself from the darkness: "Out I come feet-first, born again, ejected into the hot bright perilous world" (*LR*, 311).

The narrator's reentry into the world of experience happens, significantly, as the "final major chord of *White Christmas*" resounds from the carillon of the church. This coincidence appears to substantiate the Christian implications of More's rebirth, but it reminds us simultaneously of the secularization— in Percy's view, the impoverishment—of religion in contemporary society. Being "born again" seems to have lost its radical meaning; indeed, that may be the ironic point of Percy's painfully obvious allegory, for More's rebirth, despite its apparent symbolic importance, produces no dramatic revival of faith. Only as a representation of More's response to institutional religion does the event possess Christian meaning; his deliverance literally involves an escape from a dead church, a reminder perhaps of Kierkegaard's persistent struggle with established Christendom.

But if More's ordeal assumes false significance as a New Testament ritual of rebirth, it embodies, on another level, a revealing Old Testament motif. More makes his way out of the air conditioning duct, his dark, cool paradise, using the sword of St. Michael (removed from a religious statue) as a makeshift screwdriver. According to Milton's account of the fall, St. Michael is the archangel who escorts Adam and Eve out of the garden. But he subsequently performs a more complex task, offering the fallen couple an insight into the spiritual purpose of suffering and counseling them to learn "true patience" and practice moderation. Although More experiences no such meeting with the archangel, he does, after wielding St. Michael's sword, eventually amend his own life. He forsakes his lovers, Moira and Lola, to marry his Presbyterian nurse, Ellen, and he finally accepts the limited happiness of a more moderate and orderly existence, returning, in the epilogue, to the religion he had lost years before.

Five years after the main action of the novel takes place, More goes back to the church on Christmas eve to confess his sins, perform an act of penance, and take Communion. He offers the reader a key to the meaning of the ritual when, in an earlier passage, he speaks of his travels with Doris, his first wife, and of his delight in seeking out "some forlorn little Catholic church" every Sunday morning: "Here off I-51 I touched the thread in the labyrinth, and the priest announced the turkey raffle and Wednesday bingo and preached the gospel and fed me Christ"

(*LR*, 254). More's "touching the thread in the labyrinth" serves the mystical function of uniting mind and body: "It took religion to save me from the spirit world, from orbiting the earth like Lucifer and the angels . . . it took nothing less than touching the thread off the misty interstates and eating Christ himself to make me mortal man again and let me inhabit my own flesh and love [Doris] in the morning" (*LR*, 254). Thus at the end of *Love in the Ruins* when More takes Communion, he once again touches the vital thread which can bring the sundered self together. In Kierkegaardian terms, the mass becomes a "repetition," a moment of spiritual awareness occasioned by a sudden recovery of past experience. In ritual, More rediscovers a source of wholeness, a means of reconciling the self with itself and of continuity, a means of uniting himself with a chain of believers the first of whom were the disciples.

To disguise the conventionality of More's return to faith, Percy portrays him at the end of the novel incongruously barbecuing turkey in his sackcloth, sipping Early Times bourbon, and singing "old Sinatra songs." But the narrator's new perspective is plain enough; he now spends his time "watching and waiting and thinking and working" (*LR*, 382). Specifically, he waits for the Second Coming. When Colley Wilkes, the "super Bantu" birdwatcher, announces that the rare ivory-billed woodpecker—called the "Lord-to-God"—has come back "after all these years," More describes a second religious reverie, the counterpart of his "Spanish Christ" fantasy: "This morning, hauling up a great unclassified beast of a fish, I thought of Christ coming again at the end of the world and how it is that in every age there is the temptation to see signs of the end and that, even knowing this, there is nevertheless some reason, what with the spirit of the new age being the spirit of watching and waiting, to believe that—" (*LR*, 387). The wish remains unstated and unfulfilled. But it seems an index of More's spiritual progress that he no longer casts himself in the role of messiah. Though Christ has not yet come again, More's recovery of faith has at least granted him more peace and serenity than he has known in years. His recovery of the thread in the labyrinth has evidently mitigated his "chronic angelism-bestialism" and enabled him to relish the paradoxical freedom of life in the slave quarters.

4

While Tom More regards the sundered self alternately as a psychophysical disorder and as a spiritual malaise, he also understands the split as a product of historical processes. According to Toynbee's *A Study of History*—a work of evident importance to Percy's narrator—the disintegration of a civilization tends to manifest itself in individual and social schisms; More is thus to some extent a victim of historical destiny. But as an adherent of Toynbee's cyclical theory, the narrator also founds his hope for deliverance partially upon history itself, believing that the end of an age dominated by Cartesian thought may produce a new theory of man based on the sovereignty and wholeness of the individual. This historical sense creates a consequent ambivalence in the narrator; though he outwardly dreads the "catastrophe" threatening Western man and struggles (however ineffectually) to prevent it, he secretly longs for disaster and the new beginning it might provide.

Woven into the fabric of the novel is the narrator's persistent sense of cyclical destiny. The opening scene finds More sitting under a tree "waiting for the end of the world" and pondering the possibility that "God has at last removed his blessing from the U.S.A. and what we feel now is just the clank of the old historical machinery, the sudden jerking ahead of the roller-coaster cars as the chain catches hold and carries us back into history with its ordinary catastrophes" (*LR*, 3–4). More's ambiguity in this passage exposes the limitation of the human view of history: we are unable to distinguish "the end of the world" from one of the "ordinary catastrophes" of civilization.

Nonetheless, the roller-coaster proves a felicitous metaphor for history since its structure physically suggests the rise and fall of empire and the idea of cyclical movement which returns inevitably to the point of origin. This idea corresponds to T. S. Eliot's discovery in "East Coker":

What we call the beginning is often the end
And to make an end is to make a beginning.
The end is where we start from.

More likewise understands his existence in terms of temporal paradox: his anguished "sense of an ending" (to use Frank Kermode's phrase) is balanced against his anticipation of the age to come.

The dying age, according to More, was first ushered in by the emergence of modern science in the seventeenth century. Heralded by the *Discourse* of Descartes, this epoch reached a momentous juncture in the first World War; in "The Delta Factor" Percy baldly asserts, "The old modern age ended in 1914" (*MB*, 27). Affected by his reading of Stedmann's *History of World War I*, Tom More says of the same year: "Here began the hemorrhage and death by suicide of the old Western world: white Christian Caucasian Europeans, sentimental music-loving Germans and rational clear-minded Frenchmen, slaughtering each other without passion" (*LR*, 47). Stedmann's devastating account of Verdun leads More to observe ironically that "the slaughter at Verdun was an improvement" over the less effective warfare of the nineteenth century. Verdun epitomizes for the narrator both the potential destructiveness of technology and the futility of modern experience. For as More recognizes, these soldiers fought "without passion" not so much to annihilate each other as to destroy the deadly boredom of their own lives: "For fifty years following the Battle of Verdun, French and German veterans used to return every summer to seek out the trench where they spent the summer of 1916. Why did they choose the very domicile of death? Was there life here?" (*LR*, 190). The story of the returning troops strikes More deeply because he too senses that "the dying are alive and the living are dead," even in Louisiana.

More's vision of disintegration parallels the theories of Toynbee in striking ways. The implied relationship between the sundered self and the riven world in *Love in the Ruins* seems a fictional projection of the "schism in the soul" and the "schism in the body social" by which Toynbee identifies a disintegrating civilization. The schisms are closely related; the social dichotomy, according to Toynbee, becomes an "outward and visible sign of an inward and spiritual rift." The denizens of a crumbling culture may experience this latter split as an inner conflict between "abandon" and "self-control"; between a "sense of drift" and a "sense of sin"; or between "archaism" and "futurism." All of these responses, Toynbee argues in Volumes V and VI of *A Study of History*, reveal an absence of imagination and growth; in essence, they amount to active or passive alternatives to creative human behavior.[4] This dialectic seems fully consistent with Percy's critique of American society and Western civilization. The stereotyped Knothead proctologists and Leftpapa psychologists of *Love in the Ruins* look to the past and the future, respectively, but fail to articulate a humanly constructive response to the present.

In fundamental ways, the narrator's actions also illustrate the polarities of the "schism in the soul." That More's "disorderly life" as Don Giovanni reflects the principle of "abandon" seems clear enough; yet his battle with Art Immelmann and his subsequent marriage to Ellen represent an effort to discipline the passions and exercise a modicum of "self-control." Similarly, More is caught between a "sense of drift" and a "sense of sin"; he feels powerless to halt the "forces of evil" at large in society and to some extent participates in the decadence, but he feels guilt, finally, for his failure to "master and control the soul's own self" (in Toynbee's words), and so goes to confession.

His response to cultural crisis also reflects aspects of both "archaism" and "futurism." The narrator frequently reverts to the past when confronted by contemporary chaos: he recalls idyllic love-making with Doris, his erstwhile "Apple Queen," his horseplay with Samantha, the fated daughter, and his life in the old "auto age" before vines covered shopping plazas and the pool at Howard Johnson's turned "an opaque jade green, a bad color for pools." More feels drawn also to the Middle Ages and the unclouded moral certainty of his namesake, Sir Thomas More, who likewise dreamed of a simpler, utopian existence. And he further yearns for the prelapsarian harmony of Eden, the third focus of his archaistic imagination. With the lapsometer, he hopes to enable man "to reenter paradise, so to speak," and return in effect to an earlier, beatific phase of human history.

But More's own experience ultimately discloses the futility of archaism (Paradise Estates proves a false utopia) and causes him to look to the future for deliverance from the present. Toynbee observes that "it is only when this archaistic line of escape has been tried in vain" or rejected as intrinsically impossible that the soul will "nerve itself to take the less natural line of futurism."[5] And so More watches and waits for the end of the world, focusing his chiliastic hopes on the Second Coming. But his persistent references to catastrophe imply another futuristic solution to his problem; as noted earlier, More covertly longs for the sort of disaster that might reshape the human order and resolve the "schism in the soul."

For if More's experience has taught him anything, it is that accidents and catastrophes have the effect of confirming the wonder of existence and enabling us to "come to ourselves." An unexpected recovery of self occurs when More tries to escape his depression through suicide: "One morning—was it Christmas morning after listening to Perry Como?—my wrists were cut and bleeding. Seeing the blood, I came to myself, saw myself as itself and the world for what it is, and began to love life" (*LR*, 97). Percy's refrain—coming to one's self—seems to imply a reconciliation of mind and body, a sudden recovery of spiritual wholeness. On such terms More can accept the collapse of Western civilization—which on one level he dreads—as a potentially salutary experience. Notwithstanding its frightening aspects, disaster has the effect of making life more "real," of generating vitality, and of clarifying purposes and values. As Percy observes in "The Man on the Train," the question "what if the Bomb should fall" really misses the point of the modern predicament: "The real anxiety question, the question no one asks because no one wants to, is the reverse: What if the Bomb should *not* fall? What then?" (*MB*, 85). At least the Bomb, the threat of disaster, affords man some means of recovering the "wonder and delight" of existence. For Percy, catastrophe implies both desolation and redemption, for only through loss can we regain an awareness of the mystery of being.

To illustrate the regenerative aspect of catastrophe, Percy juxtaposes the dramatic action of *Love in the Ruins* against the steady, silent incursion of the wild vines. For Tom More, the vines furnish tangible evidence of cultural disintegration: he discovers them pushing through the rotting top of an Impala convertible, invading the bar of the Paradise Country Club, and menacing his mother's backyard. At one point he notes with apparent alarm "a particularly malignant vine" which has laid hold of a garden statue of St. Francis. However, in "The Man on the Train," Percy affirms that "the heart's desire of the alienated man is to see vines sprouting through the masonry" (*MB*, 84). One suspects that, beneath his surface concern, More too shares a secret delight in the mutability of human structures and sees the vines as a symbol of life and growth. Significantly, he uses vine imagery in the last paragraph of the novel to describe a loving embrace with Ellen: "To bed we go for a long winter's nap, twined about each other as the ivy twineth" (*LR*, 403). Although the vines initially threaten More, they finally seem to represent the possibility of regeneration in the ruins of what Ezra Pound called "a botched civilization."

Thus through historical change, More hopes to be saved from history. It is his fate (and perhaps our own as well) to live in a period of cultural breakdown, to experience the "schism in the body social," and to discover a corresponding rift in his own soul. But if the course of history is cyclical, as Toynbee (and his predecessor, Oswald Spengler) asserted, then a final collapse might well usher in a new age of creativity, growth, and spiritual renewal. Indeed, the same theory of disaster and recovery underlies the conception of *Love in the Ruins*; in "Notes for a Novel about the End of the World," Percy suggests: "Perhaps it is only through the conjuring up of catastrophe, the destruction of all Exxon signs, and the sprouting of vines in the church pews, that the novelist can make vicarious use of catastrophe in order that he and his reader may come to themselves" (*MB*, 118).

5

In the epilogue to *Love in the Ruins*, Tom More has apparently "come to himself" without the aid of a global catastrophe. Indeed, More refers casually to the crisis five years earlier as a "fiasco"; Bantu militants have been transformed by oil profits into Bantu golfers, who furiously attack the back nine clad in knickerbockers and English golf caps pulled down to their eyebrows. The political turmoil has also subsided: Knotheads have moved to "safe Knothead havens" like Cicero and Hattiesburg, while Leftpapas have flocked to Berkeley and Madison. But whatever the satiric purpose of such resolutions, the epilogue creates an idyllic perspective seemingly at the expense of the novel's integrity. In effect, More invalidates his own earlier vision of things, shifting his narrative out of the eschatological mode to create what Frank Kermode calls a "disconfirmation" of apocalypse.[6] He produces this falsification by collapsing the "riven world" theme, trivializing the social and political conflicts which had seemed so momentous. For example, the race issue ceases to matter when Percy depicts the black man as a parody of the white status-seeker, his historical predicament utterly forgotten. Tom More simultaneously advances a mawkish theory of poverty: "All any man needs is time and desire and the sense of his own sovereignty. As Kingfish Huey Long used to say: every man a king. I am a poor man but a kingly one. If you want and wait and work, you can have" (*LR*, 382). That is, differences in power, opportunity, and ideology vanish if one works hard and savors his disinheritance.

It seems clear that Percy regards the schism in the social structure as a superficial manifestation of the split within the individual. That split, "the modern Black Death . . . chronic angelism-bestialism," continues to afflict the world, but Percy's narrator has apparently found a solution. His leap into faith, which parallels developments in Percy's first two novels, seems to derive in part from the writings of Kierkegaard and Marcel. But a more likely inspiration for More's recovery of self is Toynbee's theory of "palingenesis" or rebirth. In *A Study of History*, Toynbee describes transfiguration, "illustrated by the light of Christianity," as the only authentic solution to personal fragmentation. This mystical transcendence may require a compound movement of withdrawal followed by return—a period of meditation in exile followed by a reentry into the world of men.[7] Significantly, Percy's narrator refers to the same passage early in *Love in the Ruins*: "Toynbee, I believe, speaks of the Return, of the man who fails and goes away, is exiled, takes counsel with himself, hits on something, sees daylight—and returns to triumph" (*LR*, 25). The remark is more than a scholarly allusion; it prefigures the outcome of the novel and identifies a major theoretical substructure. It suggests that even as Percy explores the problems of the sundered self and the riven world, he has in mind a specific conclusion—the "palin-genesis" of Toynbee as an archetype of redemption.

The author's conceptual design has important consequences for the representation of character. In "Notes for a Novel about the End of the World," Percy recalls with apparent approbation Flannery O'Connor's explanation for the bizarre types in her fiction: "for the near-blind you have to draw very large, simple caricatures" (*MB*, 118). Though Percy disparages "edifying" fiction, his commitment to Christian eschatology inevitably binds him to a didactic program and governs his representation of experience. Indeed, his predilection for the split-metaphor seems to reflect his desire to create "very large, simple caricatures," who, whatever else they may be, present themselves as angels, beasts, or some combination of the two. Although the technique enables him to investigate, in clinical fashion, the peculiar relationship between spirit and flesh, it leads likewise to an oversimplification of human personality. Thus, while Percy asks us to take seriously the angelism-bestialism of Tom More and supplies the salient facts of his life, the narrator remains curiously remote and fantastic; he speaks of pain but never seems to feel it. Part of the difficulty stems from metaphorical overkill, in which angelism and bestialism lose their evocative qualities, becoming mere figures in an equation. Faced with a similar problem in *Steppenwolf*, Herman Hesse rejected the simplicity of the wolf-man metaphor as a way of describing the suffering of Harry Haller:

For there is not a single human being, not even the primitive negro, not even the idiot, who is so conveniently simple that his being can be explained as the sum of two or three principal elements; and to explain so complex a man as Harry by the artless division into wolf and man is a hopelessly childish attempt. Harry consists of a hundred or a thousand selves, not of two. His life oscillates, as everyone's does, not merely between two poles, such as the body and the spirit, the saint and the sinner, but between thousands, between innumerable poles.[8]

Half-man and half-caricature, Percy's Tom More is too complex to be understood in terms of the metaphor by which he persistently attempts to explain himself.

Why then does Percy make such extensive use of the split-metaphor? Surely, one factor is the eschatological motive, the desire to represent modern man as a creature torn asunder, in need of wholeness and vision. But a more important clue may come from the metaphor Percy uses to describe his vocation: the novelist as diagnostician. Percy's characters, frequently described in physiological terms, fall readily into categories (the Knothead proctologist, the Leftpapa behaviorist, etc.); they exist not as human beings but as completely predictable organisms in an environment. Even a major character can be described as the locus of certain symptoms. That is, of course, the very truth Percy seeks to disclose—that twentieth-century man has willingly traded his soul to satisfy needs and has thus surrendered his individuality. But this revelation, the product of Percy's scientific training, his passion for ideas, and his pursuit of a "theory of man" within the context of Christian belief, comes to us finally not as the confession of a fellow sufferer but as the clinical diagnosis of an angel orbiting the earth.

WILLIAM LEIGH GODSHALK

Love in the Ruins: Thomas More's Distorted Vision

IN THE ESSAY "Notes for a Novel about the End of the World," Walker Percy discusses his ideas about a serious novel describing "the passing of one age and the beginning of another" (*MB*, 114). The novelist, Percy thinks, is a quasi-prophet who "writes about the coming end in order to warn about present ills and so avert the end" (*MB*, 101). His vision testifies "to a species of affliction which sets him apart and gives him an odd point of view. The wounded man has a better view of the battle than those still shooting" (*MB*, 101). Percy's essay, written some five years before *Love in the Ruins*, suggests his general theory about what and how the novelist who can see signs of the end should write. In *Love in the Ruins* Percy follows the essay's prescriptions, but with certain modifications. One rather improbable (and therefore intriguing) modification is that, while Percy says that the novelist as quasi-prophet necessarily speaks from an odd point of view, in this apocalyptic novel he chooses a narrator whose point of view is not just odd; it is unreliable. We see all the action from the perspective of Tom More—drunkard, psychotic, and semilapsed Catholic. Thus, though Percy planned for his third novel to embody the quasi-prophetic insights of the eschatological novelist, he chose to relate those insights through a narrator whose own vision is distorted by alcohol, neuroses, and guilt. We may understand more clearly how Percy's art works if we take a close look at the complex ways in which More distorts reality and if we speculate about the possible origins and implications of More's distorted vision.

First, More's ability to discriminate and to narrate simple facts accurately is decidedly suspect.[1] More remarks, "As best I can piece out the Colonel's rambling, almost incoherent account, the following events took place earlier this morning," and at the same time decides, "There is no reason to doubt their accuracy" (*LR*, 283). The juxtaposition of the incoherent Colonel Ringo and More's assurance is puzzling, and More himself has already described the Colonel as a much distracted old man with one eye "turned out ninety degrees" (*LR*, 282). Why should the reader believe that this overwrought old man with impaired vision is an accurate observer and narrator? The answer of course is that the reader would be wrong to do so, and More's rapid acceptance of the authority of the "rambling, almost incoherent" story gives the reader an insight into More's difficulties in assessing reality. To corroborate the Colonel's story, More acknowledges that he "witnessed the beginning of the incident" (*LR*, 283), and then admits that he thought the discharging of celebratory firecrackers was actually rifle fire (*LR*, 284). More's admission undercuts his credibility as a verifying witness and accurate narrator.

Throughout the novel, More exhibits his inability to get things straight. He tells us that Lola occupies room 205 of the deserted Howard Johnson's motel (*LR*, 8), but later when he sees a "blurred oval in the window of room 203," he believes it is "Lola" (*LR*, 46). Actually room 203 is Ellen's. Later, More writes that the Bledsoes have lived in their "Spanish stucco" house for "fifty years" (*LR*, 98), although in a later passage he says, "Yonder in the streaked stucco house dwelled the child-less Bledsoes for thirty years" (*LR*, 246). The latter number, thirty years, is correct, if we may believe More's assertion that he visited the area "as a boy while the house was a-building" (*LR*, 246). Since More is forty-five, such a visit would have been impossible had the house been fifty years old.

The reader may be amused to trace More's slips, trying to verify his assertions, calculating his accuracy in details, catching his mistakes. That Percy has underlined the inaccuracy of his narrator is hardly to be doubted. As the novel nears its conclusion, More admits that he is more than normally "confused and exhausted" (*LR*, 350). He has a hard time getting his bearings, and—"somewhat confused"—he examines the contents of his "pockets to get a line on the significance of the past and the hope of the future" (*LR*, 364). For the present, he is lost, overwhelmed by the flux of reality.

Like the equally confused Hamlet who is also confronted by a metaphysical identity crisis, More is a constant questioner. His questions seem attempts to "get a line on" the present: "Did I remember to put pistol in bag?" (*LR*, 105). "Why am I so jumpy?" (*LR*, 174). "Where are the dogs?" (*LR*, 142). "Did Max give me a shot?" (*LR*, 362). "Is it possible to live without feasting on death?" (*LR*, 374). The questions are aimed at himself, his environment, his beliefs; they apparently arise from two aspects of More's personality. First, he is basically insecure and unsure of himself. Since he lacks an integrated selfhood, everything comes to him in a questionable shape. In *The Message in the Bottle* Percy discusses the poorly integrated self and the results of that "monstrous bifurcation of man into angelic and bestial components." He explains that the fragmented person could not "take account of God, the devil, and the angels if they were standing before him, because he has already peopled the universe with his own hierarchies" (*MB*, 113). A bifurcated world not only obscures truth but also spawns illusions. The world More lives in then is both fragmented and phantasmagorical.

More's insecurity takes a second, more positive form, however, as intellectual curiosity. He never accepts an *apparent* reality without question. Paradoxically, his weakness can be his strength. As a medical diagnostician, he is a genius; as a man, he is filled with terror of an unknown and, perhaps to him, an unknowable reality. This terror leads More to a peculiar and yet not totally unique way of dealing with reality. He has a penchant for using similes; and through his use of the simile, he transforms his world into a romantically more acceptable place. The Pit scene will serve as an example of More's habit of imposing an incongruous series of romantic similes on reality: "The seats of The Pit slope steeply to a small sunken arena, a miniature of the bullring at Pamplona. . . . My one small success in The Pit might be compared to a single well-executed *estocada* by an obscure matador" (*LR*, 198). The students "roost like chickens along the steep slopes"; Max Gottlieb sits "erect as a young prince, light glancing from his forehead" (*LR*, 218), reminding us of Buddha. More enters "like a relief pitcher beginning the long trek from the left-field bullpen" (*LR*, 219). The Director is "like the ancient mariner"(*LR*, 224); Buddy Brown, "like a cowboy bulldogging a steer" (*LR*, 225); Mr. Ives, "like a jake-legged sailor" (*LR*, 231); and Helga Heine, "like Brunhilde" (*LR*, 236). The Pit is finally "like a den of vipers" (*LR*, 240).

Certainly these comparisons reflect the range and power of Percy's imagination, and they further confirm his assumption that the beauty of analogy may be "proportionate to its wrongness or outlandishness" (*MB*, 66). But from another viewpoint, they testify to Percy's consciousness that, though a linguistic analogy may, as he says in "Metaphor as Mistake," make knowing possible, it may also interfere with knowing. That seems to be what happens in The Pit scene; for the reality of The Pit is so distorted by the superimposition of romantic imagery that we cannot be sure what does happen. Certainly the scene becomes anything but what it is, a place for good-natured medical high jinks; More transforms the scene in The Pit into a possibly crucial occurrence in his nation's history—and he cannot allow himself the comic perspective.

Nor can More allow himself, insecure as he is, to take responsibility for his own disaster. When the horseplay of The Pit turns into a sexual orgy, he claims that there has been diabolical interference; Max, on the other hand, believes More's own "gift for hypnotherapy" is to blame (*LR*, 359). Apparently, no one but More has observed Art Immelmann's mass distribution of lapsometers, and we should at least consider the possibility that More has here "peopled the universe with his own hierarchies." Perhaps More's paranoia has (if you will) hypnotized him into seeing a merely irritating man as an embodiment of the devil himself. If so, vehicle has obliterated tenor, and an outlandish simile has become not a way of knowing but a way to self-deception.

Analogy seems to work similarly in More's private life as a means of denying and evading his own experience. He heightens the quotidian reality of conjugal existence by the eclectic use of religious myth. "Women are mythical creatures," he tells us. "They have no more connection with the ordinary run of things than do centaurs" (*LR*, 89). Doris, his first wife, "became a priestess of the high places," while at the same time she looks "like long-thighed Mercury, god of morning" (*LR*, 64, 65). Alistair, Doris's English boyfriend, flexes "as gracefully as Michelangelo's Adam touching God's hand . . . extending his golden Adam's hand and touching me" (*LR*, 270–71). Through his continued use of simile, More's homelife is projected as a strange concatenation of Hebrew, Classical, and Christian myth. The extraordinary will help to save him from the ordinary reality which he seems to fear and with which he cannot cope.

More's fundamental way of dealing with the pressure of reality is a variant of his transformation of the world through similes. If we are careful with the concept, perhaps we can see More's tendency to heighten, distort, and schematize reality as a mythmaking process. For example, the Myth of Foundation (which may derive from Faulkner) is basic to More's vision of the United States not as "any other country" but as a "new Eden" blessed by the deity. More imagines God saying, "it is yours because you're the apple of my eye; because you the lordly Westerners . . . believed in me and in the outlandish Jewish Event even though you were nowhere near it and had to hear the news of it from strangers. . . . And all you had to do was pass one little test, which was surely child's play for you because you had already passed the big one. One little test: here's a helpless man in Africa, all you have to do is not violate him" (*LR*, 57). Western man promptly flunks his historic examination. With More's mythic statement, compare Percy's statement in propria persona in "Notes for a Novel": "White Americans have sinned against the Negro from the beginning and continue to do so, initially with cruelty and presently with an indifference which may be even more destructive" (*MB*, 117). The baldness of Percy's statement contrasts strikingly with More's ornate myth of national loss, though the ideas expressed are similar. For More, the myth of the fall from grace stands as a buffer between him and the sordid simplicity of "cruelty" and "indifference."

If More sees American history in mythic terms, he also heightens his own past into a particular myth of death and loss—the death of his daughter and wife, his loss of direction. Samantha's death seems to have been the unbearable reality that pushed More into his role as mythmaker. Her death has become a way of finding himself; he recovers the "self" through participating in the "ordeal" of her dying. After considering her death, he asks, "Is it possible to live without feasting on death?"

(*LR*, 374). The phrasing reminds us of More's emphasis on "eating Christ," on the Eucharist, and suggests that in More's vision Samantha's death is rather closely linked with Christ's. In a way, More's concept of life-in-death and life-through-death is an extension of the Christian mythos by which the true believer gains the fullness of life through participation in Christ's sacrificial death. The old man dies; the new man is reborn. Thus More expects Samantha's death, like Christ's sacrifice, to anchor him to life. But More's myth—one might call it his obsession with the death-dealing Western civilization—fails since it precludes his full participation in life. Perhaps also it fails because More is making a false analogy, or rather, a false theology.

Similarly, More's mythologizing of his own past seems to deny him access to his immediate experience. Waiting for Moira to shower in the ruined motel, More thinks not of Moira but of "Doris, my dead wife who ran off to Cozumel with a heathen Englishman" (*LR*, 253). Holding Moira in his arms, he thinks of Samantha's first abortive date, and while he is answering Ellen's questions, he is reminded "of Samantha, who used to come home from school letter-perfect in her catechism and ask me to hear her nevertheless" (*LR*, 260, 350). No matter how More may mythologize the past, the past haunts him and keeps him from participating fully in the present. His awareness is blocked; the death myths of the past throw their shadow on his present life.

Further, it may be argued that the geography of More's world is his fictive construct, shaped by his preoccupation with the past. More remembers that he and Doris and Samantha used to travel together in the old Auto Age. On Sunday mornings, he and Samantha would leave "the coordinate of the motel at the intersection of the interstates," and descend "through a moonscape countryside" to a Catholic church in a small town. A type of Theseus seeking escape, More "touched the thread in the labyrinth." He returned to the motel "exhilarated by—

what? by eating Christ or by the secret discovery of the singular thread in this the unlikeliest of places, this geometry of Holiday Inns and interstates?" More mythologizes the landscape into moonscape and labyrinth, but more significant is the way his imagination fixes the interstates into a geometric figure of four quadrants with a motel at the center. The intersecting highways are schematized as "interstates extending infinitely in all directions, abcissa and ordinate" (*LR*, 254).

This description from the past has its echo in the present, for More *imposes the same kind of scheme on the present landscape.* Because of his attachment to the past, to his Sunday mornings with Samantha, he lifts the geometric model from a bygone time and constructs his contemporary world according to its form. Intersecting highways (Interstate 11 running north and south [*LR*, 258], and an undesignated interstate running east and west)[2] neatly quarter More's world into four symbolic parts. The very neatness of the scheme indicates that it is More's imposition, not an accurate vision of reality. The ruined Howard Johnson's motel, a focal point of the immediate action, is just inside the southwest quadrant which also contains Paradise Estates, where More lives. "The scientists, who are mostly liberals and unbelievers, and the businessmen, who are mostly conservative and Christian, live side by side in Paradise Estates," More suggests [*LR*, 15]. The symbolically and ironically named Paradise contains a soupmix of people and political opinion; because of this, it is a quadrant which lacks focus and indeed lacks drive. It is an area of abandonment—abandoned cars, abandoned motels, houses, movie theaters, churches, and so on. As a whole, Paradise lacks potency, and it is fitting that the sexually impotent Ted Tennis lives here. Although More may feel that Paradise is "an oasis of concord in a troubled land," he again deceives himself; it is an oasis in ruins (*LR*, 17).

In part the ruins are spurious. Tara seems to dominate the landscape of Paradise, "a preposterous fake house on a fake hill"

(*LR*, 181). It was built from the "original plans," that is, "the drawings of David O. Selznick's set designer" (*LR*, 279). The fraudulence of Tara suggests that life in Paradise itself is defined through incongruous images and models. But More is fascinated by the falsity; "The very preposterousness of life in Tara with Lola inflames me with love," he confesses (*LR*, 181).

As mistress of Tara, Lola is the female genius of Paradise. In each of the four quadrants, More has a woman who loves him and who symbolizes for him the central aspects of that quadrant. Lola is the auburn-haired Texas girl, the cellist who appeals to his musical-erotic. In her, More embodies his personal myth that "Music ransoms us from the past, declares an amnesty, brackets and sets aside the old puzzles" (*LR*, 339). Her mixture of music and sex is a strong potion of forgetfulness and irresponsibility. "We'll make music," she cries, "and let the world crash about our ears. Twilight of the gods!" (*LR*, 316). But Lola also represents the "Gone with the Wind" myth, a spurious southern agrarianism. "When all is said and done," Lola tells More, "the only thing we can be sure of is the land. The land never lets you down"(*LR*, 279). They are looking out over six acres of grass, hardly the kind of land to put your trust in if you wish to eat. Paradise Estates, the southwest quadrant, is a curious hodge-podge of attitudes and values. As they are embodied in the sexually attractive Lola, More finds them emotionally compelling, a possible alternative. As they are embodied in impotent Ted Tennis, More intuits their sterility.

Each of the quadrants has its natural enemy in another quadrant, and Paradise seems especially vulnerable to Honey Island Swamp in the southeast. The swamp is a misty series of savannalike islands "dreaming in the gold-green world" (*LR*, 188). Like Paradise, it is a hodge-podge of people, from "ferocious black Bantus who use the wilderness both as a refuge and as a guerrilla base from which to mount forays against outlying subdivisions" to "all manner of young white derelicts" (*LR*,

15–16). In fact, "all manner of disaffected folk" meet in the swamp (*LR*, 16). It is a variant of the pastoral world, a place to opt out of the urban world and the life that the people of Paradise stand for. Here is noncommitment, and More is attracted to this life through the brown-haired, hazel-eyed Hester onto whom More projects, with almost no knowledge of the real woman, an entire world view. "Hester is my type," More asserts, "post-Protestant, post-rebellion, post-ideology . . . reverted all the way she is, clear back to pagan innocence like a shepherd girl piping a tune on a Greek vase" (*LR*, 49). For him, she is ahistorical, standing outside the stream of history. As he later says, "she's wiped the slate clean" (*LR*, 366). More does not deny his attraction to Hester and what she stands for in his mind—"How stands it with a forty-five-year-old man who can fall in love on the spot with a twenty-year-old stranger, a clear-eyed vacant simple Massachusetts girl, and desire nothing more in this life than to move into her chickee?"—but she is the one girl to whom he is sexually attracted and with whom he does not sleep (*LR*, 55). He cannot make contact with Hester. Because of his strong sense of tradition—a sense of the past that allows him to impose his myths on a recalcitrant present reality— More cannot wipe the slate clean; he cannot follow his mythic Hester into the "gold-green world" of Honey Island Swamp.

In More's mythic geometry, this pastoral world is antagonistically juxtaposed to the suburban world of Paradise. Charley Parker's son, Chuck, who opposes his father's social ideas, lives in the swamp while his father lives in Paradise. The Bantus from the swamp apparently invade Paradise at various times, looting and burning, and after the Bantus finally become rich, they buy Paradise and live there. The uncommitted life of the swamp people stands in strange and perhaps envious opposition to the vested interests of Paradise.

In the northeast quadrant "rise the monoliths of 'Fedville,' the federal complex including the hospital . . . the medical school, the NASA facility, the Behavioral Institute, the Geriatrics Center, and the Love Clinic" (*LR*, 14). Fedville is the liberal sector, filled with scientists, who, as More sees it, "are mostly liberals and unbelievers" (*LR*, 15). The area is associated with mental aberrations, amoral sexual investigations, behavioral control systems, and finally euthanasia. In contrast to the freedom of the swamp, the emphasis here is on control of the individual and his environment; here More sees an unrestricted modernism which he helps with his scientific discoveries, but which he decries as a religious man.

A West Virginian with short blond hair, Moira Schaffner is More's girl in Fedville. At first she is an assistant in the Love Clinic; later she becomes the nurse (and still later the wife) of Buddy Brown, More's licentious alter ego. Moira (the Greek "Fate") embodies More's vision of love—modern romantic love. "She's a romanticist. . . . She lives for what she considers rare perfect moments," perhaps vaguely remembering Robert Browning, the poet of "Love Among the Ruins" (*LR*, 130). For Moira, the old-fashioned sexual inhibitions are gone: "How prodigal is she with and how little store she sets by her perfectly formed Draw-Me arms and legs" (*LR*, 259). Unlike More's Hester, she requires a historical setting for her love. "She likes to visit ghost towns and jungle ruins," for "ruins make her passionate. Ghosts make her want to be touched" (*LR*, 130, 133). Of course More realizes that her historical romanticism is commonplace and thoughtless. "Moira, who is twenty-two and not strong on history, thinks that the great motels of the Auto Age were the haunt of salesmen and flappers of the Roaring Twenties" (*LR*, 134). Moreover, she gets the name of the romantic Roman city wrong; she misquotes Edward FitzGerald, considers Mantovani classical, and holds Rod McKuen as her favorite poet (*LR*, 133, 135, 253). The spuriousness of her romanticism rivals the spuriousness of Lola's "Gone with the Wind" agrarianism, but as More is enamoured by the preposterousness of

Lola's myth, so is he equally in love with Moira's fantastic romanticism. It is More himself who selects the ruined Howard Johnson's as their place of assignation, thus accepting (if only ironically) Moira's mythology. Her past is an urban past made up of flappers and salesmen meeting in lonely motels; Lola's is of an agrarian, gentile South. With Lola and Moira, More seems to be attempting a parodic "kind of 'historical therapy' . . . a recapture of the past and one's self" (*LR*, 43). Since he realizes the speciousness of these mythic pasts as well as their attractiveness, his attempts are half-hearted and unsuccessful. He cannot give himself wholly to either.

The northwest quadrant contains the town, a fairly small Louisiana town, where More maintains his office. "By contrast with the swamp, the town has become a refuge for all manner of conservative folk," More believes (*LR*, 16). Leroy Ledbetter's Little Napoleon tavern is in town, and here More sips toddies with his old friends. The flavor of the town is perfectly captured when Victor Charles helps More into the tavern. Victor has played the Good Samaritan, helping More out of a ditch into which he had drunkenly fallen. As Victor supports him, More is party to a subtle interracial violation: "I should have either dismissed him outside or held on to him longer," More explains. "As it was, letting go Victor when the bar was within reach, I let go a second too early, so that Leroy Ledbetter turning toward me in the same second, did not see me let go but saw Victor just beside me and so registered a violation. Not even that: a borderline violation because Victor was not even at the bar but still a step away" (*LR*, 150). While the scientists are busy recording data electrically in Fedville, the townsfolk are just as busy recording another type of data. The measurements are subtle and traditional, and More can understand these findings as easily as he can interpret scientific data.

Although born in Japan of Georgia missionaries, the dark-haired Ellen Oglethorpe embodies this basically conservative tradition. She "is a beautiful but tyrannical Georgia Presbyterian. A ripe Georgia persimmon not a peach, she fairly pops the buttons of her nurse's uniform with tart ripeness. She burgeons with marriageable Presbyterianism. . . . Her principles allow her a kind of chaste wantonness" (*LR*, 155). In contrast to the too-liberal Moira, Ellen is a twenty-four-year-old virgin. Her aunt admonishes her: "think of yourself as a treasure trove that you're guarding for your future husband" (*LR*, 335). She wants More to live up to the best that's in him, and, like a good Presbyterian, feels what he needs is "good hard work" and (she hesitates to say) a wife (*LR*, 365). If Hester represents a thoughtless present, and if Moira and Lola represent specious pasts, Ellen emphasizes the responsibilities of the present to the future.

The town and Fedville are natural antagonists in More's world. On the Fourth of July, the townspeople meet at the football field for a celebration, and the deputy sheriff reports, "They talking about marching on the federal complex" (*LR*, 322). According to one townsman, Fedville is filled with "commonists, atheistic scientists, Jews, perverts, dope fiends, coonasses" (*LR*, 322). The conservative town and liberal Fedville are as at odds as Paradise and the swamp. "It's the town people fighting the federal people" (*LR*, 305).

More sits at the omphalos of his projected four-part world when we first see him in the novel. "This spot, on the lower reaches of the southwest cusp, was chosen carefully," he says. "From it I command three directions of the interstates and by leaning over the lip of the culvert can look through to the fourth, eastern approach" (*LR*, 4). Symbolically More places himself at the center of his world, and as Ellen points out, More's "shelter"—the motel—is "convenient to town, Center, and Paradise" (*LR*, 321). In More's view, he is indeed at the center of the historical crisis he believes to be happening in 1983. His geometric schematization of reality mirrors this belief.

From this survey of More's world, we see that he is the product of a secular age, and his problems, although spoken of in religious terms, are often secular in nature. The moral landscaping that More does is not along spiritual lines, but political —moderate, radical, liberal, and conservative. Religion is a secondary consideration, and it is not the veil of the temple which is rent, but the Rotary banner: "Is it the truth? Is it fair to all concerned? Will it build goodwill and better friendships?" (*LR*, 9).

For what he believes to be the disintegrating secular world, More projects himself as the neo-Christ, the modern savior. Drinking at the Little Napoleon, More sees his image in the bar mirror. "In the mirror there is a dim hollow-eyed Spanish Christ," More fantasizes. "The pox is spreading on his face. Vacuoles are opening in his chest. It is the new Christ, the spotted Christ, the maculate Christ, the sinful Christ," and it is of course Thomas More. When he sees himself as the "new Christ [who] shall reconcile man with his sins," More's habit of imposing myths approaches blasphemy (*LR*, 153). But in the present time of the novel reconciling men through love seems a less appropriate means than curing them through methodology; thus More is more likely to trust the fate of Western Man to his lapsometer. Between Christian love and scientific control, between a free gift and an imposed solution, More finds the second alternative more congenial. He considers his article for *Brain*, which explains the use of the lapsometer, as "perhaps even epochal in its significance." With the lapsometer in hand, "any doctor can probe the very secrets of the soul, diagnose the maladies that poison the wellsprings of man's hope. It could save the world or destroy it" (*LR*, 7). Salvation will now be in the hands of the doctors, not the priests. More sincerely believes his invention to be of crucial importance, and dreams of receiving the Nobel Prize for his work.

More distorts the importance of his gadget, and one way

Percy puts More's vanity into context is through Mr. Ives, who has deciphered the Ocala frieze. Among other things, Dr. Brown finds Ives to be suffering from senile psychosis, psychopathic and antisocial behavior, and aphasia. "Despite extensive reconditioning in the Skinner box, the patient continued to exhibit antisocial behavior," Brown reports (*LR*, 223). Nevertheless, Ives, through a great deal of painstaking research in "the Franciscan files in Salamanca" and in Tampa, Florida, has mastered proto-Creek and deciphered the frieze (*LR*, 230). His explanatory article will appear in "next month's Annals." Part of his evidence is "a crude coin . . . like a ten-dollar gold piece," which he is chary of giving up (*LR*, 231).

More and Ives—both accused of madness and antisocial behavior, both refusing to be reconditioned by the Skinner box, both private researchers, both widowers—feel that they have made their ultimate contribution to their respective areas. The difference is that Ives has really deciphered the Ocala frieze; it is questionable if More has invented a gadget which will cure Western man. By implication Percy asks the reader, "Could it be that More's work will be, in reality, less influential than Ives's?" Colley Wilkes puts More's research into proper empirical framework when he tells him: "I'm convinced you're on the right track in your stereotactic exploration of the motor and sensory areas of the cortex. This is where it's at" (*LR*, 389). More's lapsometer is a specialized tool for exploring the uses of the brain; but More snaps back, "What concerns me is angelism, bestialism, and other perturbations of the soul" (*LR*, 390). Wilkes and his wife are nonplussed. These things may interest More (as they interest Walker Percy), but they are not to be measured in the laboratory. More cannot see the incongruity between his end and the means he has selected; he would like to see himself as the new Christ who can use gadgetry to bring a scientific means of grace to a secular age. Because he is in the

habit of randomly projecting diverse myths, More cannot see
that these two myths—the one of God's grace, the other of man's
scientific control—are mutually exclusive.

Ironically, even while More wants to save his age, he wishes
to destroy himself. He has attempted suicide by slashing his
wrists, and though he has almost killed himself in the past by
drinking gin fizzes, he still drinks them—at a time when he
feels that he needs his full faculties. Generally courting danger,
he dwells on scenes of destruction, on Verdun and other battlefields. The deaths of his wife and child are constantly in mind.
The Tom More we see throughout most of the novel is a man
preoccupied with destruction. Given More's preoccupation, it
is not surprising that he sees an apocalyptic world which is
ready to explode. He projects himself onto the world. As he
says, catastrophes are comforting to him; it is the everyday
world that he finds hard to face.[3] The myth of the apocalypse
seems ready-made for his underlying pessimism.

The myth of diabolical intervention is equally important to
More, since he does not want to be responsible for any misuse
of the lapsometer. Indeed, More refuses to accept responsibility
for himself or for his world. When Lola asks him to stay with
her at Tara, he tells her, "I have, ah, other responsibilities," and
adds subvocally, "Such as two girls in a motel room" (*LR*, 278).
The point is that More has no sense of responsibility. In the
midst of what he sees as an apocalyptic disaster, More is holed
up in a motel for less than moral reasons. He refuses to take a
truly active part in trying to save his world.

Because More cannot accept his responsibility, Art Immelmann enters. Art may be more than a figment of More's unstable mind; but he is certainly both a convenient scapegoat
and a projection of More's destructive propensities. More's col-
leagues sensibly see that More himself is responsible for the
orgy in The Pit. Max points out that More has taken "four hundred overworked dexed-up strung-out students at the end of

the year" and used hypnosis on them; Stryker sees the lapsometer as "an extremely effective objective correlative" (*LR*,
359). Of course, More would like to blame "diabolical abuse"
(*LR*, 389), that is Art Immelmann. But even if he is the devil incarnate, Art explains that he is essentially powerless. "We never
'do' anything to anybody," he tells More. "We only help people
do what they want to do. We facilitate social interaction in order to accumulate reliable data" (*LR*, 363). Art merely helps
More do what he basically desires to do. Before Art's arrival,
More tells Max, "I've got to get this thing mass-produced and
in the hands of G.P.'s" (*LR*, 115), and Art later only slightly increases the scope of More's original plan: "We're prepared to
fund an interdisciplinary task force and implement a crash
program that will put a MOQUOL in the hands of every physician and social scientist in the U.S. within one year's time"
(*LR*, 169). In either case, the plan is extremely dangerous if the
lapsometer has the capacity to "destroy" the world as More
claims. It is no tool to be trusted at random to every doctor and
social scientist in America. Art really becomes a projection of
More's own irresponsibility and pride. More wants the Nobel
Prize for his work, and Art promises to get it for him. Even Art's
slightly old-fashioned manners and dress seem to mirror an
essential part of More, the old-fashioned gentleman doctor. In
narrating his story, More radically distorts Art's passive function in the action.

In the scene dated "7:15 P.M. / July 4," More recapitulates
the antagonisms and the desires of his story. Wrapped in smoke,
with whiffs of brimstone, noxious vapors, and fog, the scene is
much like a movie montage or a nightmare, and the reader
may feel that a good part of the action takes place in More's
confused head. But three important things happen in this
strange scene. First, Ellen reports, "There was no real trouble"
(*LR*, 366). The Bantus "faded away," as if they were simply dark
figures of paranoia in a diseased mind (*LR*, 365). More's myth

of apocalypse fades with them. Second, More rejects Art Immelmann, and the rejection of Art becomes important for More as a rejection of his own pride and irresponsibility. Third, More goes home with Ellen, and by so doing, seems to reject an illusory world and accept a real one. The next time we see him, he is hoeing collards in his kitchen garden. The enclosed patio in Paradise is exchanged for a workaday vegetable garden in the slave quarters.

In the novel's coda, "Five Years Later," More has changed, though he has not been utterly reclaimed from his vanity. He still believes that his gadget can save the world—if he can get it right—and that there is "some reason" to await the imminent apocalypse (*LR*, 387). But, with a few minor exceptions, the romantic similes are gone along with the confused questioning of the earlier action. More feels that a new age has come. "Now while you work, you also watch and listen and wait. In the last age we planned projects and cast ahead of ourselves. We set out to 'reach goals.' We listened to the minutes of the previous meeting. Between times we took vacations" (*LR*, 381–82). Formerly, More dredged up myths from the past and awaited the future apocalypse. By distorting reality, he failed to live and love *in the real world* and was indeed a soul divided from its body. Now he again has a wife and children, and is coming to know himself as an integrated person.

Father Smith's final words to More are important advice. We must think about things "like doing our jobs, you being a better doctor, I being a better priest, showing a bit of ordinary kindness to people, particularly to our own families . . . doing what we can for our poor unhappy country—things which, please forgive me, sometimes seem more important than dwelling on a few middle-aged daydreams" (*LR*, 399). The middle-aged daydreams are not only More's lecherous thoughts about Mrs. Prouty, the flirtatious Sears salesperson. They also include his distorted vision—a daydream—of himself and his world.

Moreover, his earlier vision of apocalypse is undercut by Victor Charles who is running for Congress. "I got the Bantu vote," Victor claims (*LR*, 401). Chuck Parker is working for him among the swamp people; Max Gottlieb, among the liberals; Leroy Ledbetter, among the conservatives; and Victor wants More's help with the Catholics. More joins Victor's political team. More's lapsometer is not needed to save the political fabric of Louisiana and the nation, nor are his various mythologized attempts to translate his world out of itself. Some far more commonplace and traditional political wisdom seems to have done the job.

But perhaps the myths More has used and needed are *there* in the texture of his world. Perhaps Lola, Moira, Hester, and Ellen are *indeed* embodiments of American myths of agrarian stability, the grandeur and vitality of the past, the saving power of music and love, the Edenic and unspoiled country, the efficacy of work. Perhaps a sense of apocalypse does hover over a divided nation. Perhaps then the myths are not completely imposed by More, but simply seen by him in his role as vatic shaman. Nevertheless, Percy shows us these myths operating in the mind of a mentally disturbed man. As a psychotic psychiatrist, More is continually advising, "Physician heal thyself." He is both diagnostician of and participant in the disease, and he has the same relationship to the larger disease, the malaise of Western man. There is a resulting ambiguity in More's vision; for as it reveals the basic problems, it also obscures them by distortion. Arthur Kopit's statement on the American propensity for mythmaking is surely apropos here: "The danger isn't what happened, but the way in which we changed what happened into a *fable*."[4] And John Lahr later notes that the American "need for oversimplification encourages myth." More the seer is also More the simplifier, the schematizer, the fabler. Our myths, Percy seems to imply, are a part of the malaise, part of our inability to confront reality in a positive, clear-sighted way and to deal with it as it is. By diagnosing More, we come to understand our own habits of verbal distortion and romantic mythologizing, our own propensities to rely almost superstitiously on science rather than humanely and responsibly working out our spiritual salvation. More never completely frees himself from his mythologized world, but at the end of the novel, he is slowly working toward a clearer vision. Implicitly, Percy instructs us to do the same.

THOMAS LECLAIR

Walker Percy's Devil

IT IS SATURDAY afternoon, July 1, 1983, and Dr. Tom More sits in his office thinking: "If only my lapsometer could treat as well as diagnose" (*LR*, 165). *Don Giovanni* plays, lightning flashes, and Art Immelmann, Walker Percy's devil, appears. He's an odd-looking fellow, curiously old-fashioned. His "old-style flat-top haircut," white shirt, and neat dark trousers make him look like "a small-town businessman in the old Auto Age" (*LR*, 166). In bureaucratic jargon he promises Dr. More funding for his lapsometer. More balks at the contract. But two days later, Immelmann raises his stakes: he offers the disappointed doctor the ionizer that will make the diagnostic lapsometer therapeutic. Weakened by the brain massage Immelmann gives him with the new device, Tom More succumbs to the devil's temptation. It is only after several days of devilish chaos roiling toward apocalypse that More repudiates Immelmann and recovers himself and, just possibly, the world. In this retelling, the devil loses and, with God's grace and the help of St. Thomas More, man wins.

Percy's devil is a modern avatar of the Faust and Don Juan myths so prominently alluded to in the novel, but the details of Immelmann's appearance and method also owe much to the devil in Dostoyevsky's *The Brothers Karamazov*, a book that helped lead Percy into a systematic study of existentialism. The ideas and terms that Percy borrows from existential novelists like Dostoyevsky and Sartre and from the philosophers Kierkegaard, Heidegger, and Marcel give his fiction an interesting allusiveness and, at times, a real philosophical depth. However, in *Love in the Ruins* the way Percy uses existential ideas—the form of their presentation—is at odds with the existentially influenced aesthetic he has articulated in interviews and essays. While *Love in the Ruins* is the work of a ranging intellect and observant eye, I think it is the least successful of Percy's four novels. Its weakness is a disturbing incongruity between intelligence and imagination, an incongruity I hope to demonstrate by identifying several important existential sources of the book and by showing how the ideas they supply are embedded in a narrative form Percy once attacked as obsolete. I call this essay "Walker Percy's Devil" because Art Immelmann represents both Percy's philosophical allusiveness and the aesthetic inconsistency of the novel. Immelmann's temptation of Tom More is the internal analogue of Percy's temptation by an old-fashioned art. Briefly put, Walker Percy's devil is the attempt to render existentialist material in an unexistentialist novel form.

The primary terms in which Percy presents Tom More's psychological condition are angelism-bestialism—terms derived from Maritain's *The Dream of Descartes*. Tom More has both a Faustian abstractive pride and a Don Juanian absorption in carnality, and his fall issues from both. Immelmann promises a hedonistic life and encourages More to "'Develop your genius'" (*LR*, 364). While the latter can be read as a call to scientific pride, it is also more specifically an allusion to a Kierkegaardian essay, "Of the Difference Between a Genius and an Apostle," that Percy has said "was more responsible than anything else for my becoming a Catholic."[1] Kierkegaard wrote the essay to combat his contemporaries' tendency to speak of Christ as a profound thinker or of Paul as a clever stylist rather than as figures with a wholly different kind of authority, that of the "absolute paradox" of divine appointment. The genius, despite his knowledge and appeal, is necessarily limited to the sphere of immanence. His message has its own intrinsic authority to be evaluated aesthetically or ethically; thus his originality is soon assimilated by history. The genius has a "humorous self-sufficiency": "the unity of a modest resignation in the world and a proud elevation above the world: of being an unnecessary superfluity and a precious ornament."[2] The Apostle, says Kierkegaard, has his authority from God; his message remains news because of its transcendent nature and authority. The Apostle cannot prove physically that he has authority. Others must be related to him in faith, for he is an unprepossessing man, not an ornament. In one of his attacks on "Christendom," Kierkegaard extends the Apostle category to include the Christian: "a genius is nature's extraordinary, no man being able to make himself a genius, whereas a Christian is freedom's extraordinary," a simple man who follows the divine "Pattern" in lowly form.[3] For Kierkegaard the genius was born not made, but anyone could make himself a Christian by exercising his freedom. Although the term *Apostle* goes back to the beginnings of Christianity, Kierkegaard's emphasis on subjectivity and freedom give the term an existential quality.

Tom More introduces himself as a genius, a man who can "discern not this thing or that thing but rather the connection between the two" (*LR*, 26). Very early in the novel he announces "I am a physician, a not very successful psychiatrist; an alcoholic, a shaky middle-aged man subject to depressions and elations and morning terrors, but a genius nevertheless who sees into the hidden causes of things and erects simple hypotheses to account for the glut of everyday events; a bad Catholic; a widower and cuckold" (*LR*, 11). More prides himself on being a mad genius, a man who makes breakthroughs in the asylum rather than the laboratory. His personal life is marked by, in Kierkegaardian terms, "modest resignation" from the decorum of the medical profession and by "proud elevation" above his fellow geniuses in the novel. Although More says he believes in "the whole Thing, God Jews Christ Church" (*LR*, 106), he identifies himself in what Kierkegaard calls aesthetic terms and takes his authority from his intelligence rather than his faith. His lapsometer is the physical proof of his genius. Although it can diagnose the ills of postmodern man and can, with the attached ionizer, adjust people to their environment, the lapsometer is limited to the immanent. It cannot save—and might well help to damn—those it "cures." It almost damns the genius who has invented it and whose faith it nearly replaces.

Tensed between the call of genius and the meaning of faith, Tom More lives two half-lives—he orbits the world in abstraction and scampers its surface in carnality. In this condition he is ripe for the devil's temptation: the assurance of genius and the lure of the "musical-erotic" (*LR*, 364). Immelmann is not a majestic force that tempts More into a titanic struggle against God. Instead, he represents himself as a charitable man who wants to give More the fame he deserves and wants to aid an America in psychic and social trouble. Actually Immelmann is a cause of conflict and a spokesman for further despair—the despair of not being aware of despair that Percy, with Kierkegaard, believes is the worst. "'We are speaking here,'" says Immelmann, "'of happiness, joy, music, spontaneity, you understand. Fortunately we have put behind us such unhappy things as pure versus impure love, sin versus virtue, and so forth'" (*LR*, 214). Finished with impurity and sin, Immelmann's new man can settle into a blur of modern happiness.

Immelmann's forebear is the devil in *The Brothers Karamazov* who describes himself as follows: "'Mephistopheles declared to Faust that he desired evil, but did only good. Well, he

can say what he likes, it's quite the opposite with me. I am perhaps the one man in all creation who loves the truth and genuinely desires good.'"[4] Dostoyevsky's devil says he helps men by
keeping alive conflicts that allow them to see how lucky they
are. But what the devil would really like to do is forget spiritual problems and settle into an ordinary life in "'the form of
some merchant's wife weighing eighteen stone.'" He comes to
Ivan, Dostoyevsky's "genius," much as Immelmann comes to
More—as a shabby, out-of-fashion traveler with an amiable,
slightly vulgar manner. His concerns are this-worldly, the
problems of the body. He complains, in a passage Percy must
have found apposite, that the medical faculty "'can diagnose
beautifully; they have the whole of your disease at their fingertips, but they have no idea how to cure you.'" He forecasts,
using Ivan's thoughts as Immelmann uses More's discovery of
heavy sodium, that man will extend "'"his conquest of nature
infinitely by his will and his science"'"[5] This "good-natured
gentleman" is an externalization of Ivan's ideas as Immelmann
is a facilitator of More's already formed desires. Dostoyevsky's
devil is unnamed and, it is suggested, the product of Ivan's
brain fever. He does not offer a specific temptation, unless convincing Ivan of his unreality is a temptation, and he offers no
reward. However, through this devil Dostoyevsky portrays an
image of hellishness that Percy finds worth recalling, for in his
discounting of spiritual issues Ivan's devil encourages both sin
and an existential inauthenticity. Although Dostoyevsky's devil
and Percy's Immelmann do appeal to conventional pride, their
call is not to rebellion but to spiritual amnesia and to an idea
of happiness that is despair. By modeling his devil on Dostoyevsky's, Percy makes Immelmann both a traditional Christian
tempter and an existential "salaud."

   More's banishing of his devil is less than heroic. It comes
very soon after he realizes that his despairing over Samantha
may have been a self-indulgent "feasting on death" (*LR*, 374),

but the immediate motivation is to protect (for himself?) nurse Ellen; the actual dissolving of Art Immelmann comes through Tom More's mumbled prayer to his ancestor the saint. It is in the epilogue, five years later, that Percy develops his hero's recovery. Although some readers have complained about the sentimental patness of this section, it is consistent with the assumptions and progress of the book: if the novelist wants to put the devil in his novel and have his hero defeat him, then a storybook ending is not out of place. A passage from Kierkegaard's *Training in Christianity* summarizes the quality of life in the epilogue: "everyone for himself, in quiet inwardness before God, shall humble himself before what it is to be in the strictest sense a Christian, admit candidly before God how it stands with him, so that he might accept the grace that is offered to everyone who is imperfect, that is, to everyone. And then no further; then for the rest let him attend to his work, be glad in it, love his wife, be glad in her, bring up his children in joyfulness, love his fellow men, rejoice in life. If anything further is required of him, God will surely let him understand."[6]

Kierkegaard's understanding of what it is to be a Christian is essentially repeated in *Love in the Ruins* by the unlikely cleric Father Smith. "A gray stiff man" (*LR*, 139), Smith is entirely unremarkable, a nearly anonymous man with an anonymous name. But Father Smith, like plain Father Boomer in *The Last Gentleman*, is the agent of God's news. Following Kierkegaard, Percy is illustrating that the knight of faith need be "no genius."[7] As a fire warden, Smith watches and waits for what Percy calls "news from across the seas" in *The Message in the Bottle*. When in the asylum with More, Father Smith doesn't concentrate on the loss of his own powers but complains about the channels of spiritual authority being jammed: the word is not getting through to him. He doesn't attempt to prove his worth through skillful dialectics and doesn't argue theology; he functions as a witness and an apostle. At the end of the novel

Father Smith's obtuseness bothers Tom More, but the priest's theology is firm, his advice to More sound, and his church has the apostolic look of the early Christian catacombs. It is to this church that More must come to complete his recovery. What is restored to More in the epilogue is the ability to wait in faith and to feel wonder—the habit of mind that opens up genius to the possibility of apostleship; for if Smith shows that genius is not required for faith, More evidences that genius, so long as it retains the capacity to wonder, does not preclude faith.

Genius, devil, and apostle—each of these central concepts has an existential source. Yet the form Percy chooses for *Love in the Ruins* is disappointingly conventional and inconsistent with the existentially influenced aesthetic he has said he works from. A futuristic novel, *Love in the Ruins* is constructed like futuristic novels of the past. Characters are motivated and events are plotted. Time and space are quite conventionally handled. Although contemporary facts are amusingly distorted, the satire is neither very subtle nor imaginatively prophetic. The narrator shows signs of unreliability, but Percy does not choose to make More's befuddlement structurally central. Percy is not embarrassed, as Barth says he is, to build the Chartres Cathedral again.[8] Does the novelist function under some imperative of originality? Perhaps not. But Percy early in his career thought it necessary to change the structure of fiction to correspond with the changed nature of the world and his ways of thinking about it. He said that "there is a disintegration of the fabric of the modern world which is so far advanced that the conventional novel no longer makes sense."[9] Percy reaffirms this apocalyptic belief in the opening essay in *The Message in the Bottle*, where he states that the modern world is ended and that we need a new theory of man for a new age. The subtitle of *Love in the Ruins, The Adventures of a Bad Catholic at a Time Near the End of the World*, may even suggest that a philosophical apocalypse has happened, that the "Time Near" is *after the fact*. Yet, despite his sense of radical social changes and radical philosophical needs, Percy does not extend his radicalism to literary form.

In several of his interviews Percy states some of the principles of the existential novelist who will best respond to this new world. Basically, Percy explained to Carlton Cremeens, a novelist "should be concerned with what is the case in the world, the facts, the richness, the intricacy and the variety of the way things are."[10] He begins with man in a situation: "I'm concerned with a certain quality of consciousness put down in a certain place and then seeing what kind of reaction takes place between a character and his environment and the people he meets." For the novelist exploring and discovering reality in his fiction, "telling a story and putting characters together so that something is going to happen" will be secondary. Percy further insisted that the novelist must avoid the "temptation to understand the [social] issues of the times in terms of sociology, in terms of abstractions." Without "writing in enigmas and acrostics," the novelist will make his philosophy "part and parcel of the novel, and there's no illustrating of theses."[11] The novelist as phenomenologist of man in a concrete situation will tell the reader "something he already knows but which he doesn't quite know he knows"[12] in an indirect way and will, at all costs, avoid the edifying. If he successfully articulates the not quite known but shared condition of alienation, the result will be its reversal through the joy of naming. Such comments reflect Percy's existential reading and thinking; they are often accompanied by references to Sartre and Camus, two novelists whom Percy readily recognizes as influences on his aesthetic.

Although neither *The Moviegoer* nor *The Last Gentleman* is strictly experimental, Percy follows the principles quoted above rigorously and successfully in *The Moviegoer* and, with somewhat wider and looser application, in *The Last Gentleman*. *Love in the Ruins*, while suggesting thematically that all conventions are being overturned, nevertheless retains stylistically a conventional aesthetic. *Love in the Ruins* begins with a familiar Percyian consciousness set down in a situation, the unwanted greening of America, that soon becomes a plot. As the novel progresses, More becomes less a meditative consciousness than a stimulus-response creature who tramps back and forth through the novel's four days. Action becomes plotted and predictable, and thus at odds with Percy's notion of fiction as exploration and discovery. The last half of the novel is dominated by dialogue and descriptions of action, action more externally exciting than internally revelatory. The novel's conventional cinematic quality diminishes the "richness, the intricacy and the variety of the way things are," qualities Percy told Cremeens were essential. There are an artificial intricacy of plot and a superficial variety of people without the parodic extremity Pynchon uses to set his plotted and peopled fiction apart from its conventional "models." *Love in the Ruins* is essentially an adventure story with the expected physical threats, suspense, and beautiful women. In *Nausea*, a book Percy much admires, Roquentin recognizes the inauthenticity of "adventures" and "perfect moments." In *Love in the Ruins* Tom More sees through Moira's need for adventure and "perfect moments" (*LR*, 130), yet Percy seems too fond of such moments himself to prune them from his novel. The book is more dogmatic than *The Moviegoer* or *The Last Gentleman*, but the problem is not so much whether Percy has the authority to be edifying as whether his satire is equal to the complexity and artistic achievement of the comedy in his first two books. I don't think it is. While *Love in the Ruins* may be a book Percy needed to write as a logical extension of the movement toward Catholicism of his earlier novels, what he sacrifices—and what *The Moviegoer* has—are the "resistance to recuperation" and "opacity" that Roland Barthes and other French critics find admirable (and existentially consistent) in new fiction. As a Christian satire and entertainment, *Love in the Ruins* works. As an existential exploration of a consciousness in a place, it is crowded with problem people rather than mysterious persons and things.

The malice from which Percy admittedly draws some of his creative energy, in combination with the book's emphasis upon action, results in character simplification. Minor characters in *The Moviegoer* and *The Last Gentleman* threaten to fold into caricature. In *Love in the Ruins* many of the minor characters become the abstractions Percy warned himself against—exemplary figures of various social, political, philosophical, or scientific persuasions. Although Ted Tennis, Father Kev, Colley Wilkes and others are skillfully made satiric objects, there is a simplification in this satire that is at odds with Percy's existential notions and his marvelous ability to register mystery. Sartre objectifies the fools in *Nausea*, but I think Percy's energy in *Love in the Ruins* (and later in *Lancelot*) finds the satiric exaggeration of personal traits and ideas the easy channel to take. Percy doesn't tell the reader something he doesn't quite know. Rather, he recapitulates what the reader knows and therefore easily savors the wit of.

Percy sees the novelist-novel-reader relation as an extension of the basic human language act of naming. In naming, a thing is symbolized not just for the namer but also, whether present or not, for the other person; it is an intersubjective process. Since the novelist as namer comes to the world late (in contrast with the child namer), he must use, as Percy writes in "Notes for a Novel," "every ounce of cunning, craft, and guile he can muster from the darker regions of his soul" (*MB*, 118) to give freshness and authority to his naming. If he is also a Christian writing about the many-mouthed words *grace* and *redemption* then his task is doubly difficult. What Percy does stylistically in *Love in the Ruins* is parody much of the bogus naming —scientific, mystical, and popular—that clamors in our ears. His devil speaks in the hoariest of clichés. But here again, so much of the linguistic thrust of the book is negative that the new positive naming is secondary. Despite recognizing the dangers of a used-up vocabulary, Percy borrows rather than invents his central terms, *angelism-bestialism.* He also has Tom More think and talk in old or borrowed language: "other fish to fry," "a certain emotion," his lovers' "charms." More's occasional genteel clichés set him apart from the users of new clichés, but the fact remains that the novel is largely composed of devalued language. The apostle has the authority to pronounce the old words because they announce the same radical news. The novelist has to imagine new names. But between the parodic and the borrowed, there is little space in *Love in the Ruins* for Percy's imagination to invent.

The problems *with* the novel are succinctly represented *in* the novel by the relation between Tom More and Art Immelmann. More has ideas and can diagnose, but his "breakthrough" is only partial. He stops experimenting and depends on old-fashioned Art Immelmann for the working physical form of his invention, the ionizer that (like literary form) makes it possible for ideas to affect people. More is philosopher Percy tempted by the literary sure thing—the futuristic and satiric adventure. Immelmann offers More fame, a chance to do good for others, and the conventionalized joy of love in the ruins. Percy's artistic temptation closely parallels these three attractions, for in *Love in the Ruins* Percy tends toward popularity, edification, and conventionality of form. Percy's devil as a writer, then, is his betrayal of his own literary faith to a shopworn literary cliché from H. G. Wells, Aldous Huxley, and Robert Nathan that Percy identified in "The Man on the Train." The novel is thus a metafiction, a fiction about itself that hints at its weaknesses. The devil is old-fashioned Art / art.

Percy has made *Love in the Ruins* accessible to a large number of readers and has clarified his religious position, but at the expense of a philosophically and aesthetically consistent fiction. I have called Percy's tending toward popularity, edification, and conventionality of form his devil because these qualities correspond with Art Immelmann's temptation of Tom More and because they deprive us of the best in Percy—a philosophical rigor, subtle irony, precise wonder at the world, mixture of levels of discourse, a conception of the novel as a phenomenological exploration—qualities found most prominently in *The Moviegoer*. Perhaps Percy thought his technique in *Love in the Ruins* was innovative. Perhaps he thought the satiric commentary was worth an artistic sacrifice. He has said that his "interests in writing are not primarily literary" and seems to have little sympathy for those writers, like John Barth and Ronald Sukenick, whose apocalyptic sense is more literary than social or philosophical.[13] Despite knowing more about language than other novelists, many of whom make it their subject, Percy chose to go on telling stories with ideas inside. *Love in the Ruins* is a good story, yet one comes to wish Percy had imagined through to a form that would have transmuted his enormous intelligence into some supreme verbal fiction. Perhaps one shouldn't complain about what he doesn't do, shouldn't look for devils. It's just that his essays, his interviews, and *The Moviegoer* make a promise that is unfulfilled or, more accurately, a promise not quite made, yet still somehow unkept.

WELDON THORNTON

Homo Loquens, Homo Symbolificus, Homo Sapiens: Walker Percy on Language

WALKER PERCY has written, in addition to four novels, some three dozen essays and reviews. These include fifteen linguistic and philosophical essays written over the past twenty years and gathered in *The Message in the Bottle* (1975).[1] Percy's essays are interesting for several reasons. For one, they give us another perspective on the sources and concerns of the novelist. Our pleasure in reading the essays comes in part from the echoes and reverberations we hear from the novels, and from finding that objects of satire or of admiration for Percy the novelist may be viewed differently by Percy the essayist. The essays are valuable too because they show an intelligent, articulate nonspecialist probing the methodological inconsistencies and blind spots of several disciplines. One of Percy's concerns is the depletion of our experience caused by our willingness to let specialists tell us what to think and how to feel. But Percy insists that a topic such as language is much too important to be left to the linguists. But he does not simply criticize the linguists' shortcomings: running through his essays is a pattern of ideas worth consideration in their own right. Finally, the essays collected in *The Message in the Bottle* are revealing even in their imperfections and inconsistencies, for these arise from Percy's honesty and venturesomeness, and they reflect the complexity of the problems we face.

The foundation of Percy's thought is his awareness of the uniqueness of human language, the qualitative difference between signs and symbols, between animal communication and human language. Signs, Percy contends, are simply physical; symbols involve an aspect of meaning that cannot be dealt with through physical cause and effect. He begins with this distinction; he returns to it repeatedly, and on it he builds several related ideas. One of these is his belief that, for all the mystery inherent in the acts of speaking and responding, we can by a truer, more sufficient empiricism develop a linguistics and an anthropology that can give an account of these acts. This belief arises from his conviction that, while the denotative relation between a word and its referent is not causal, it does have a physical dimension that can be observed and described. The act of speaking a word involves sounds and physical articulations, and it also involves observable interpersonal relationships between the speaker and the hearer. Indeed, in some of his essays, Percy outlines the general features of the interpersonal "symbolic behavior" involved in speaking and responding. This belief that denotation—the relationship between word and referent—is both intentional and physical Percy elaborates into the idea that all human knowing comes about through our comparing a symbol and its referent, and this he develops into a theory of metaphor. He also contends that a study of the behavior surrounding symbolic acts such as naming provides an entry into the problem of intersubjectivity, *i.e.*, of how individual minds relate to one another. He even insists that intersubjectivity is an integral part of language—that without two persons, a namer and a hearer, language could not exist. Since these ideas are interrelated in Percy's mind and interwoven among his essays, my plan here will be to present Percy's basic ideas by quoting from whatever essays best illustrate them. I will then turn to some essays that deserve individual scrutiny, and to certain problematic points about Percy's thought.

Percy's insistence on the uniqueness of language accounts for his ubiquitous references to Susanne Langer and to Helen Keller, for these two served as midwives to this idea in Percy's mind. Percy's first serious essay, "Symbol as Need" (1954), was a review of Langer's *Feeling and Form*, in which he expresses his delight that this erstwhile positivist has been driven to assert the qualitative difference between signs and symbols. Exulting in Langer's agreement on this point with St. Thomas and Maritain (an example of "thinkers converging on the same truths from opposed positions . . . unaware of the other"), Percy says,

For once and for all, we hope, Mrs. Langer has made clear the generic difference between sign and symbol, between the subject-sign-object triad and the subject-symbol-conception-object tetrad. Signs announce their objects. Thunder announces rain. The bell announces food to Pavlov's dog. When I say James to a dog, he *looks* for James; when I say James to you, you say "What about him?"—you *think* about James. A symbol is the vehicle for the conception of an object and as such is a distinctively human product.[2] (*MB*, 292–293)

Percy did not learn this distinction from Langer, but he finds her expression of it a satisfying confirmation of his own basic conviction, and he refers to it repeatedly.

If Langer's discussion of sign and symbol is important for Percy, Helen Keller's description of her discovering language is trebly so. He refers to this event in almost every one of his essays, and in "The Delta Factor" he quotes her account in full and acknowledges it as the source of his own "discovery" of the triadic structure of the symbolic act (*MB*, 3, 30, 33–40). Miss Keller describes an experience when she was six years old, when she first realized that her teacher's spelling out w-a-t-e-r in one hand while water flowed over the other, was not a command or a physical sign for water, but that it *meant* water:

As the cool stream gushed over one hand, she spelled into the other the word *water*, first slowly then rapidly. I stood still, my whole attention fixed upon the motion of her fingers. Suddenly I felt a misty consciousness as of something forgotten—a thrill of returning thought; and somehow the mystery of language was revealed to me. I knew then that "w-a-t-e-r" meant the wonderful cool something that was flowing over my hand. That living word awakened my soul, gave it light, hope, joy, set it free! (Percy quotes in "The Delta Factor" [*MB*, 34–35] from Keller's *The Story of My Life* [New York: Grosset & Dunlap, 1902], 23–24.)

This is a stirring description of a momentous event. We hardly feel that Percy exaggerates its importance when he says, "For a long time the conviction had been growing upon me that three short paragraphs in Helen Keller's *The Story of My Life* veiled a mystery, a profound secret, and that, if one could fathom it, one could also understand a great deal of what it meant to be *Homo loquens*, *Homo symbolificus*, man the speaking animal, man the symbol-monger" (*MB*, 30). In any event, for Percy the difference between an animal's response to a sign, and man's to a symbol, is crucial. All of his essays are attempts to articulate this distinction or to show us how absurd it is that we have lost sight of what is implied about our nature by every word we speak.

Percy is convinced that exploring the implications of man's unique capacity for language can be of inestimable value in freeing us from our present cultural malaise. Percy finds that no adequate theory of man has emerged to take the place of the traditional revealed Judaeo-Christian view; and he attributes that fact to the inability or failure of modern science, philosophy, linguistics, and anthropology to give language the kind of attention it deserves. This failure serves as a starting point for many of his essays, for Percy frequently begins by asserting the inadequacies of current methodologies to deal with the question of meaning. Generally he does this by foiling two opposed approaches, such as idealism and empiricism, and claiming that the all-important question of meaning is neglected by both and allowed to fall between them. In "Symbol as Hermeneutic in Existentialism," for instance, Percy begins by comparing Anglo-American empiricism with European existentialism, charging both with a "failure to make a unifying effort toward giving an account of all realities" (*MB*, 277). He finds the former needing a "genuinely empirical framework" that will permit insight into the reality of existential traits it now ignores; the latter needs "deliverance from Kantian subjectivity" (*MB*, 279). Then he asserts, typically, that the basis of their potential meeting lies in the study of language: "The necessary bridge from traditional empiricism to existential insights may have already been supplied—unwittingly, and from the empirical side of the gulf —by the study of that particular human activity in which empiricism intersects, so to speak, with existentialism—language" (*MB*, 279–80). Percy then elaborates the inadequacies and inconsistencies of these traditional approaches, asserts the uniqueness of symbolization, and reaffirms that a more complete empiricism will enable us to deal with it.

Percy's use of the term *empiricism* requires some comment, for he uses it equivocally. He often contrasts idealism and empiricism in a way familiar to any student of Western philosophy since Locke. In that context, idealism means the approach of Descartes and Leibniz; empiricism means the approach of Locke and Hume. Percy criticizes idealism for remaining confined within its definitions and deductions and "letting the world get away" (*MB*, 33). He criticizes empiricism for not pursuing its own methodology radically enough, thus limiting itself to sensations instead of including all the phenomena of experience. According to Percy, Cassirer, the idealist, would keep man "securely locked up inside his own head" (*MB*, 33). Skinner is at least on the right track in his insistence on looking at tangible, empirical evidence; all he needs is an expansion of this approach into a more radical empiricism. This belief in a continuity between traditional empiricism and "phenomeno-logical" empiricism is the basis of Percy's assertion that, be-tween idealism and empiricism, he prefers the latter. But in this we see his equivocation—an easy and tempting one for the modern mind. Percy assumes, apparently unawares, that there is a continuity of method between the empiricism of Hume and the "genuine" empiricism he calls for that would do justice to the phenomena of human experience, *i.e.*, to willing, hoping, judging, etc. In fact there is no such continuity, as Hume or Skinner would be quick to point out.

In other of his essays the methodological rift Percy exposes falls along slightly different lines, but repeatedly he foils a nar-rowly empiricist approach against an idealist or mentalist ap-proach and claims that their reconciliation lies in the proper study of language. In "Semiotic and a Theory of Knowledge," Percy shows semiotics to be schizophrenically divided into semantics, symbolic logic, and behavioristics—studies that fail to make contact with one another and that neglect the central problem of meaning. In "Symbol, Consciousness, and Intersub-jectivity," focusing on the problem of intersubjectivity, Percy sets the "explanatory-psychological" approach of George H. Mead over against the phenomenology of Husserl, again pro-posing that an entry into the problem is afforded by something they both claim to study—language. In his most recent essay, "A Theory of Language," the behaviorism of Skinner and the Cartesian mentalism of Chomsky are similarly contrasted.

Percy reveals the antinomy inherent in the scientist's or be-haviorist's inability to give an account of what he himself is doing when he develops hypotheses, makes assertions, and ar-gues about these with his fellow scientists. The essay "Culture: The Antinomy of the Scientific Method" is devoted largely to exposing what Percy considers a self-contradictory situation in contemporary studies of myth, language, and science: all cultural activities, including myth, language, and science, are assertory—*i.e.*, they state, they contend, they convey meaning—yet the functional methodologies practiced by these fields can give no account of assertory phenomena. The result, says Percy, is an obviously self-contradictory situation: "a practicing scientist who reports his findings in journals and his theories in books—and who denies the possibility of a public realm of intersubjectivity" (*MB*, 232–33).

Typically, then, Percy's subject, as he says in "Symbol as Need," is "the disastrous effects of the mind-matter split" (*MB*, 292), and he proposes a radically empirical study of language and of the behavior surrounding acts of speaking as the bridge between the two. Percy realizes, though, that it is difficult to develop a methodology for studying the behavior surrounding language that is capable of vindicating his views and convincing those who might disagree. The starting point for Percy is a unique human capacity, which issues in a certain kind of experience and behavior. But others look at the same overt behavior Percy sees and see nothing remarkable at all. Where can we find a starting point acceptable to all, one that does not itself beg the question we deal with? As Percy acknowledges, "Start with God and man's immortal soul and you've lost every reader except those who believe in God and man's immortal soul. [But start] with B. F. Skinner and man decreed as organism who learns everything he does by operant conditioning, and you've lost every reader who knows there is more to it than that and that Skinner has explained nothing" (*MB*, 18).

But while he keenly appreciates this discrepancy, Percy believes that we could solve the dilemma, bridge the gulf, through a truly empirical study of language and of symbolic behavior. Percy emphasizes that naming is an act with a physical dimension—that language is not sheerly mental but consists in part of sounds, of energy exchanges, of observable physical phenomena; similarly, it is important for Percy that how people interact with one another through language is susceptible of observation and generalization.

These beliefs are the source of Percy's surprising claim to feel more affinity with empiricists and behaviorists than with phenomenologists and idealists—surprising at least to those who would see Percy as a disciple of Kierkegaard or Marcel. Percy tells us (in "Symbol, Consciousness, and Intersubjectivity") that he finds George Mead a safer starting point to study intersubjectivity than Husserl (*MB*, 266), and in "The Delta Factor" that Skinner is a better ally than Cartesian-mentalist Chomsky (*MB*, 33–34). These alliances and this faith in the virtue of a broader empiricism reflect Percy's belief that we will never heal the Cartesian cicatrix until we grasp the inextricability of mind and matter manifested in the fact that a sound, a vocable, can, when spoken by *Homo sapiens*, achieve meaning.

This leads to another basic tenet in Percy's thought—that the denotational relationship between symbol and referent is not casual but intentional, and that the symbol contains within itself, *in alio esse*, the thing that is symbolized. This is the key to the triadic theory of meaning Percy explores in several of his essays. The term *triadic* derives from a contention of C. S. Peirce that Percy feels has been neglected even by those who claim Peirce as mentor. Peirce contends that there are two kinds of natural phenomena, dyadic and triadic. Dyadic phenomena involve physical forces only; triadic phenomena involve meaning. All dyadic events can be resolved into causal relations between pairs of particles; in "Toward a Triadic Theory of Meaning," Percy quotes Peirce to show that triadic events involve an added dimension of meaning and are not "in any way resolvable into actions between pairs" (*MB*, 161). Peirce also says that an "index [or sign] is physically connected with its object . . . but the symbol is connected with its object by virtue of . . . the symbol-using mind" (*MB*, 162; ellipses in Percy), and more pointedly, "Every genuine triadic relation involves meaning" (*MB*, 161).

Percy is delighted to find such pointed statements on this issue by one of the most respected philosophical methodologists of the past hundred years, and he stresses that semiotics, for all its claim to derive from Peirce, has neglected this basic distinction and has tried to construe all relationships, including that of denotation, as dyadic. This reductionism has put some semanticists in anomalous positions—Ogden and Richards having to call denotation an "imputed" rather than "real" relation; Stuart Chase's feeling it necessary to remind us that we cannot eat the word *oyster*; and Korzybski's frustrated protestation that the utterance "This is a pencil" involves an intolerable identification of object and vocable, and his insistence quoted in "Semiotic and a Theory of Knowledge" that "'Whatever you say the object is, well, it is not'" (*MB*, 262).

Percy agrees with Peirce that the symbol-referent relation is not physical but intentional. But this does not mean it is sheerly mental; it does have a physical aspect, which is the basis for the possibility of approaching linguistic acts empirically and learning how the symbol works and how human beings know. In the act of naming, of speaking, a "sensuous symbol," *i.e.*, audible sounds constituting a word, are linked with their object in a relation of denotation by the speaker. This simultaneously physical and intentional event is, Percy acknowledges, mysterious, but it is the prototype of human knowing. It is a pairing, in some sense an identification, yet not an identity. The semanticists say the referent is conceived through the vehicle of the symbol; Percy, preferring Scholastic language says, in "Semiotic and a Theory of Knowledge," "the symbol has the peculiar property of containing within itself *in alio esse*, in another mode of existence, that which is symbolized" (*MB*, 261). The speaker *intends* the thing and thus comes to know it and to validate it, by laying alongside it the word-symbol through which we know it. This simultaneously physical and intentional relationship cannot, Percy says, be reduced to cause and effect or to stimulus and response. As Percy asserts in one compact statement:

The thing is intended through its symbol which you say and I can repeat, and it is only through this quasi identification that it can be conceived at all. Thus it is, I believe, that an empirical and semiotical approach to meaning illumines and confirms in an unexpected manner the realist doctrine of the union of the knower and the thing known. The metaphysical implications of semiotic are clear enough. Knowing is not a causal sequence but an immaterial union. It is a union, however, which is mediated through material entities, the symbol and its object. Nor is it a private phenomenon—rather is it an exercise in intersubjectivity in which the Thou serves as an indispensable colleague. Both the relation of intersubjectivity and the intentional relation of identity are real yet immaterial bonds. (*MB*, 263–64)

In "Metaphor as Mistake" Percy elaborates this idea that the symbol, graspable simultaneously by ear and eye and by mind, is nucleus and prototype of human knowing. There he quotes one of his favorite statements from Gabriel Marcel, that when we ask what something is—what for example a given flower is—we are paradoxically more satisfied by some mere name than by a precise botanical classification or a definition. So, Percy contends, there is something wonderfully pleasing about being told that a bird is a "Blue-dollar hawk," and we are disappointed later to learn that the correct and more descriptive name is "Blue darter hawk." The latter term pragmatically describes the bird; the former gives us something to "lay alongside" it whereby to grasp it more fully: "Blue-dollar is not applicable as a modifier at all, for it refers to a *something else* besides the bird, a something which occupies the same ontological status as the bird. Blue darter tells us something about the bird, what it does, what its color is; blue-dollar tells, or the [hearer] hopes it will tell, what the bird *is*" (*MB*, 71–72). At the conclusion of this article Percy defends his view of "metapor as mistake" and links it with his ideas about the denotational relation and about human knowing:

This "wrongness" of metaphor is seen to be not a vagary of poets but a special case of that mysterious "error" which is the very condition of our knowing anything at all. This "error," the act of symbolization, is itself the instrument of knowing and is an error only if we do not appreciate its intentional character. If we do not take note of it, or if we try to exorcise it as a primitive residue, we shall find ourselves on the horns of the same dilemma which has plagued philosophers since the eighteenth century. The semanticists, on the one horn, imply that we know as the angels know, directly and without mediation (although saying in the next breath that we have no true knowledge of reality); all that remains is to name what we know and this we do by a semantic "rule"; but they do not and cannot say how we know. The behaviorists, on the other, imply that we do not know at all but only respond and that even art is a mode of sign-response; but they do not say how they know this. But we do know, not as the angels know and not as dogs know but as men, who must know one thing through the mirror of another. (*MB*, 81–82)[3]

Other aspects of this triadic theory of meaning and of what Percy means by an empirical study of symbolic behavior are explored in "The Symbolic Structure of Interpersonal Process" (1961) and "Toward a Triadic Theory of Meaning" (1972). In these he contends that the vexed problem of intersubjectivity can be approached by our attending to what actually occurs when people converse. In the earlier essay, Percy, in addition to challenging the behavioristic theory of interpersonal process (in effect a nontheory), also tries to outline the generic traits of symbolic behavior and to illustrate their relevance for understanding therapist-patient situation. Percy claims here that "the generic traits of symbolic behavior are not 'mental' at all. They are empirically ascertainable and have indeed been observed often enough" (*MB*, 195–96), and he says "it would be quite possible to defend the thesis that Buber's analysis of human existence and human relations is also empirical in the broad sense of the word" (*MB*, 197). As evidence for his contentions, Percy cites the opinions of psychiatrists such as Ruesch and Jaffe that interpersonal processes are not reducible to organism-environment processes, and he cites Schachtel's idea that children show an "autonomous object interest" distinct from need satisfactions and wish fulfillments (*MB*, 196). He also mentions Buber's categories of "distance" and "relation" as representing unique but observable modes of human interaction. Of all such modes of experience he says that they are "neither random nor reducible characteristics of human behavior. They are rather among the prime and generic traits of the highly structured meaning-situation found in symbolic behavior. What is more important, these traits are ascertainable not by a philosophical anthropology . . . but by an empirical analysis of language events as they are found to occur in the genetic appearance of language in the encultured child, in blind deaf-mutes, and in the structure of everyday language exchanges" (*MB*, 197).

In illustration of his belief that we can study "the structure of everyday language exchanges," Percy describes certain generic features of the "symbolic behavior" they involve: that such behavior occurs in and presumes an intersubjective community; that symbol-using creatures inherently project a meaningful "world," whereas sign-using animals exist in a physical "environment"; that the speaking being, having projected this world, cannot forgo decisions about how he will live in it; that a sentence is not simply a syntactic structure or a physical response, but a mode of assertion, and as such it is "open to a rich empirical phenomenology that is wholly unprovided by what passes currently as semantics" (*MB*, 205). Percy typically denies that recognizing these traits of symbolic behavior involves him in the high-flown categories of existentialism or phenomenology; to say that we live in a world that requires decisions is not to invoke existentialist *Dasein*: "It is no more than a working concept arrived at through the necessity of giving an account of the organism who participates in symbolic behavior" (*MB*, 204).

The most interesting and concrete portion of this 1961 essay is an illustration of this "rich empirical phenomenology." Taking as starting point a brief exchange between a therapist and a patient, Percy develops an analysis focusing on the complex kinds of role-playing, of assertion, of "world projection," and of being-in-the-world that can maintain in even a brief instance of symbolic behavior. To the patient's description of a sexual encounter in a dream, the therapist replies "Horrendous! (Pronounced heartily with a *j*: horrenjus!)" (*MB*, 207). Percy develops a subtle analysis of this exchange, showing in part how the "exaggerated vaudeville-British propriety" of the pronunciation puts the patient at ease and joins the two in "good-natured deprecation of the Puritan streak in our culture," but does not contravene the therapist's underlying objective stance.

Percy is working of course from a fictional account, and all of his attributions of motive and attitude to therapist and to patient are hypothetical so that he produces something closer to what we expect in a novel than in an account of psychological behavior. But his analysis begins with a believable exchange betwen patient and therapist and moves to a tangible, believable analysis. The rigorous behaviorist might object that all of this is suppositious and that the motives and modes Percy posits would, even in an actual situation, be inferred and unprovable. But Percy's examples show convincingly that the qualities he deals in are tangible and experienceable, and that any analysis of human behavior leaving out such aspects is sorely incomplete.

In a 1972 essay, Percy provides another more organized but less fully illustrated discussion of this topic. The main contention of "Toward a Triadic Theory of Meaning" is that the basic unit of language is the sentence, which involves a coupling of a class of sounds with a class of things into a relation not isomorphic with any world-relation. Percy also proposes that considering sentences as triadic behavior involves us in a set of parameters different from those relevant to dyadic relationships. These include (as we saw earlier) a qualitative, meaningful *community* or *world* in which the sentence is uttered (this may for any series of utterances be a constant or a variable); the *medium* of the sentence (*i.e.* , whether "I need you" is said by lover to lover or by the president to a television audience); and the *normative dimensions* of the sentence. This last relates not simply to whether the sentence is true or false, but to whether it is literal or metaphoric, perfunctory or revelatory, sincere or insincere, etc., Percy's point being that several species of "normativeness" enter into every human utterance. He also explains that the receiver of a sentence may mis-take it in a variety of ways, by mis-taking any of the parameters mentioned above. He can, for instance, mis-take the qualitative world, or the normative mode of the sentence, and Percy gives examples of these from therapist-patient exchanges, where such large-scale errors are particularly likely.

Later in this essay, however, Percy acknowledges a large question that must continually be in the mind of the writer and the reader; he questions the possibility of a methodology for studying symbolic behavior:

So here is the real question, or rather the main specter which haunts every inquiry into language as behavior. Granted the shortcomings of the two major methodological approaches to the talking patient—the analytical-psychical and the organismic-behavioristic—is not the sole remaining alternative the novelistic? Instead of "novelistic" we could say phenomenological, for the novelist must first and last be a good phenomenologist, and to most behavorial scientists phenomenologists are closer to novelists than to scientists. But is it not the case that when all is said and done and all theories aside, what happens is that the therapist gets to know his patient pretty well, understands him, intuits him, can talk with him and about him—and that behavioral theory can never say much about it? (*MB*, 186)

Percy explores this further and suggests that we should not yet conclude that a theory of symbolic behavior is impossible. But as we shall see, the question he acknowledges here raises issues central to his purposes as an essayist, and surfaces in other ways in other essays.

Percy's "A Theory of Language" (1975) deserves special attention for several reasons. Here he ventures more specifically into linguistic theory than he has done before, challenging the adequacy of transformational grammar and outlining his own alternative theory of languge. Also, this essay illustrates in another way the perhaps insurmountable difficulties Percy acknowledged at the end of "Toward a Triadic Theory of Meaning." For one, it is doubtful that anyone who does not share Percy's presuppositions will feel that he gives an adequate account of how meaning gets incarnated into a sentence. For another, Percy does something in this essay that seems surprising indeed in view of his own earlier statement, something that testifies eloquently to the frustration bred by trying to bridge the gap between utterance and meaning, between mind and brain: he points to a portion of the brain that he suggests may be the neurophysical substrate for the triadic structure of the symbolic act.

Noting again the bifurcated situation in current linguistic theory, Percy contends that contemporary "linguistic theory has not yet reached the level of explanatory adequacy of, say, seventeenth-century biology" (*MB*, 301). Turning more specifically to transformational grammar, he says that it fails as an explanatory theory of language, "because it violates a cardinal rule of scientific explanation, namely that a theory cannot use as a component of its hypothesis the very phenomenon to be explained" (*MB*, 304). Elaborating this, he says,

So it will not do for an explanatory theory of language which must presumably account for the utterance and understanding of a sentence or "surface structure" to hypothesize a "deep structure" as its

source when deep structures are themselves described as "kernel sentences" (Chomsky) or "underlying propositions" (Chomsky), when in
fact it is the phenomenon of sentence utterance itself in whatever form,
kernel sentences or propositions, that is unique among species and
therefore, one would think, the major goal of theorizing. (*MB*, 304)

Of the idea of a "Language Acquisition Device" (LAD), which
Chomsky offers as part of a schema to account for the child's
learning language, Percy says, "this schema is in no sense an
explanatory model. It is no more than a statement of the problem under investigation. The 'LAD' appears to be a black box
whose contents are altogether unknown" (*MB*, 302).

Percy's central criticism of transformational grammar, then,
is that it has no explanatory power because it "in effect posits
syntax as an underivable and therefore unexplainable given"
(*MB*, 305). Percy moves to correct this by asserting that whatever Chomsky's "LAD" may be, its central component is not
syntactical, but semological-phonological; it links or couples a
class of objects with a class of sounds. The basic sentence has
the form "S (is) P," and this structure is implicit in the one-
word naming sentence in which the child first names any element in his experience. For Percy then the genetically prime
component of language is a semological-phonological linkage,
not a syntactic structure. This, he feels, has the advantage of
being founded upon a general semiotic (*i.e.*, theory of the relations between people and signs and things) and thus treating
syntax as but one dimension of sentence theory (*MB*, 307). The
emphasis upon a sound-object coupling, Percy says, also ac-
cords better with the ontogenesis of language in children than
does generative linguistics; it allows the possibility of finding a
neurophysiological correlate of the model; and it permits the
assimilation of linguistic theory to a more general theory of all
symbolic transformations (*MB*, 307–308).

Percy then traces the stages of language acquisition in the
child through the naming stage, to the stage characterized by

two-word constructions of the "pivot-open" type (*e.g.*, my sock, my boat, my fan, etc.), to the differentiation of the pivot class, and into "open-open" constructions. His contention here is that his semiotic-grounded sentence theory deals more adequately with the phenomena of naming and speaking than does any merely syntactical theory. Though theoreticians of language often neglect the one-word naming phase of language acquisition in children to push on to the phrase stage, Percy contends that naming is the unique act, and that even one-word naming utterances are, semiotically, complete sentences. Percy does, however, distinguish two stages of language acquisition: in the first (the naming stage) the child "couples" semological and phonological elements into what Percy calls a "semophone"; in the second the child "couples" semophones into NP-VP (*i.e.*, noun phrase-verb phrase) sentences.

Later in "A Theory of Language," Percy invokes Peirce's theory of abduction in an attempt to offer a more tangible theory of meaning. (Briefly, abduction is Peirce's term, correlative to both induction and deduction, for the human faculty for developing explanatory theories from facts and deductions.) Percy invokes the idea in justifying his own theory of language, but as he uses it, abduction amounts simply to (1) an acknowledgment of this unique human faculty (itself unexplained), and (2) an invoking of the principle of economy in proposing any explanatory model.

Under the aegis of abduction, Percy does something surprising: drawing on the image of the "couplings" that occur in the basic sentence form, he suggests the possibility of a neurophysiological correlate for this coupling process. In view of its function, Percy suggests that this physiological structure should be recently evolved in the human brain and either absent or rudimentary in the highest primates, and that it should be "structurally and functionally triadic in character, with the 'base' of the triad comprising what must surely be massive interconnections between the auditory and visual cortexes" (*MB*, 326). Drawing on the work of Norman Geschwind, Percy suggests that he can identify the sought-for structure: "the human inferior parietal lobule, which includes the angular and supramarginal gyri, to a rough approximation areas 39 and 40 of Brodmann" (*MB*, 326).

Percy makes this suggestion tentatively: he claims this physiological structure as no more than the correlate of the process he describes, and he acknowledges that the "coupler" remains a complete mystery. But clearly this idea of a physiological correlate has a value for Percy, and just as clearly it focuses for us certain problems in Percy's theories, not the least of which is a confusion between the triadic relationship involved in meaning and the shape of the physical structure. But the basic problem is whether Percy, or anyone, can give an explanatory account of meaning, of how symbolization works.

The virtue of Percy's essays is the clarity with which they expose the gaps and inconsistencies in certain contemporary methodologies; they make us aware of how basic the problem of meaning is and how inadequately it is handled by linguistics and psychology. Percy's criticism of Chomsky's syntactics and of the LAD is, quite correctly, that it either presumes an answer or offers a non-answer to the basic problem. But does Percy's insistence on a semological-phonological coupling and his suggestion that the event occurs in the parietal lobule do any more? Even if we agree with Percy that a theory of language must acknowledge a coupling of a class of objects and a class of sounds, and that the basic unit of language is a sentence of the "S (is) P" form, we still feel that all Percy offers is a more specific description of the problem, not an "explanation" of how it works. It is of great value to look clearly at the problem, but the closer we look the more we realize that there is a mystery here that no one has yet explained. And Percy's attempt to find some physiological base for the intentional act not only fails to explain anything, but seems to compromise what Percy himself had earlier contended. In his essay "Culture: The Antinomy of the Scientific Method" Percy said:

We can observe the overt behavior of a physicist as he goes about setting up his apparatus and making measurements. But even if we had an exact knowledge of the colloidal brain events which occur in each case, these events can never be coterminous with the assertions *This is grass* and $E=mc^2$. It is possible to say this, not because of our present knowledge of brain events, but because no space-time event, however intricate, no chemical or colloidal interaction, no configuration of field forces, can issue in an assertory event. As Cassirer put it, there is a gap between the responses of animals and the propositions of men which no amount of biological theorizing can bridge. (*MB*, 219)

Earlier in "A Theory of Language" Percy had compared current linguistic theory with seventeenth-century biological theory, and he points to the breakthroughs achieved by Harvey's comparing the heart with a pump and Malphigi's comparing the kidney to a filter, apparently hoping for something analogous in modern language theory. But for all his hope that a radical empiricism can cast some light on this, Percy cannot himself lead us out of the labyrinth.[4]

One other of Percy's essays deserves to be considered separately. "The Message in the Bottle" was published in 1959, but its importance for Percy is shown by his using its title for this collection of essays. Its importance for us is that it sharply focuses certain questions and inconsistencies that run throughout Percy's thought.

The essay is preceded by two epigraphs, one from St. Thomas, the other from Kierkegaard. The first says "The act of faith consists essentially in knowledge and there we find its formal or specific perfection"; the second says "Faith is not a form of knowledge; for all knowledge is either knowledge of the eternal, excluding the temporal and the historical as indifferent, or it is pure historical knowledge. No knowledge can have for its object the absurdity that the eternal is the historical." Taking these as his starting points, Percy tries to argue, with Thomas and against Kierkegaard, that there need be no radical severance between faith (*i.e.*, those matters of deep personal concern to us), and knowledge (*i.e.*, those things demonstrable by some accepted methodology). In pursuing this aim, Percy touches upon several issues fundamental to his own world view. The most important of these are whether man's present malaise is the result of something that has occurred in the Western mind in the past few centuries, or whether it is generic to the human situation; and whether knowledge can ever significantly be brought to the support of faith. Is man's plight of local origin and susceptible of solution through a limited, reasonable program, or is it radical and approachable only by means that grasp our whole being and reorient us?

In this essay, Percy proposes to divide propositions not into the traditional categories of analytic and synthetic, but into "knowledge *sub specie aeternitatis*" and "news." The distinction relates not to logic or epistemology but to the relevance of the proposition for the hearer's "predicament." If it is relevant, it is news; if not, it is knowledge. Percy further contends that in addition to being relevant to the hearer, news is not deducible, repeatable, or confirmable at the time of hearing. The hearer must respond to the news and must therefore "act by a canon of acceptance which is usable *prior* to the procedure of verification" (*MB*, 133). This is not to say, however, that there are no controls over whether the hearer assents to the news. Whether and how the hearer responds is not, Percy stresses, purely arbitrary; it does not fly in the face of reason. The canons of acceptance involve (1) the relevance of the news to the hearer's predicament; (2) the credentials of the newsbearer; and (3) the possibility of the news. This third criterion is particularly important in that it keeps the "news" in some kind of congruence with reality and with knowledge. For Percy's further purpose is to argue (with Thomas and against Kierkegaard) that there need be no radical severance between faith and knowledge. Percy acknowledges that Kierkegaard made, even exulted in, such a distinction, but he stresses that Thomas did not. For Thomas, scientific knowledge is that "in which assent is achieved by reason"; knowledge of faith is that "in which scientific knowledge and assent are undertaken simultaneously" (*MB*, 145). Percy affirms the continued possibility of the second.

In siding with Thomas rather than Kierkegaard, Percy is saying that there need be no severance, much less opposition, between "news" and "knowledge"—that it should be possible to support assent by knowledge rather than to regard the two as antagonistic. This belief in the value of reason is consistent with and lies behind Percy's aims as an essayist. In particular it lies behind his contentions that a sufficiently thorough empiricism can lead us into a methodology capable of dealing with the question of meaning, and that there can be a methodology for articulating the symbolic aspects of behavior. For Percy in this role as essayist, it seems that man's present malaise is largely a matter of cultural and intellectual events of the past few hundred years that eroded the traditional Judaeo-Christian view of man, and that when corrected will permit our return to some such happy union of methodology and faith.

But this sanguine hope tells only a part of Percy's story, and probably the smaller part. In his novels, in his essays—even in the very essay we are discussing—there are signs that Percy is more Kierkegaardian, less Thomistic, than he would claim. Throughout Percy's work, some of his most virulent satire is directed at those approaches to man's malaise that miss the point so badly because they are so simplistically, so offensively, reasonable. Also, Percy is extremely adept, in fiction and in expository prose, in evoking man as castaway, as radically alienated, and as needing some major reorientation, perhaps even some awareness of his own alienation. In these instances, we find it hard indeed to believe that Percy is talking about a problem localized in Western culture since Descartes, or one susceptible of solution by any rational methodology. We wonder what would be the effect on Percy if Chomsky and Skinner were to accept this triadic theory of meaning and begin to expound it. Would the result be to make Percy joyous, or heartsick? If the idea that sign and symbol are qualitatively different, the idea that human language is unique, were accepted by philosophers and linguists, would this bring man, or us as individuals, out of our plight as castaways? I doubt it, for it seems unlikely that our malaise can be cured except by a personal response such as no expository essay, no received methodology, however radically empirical, can bring about.

Percy is, as are we all, a man divided, but he has wrestled with the division more vigorously and expressed it more articulately than most. One deep reflection of this is his dual role as essayist and novelist. The two modes are not even directed at the same audience, not because the novels are fictive and the essays philosophical—many readers can span that gap with little difficulty—but because his essays are directed to those like-minded souls who wish for some reasonable expression of what they know to be true, while his novels are aimed at those who require more drastic therapy. For in his novels Percy hopes to "save" his readers in something like the traditional sense—he hopes to achieve an experiential shock and reorientation that no essay however reasonable and persuasive can accomplish.

The primary value of these essays lies in their attempt to win certain basic questions about language, about meaning, about human nature, back from those specialists who have claimed them but neglected them. In his fine essay "The Loss of the Creature" (1958), Percy convincingly illustrates the depletion of our experience engendered by our surrendering to the authority of specialists in so many spheres of life. Percy's essays aim to reclaim certain basic questions from the specialists' province. These essays are valuable also for their proposing the formal study of interpersonal symbolic behavior and outlining its rudiments. And while I personally would regret seeing Percy himself turn his energies fully into this channel, his suggestions do deserve developing into a full-scale phenomenology of symbolic behavior. Finally, as I suggested earlier, these essays are valuable even in their equivocations and inconsistencies, because they testify to the scale of Percy's attempt and to the depth of the problems we face.

WILLIAM H. POTEAT

Reflections on Walker Percy's Theory of Language:

Or, It is Better to Stay with Helen Keller at the Well-House in Tuscumbia, Alabama, Than to Venture To Mars and be Devoured by the Ravening Particles

WALKER PERCY'S sensibility captures and holds our attention because it embodies a plexus of puzzles. One of the puzzles is this: how does it happen that a writer so absolutely right in all his philosophical instincts should, when he undertakes to give them explicit embodiment in the medium of an essay, betray his own deepest insights? In order to answer that question, I wish to undertake a serious look at Walker Percy's theory of language, set forth in *The Message in the Bottle*, in the context of his vocation as a writer and critic. I should like to avoid any appearance here of arguing *ad hominem*; and I wish to take "A Theory of Language" with the absolute philosophical seriousness it both requires and deserves. While however carrying out this straight-forward task in familiar ways, I wish to retain as its background the image of Percy as a paradigmatic case of the dropout from the "old modern age" who has turned critic of that age. For I shall be suggesting that dropping out is the most radical philosophic feat; that only men of the most complex sensibility—more complex than that of most professional philosophers—are inclined to do so; and that no one can consistently succeed, since it is analogous to carrying through the Cartesian program of sundering oneself from one's roots.

At the outset the reader should know of three general premises that shape these reflections. I shall make a defense only of the second and will elaborate but not defend the third.

First, I believe that the Walker Percy phenomenon can be fruitfully examined only if we realize that the existence-sphere in which he appears is irony: he is not serious in the same way about the practice of the art of fiction as is, say, Saul Bellow; nor is he serious in the same way about doing philosophy as was Charles Saunders Peirce, or even William James, one of whom he admires, the other of whom he resembles. Academic critics neglecting Percy's ironic pose, will, I suspect, find his novels at once clever and profound but aesthetically incomplete. Academic philosophers, in a generous mood, will certainly find *The Message in the Bottle* pleasant reading, provocative at points, but not really "professional." At bottom, these two sorts of criticism come to the same thing. It is as if both the novels and the essays are the works of pseudonymous authors. What does it mean to say this? It means that neither were written as ends in themselves, but were written to serve other, undisclosed ends. The works in which Percy overcomes his irony and becomes "serious" are yet to come. I myself shall feel no loss if they never do.

Second, Percy's philosophy of language especially as embodied in "A Theory of Language," is, I want to say, at bottom, or at the crux, *profoundly* confused. I do not mean hopelessly, utterly, or trivially confused. I mean confused as the result of exigent, original, and polemically deadly thought, confused in such a way as to require a sober and concentrated effort to understand its nature; I mean that his confusion is of a kind that, when it is understood, will shed a special kind of light, for it is not just the product of the eccentricity of one man vis-à-vis his own time, singular though he be, but the embodiment of the truncated radicalism of the criticism of a whole cultural atmosphere summed up in Percy's own name for the age beyond which we now live, "the old modern age."

Third, Percy's profoundest and most original contribution to the philosophy of language and to a theory of man is to be found not in those essays in which he is being dialectically most explicit and rigorous, as in "A Theory of Language," but in those in which he is being least so, as in "The Delta Factor." As to Percy's seriousness, it appears less in his own than in another's words. The epigraph to *The Last Gentleman*, for example, is from Romano Guardini: "Loneliness in faith will be terrible. Love will disappear from the face of the public world, but the more precious will be the love which flows from one lonely person to another."

1

Percy opens *The Message in the Bottle* with "The Delta Factor," the fulcrum of which essay is his discovery of the clue, in three short paragraphs of Helen Keller's *The Story of My Life*, to man's "breakthrough into the daylight of language" (*MB*, 3). That breakthrough parallels the original emergence of *Homo Symbolificus*. Presenting man as symbolmonger, Percy hints broadly about the larger purpose which a theory of language is meant to serve: it is to be the philosophic ground of a theory of man.

It is his assumption that current theories of language are untenable and that "man's theory about himself doesn't work any more" either (*MB*, 19). An investigation of the phenomena of speech may perhaps shed light upon the question as to why men "prefer bad environments to good, a hurricane on Key Largo to an ordinary Wednesday in Short Hills" (*MB*, 27). Percy knows that, "A theory of man must account for the alienation of man" (*MB*, 23); but the theories of the "old modern age," obsessed by seeking ever more ingenious explanations of this alienation either in the organism alone or in the environment alone, are clearly bankrupt. Percy then wonders: "Is there any other way to understand why people feel so bad in the twentieth century and writers feel so good writing about people feeling bad than in terms of the peculiar parameters, the joys and sorrows of symbol-mongering?" (*MB*, 45).

The investigation of *Homo Symbolificus*, then, is to be the source of a new theory of man, of what used to be called a "philosophical anthropology." It is to be a view of man's place in the cosmos, an answer to the question by Pascal at the beginning of the "old modern age," asked by him with the special pathos of this question in that age: "For in fact what is man in nature? A nothing in comparison with the infinite, an All in comparison with the Nothing, a mean between nothing and everything. . . . the end of things and their beginning are hopelessly hidden from him in an impenetrable secret." [1]

Percy, of course, entertains no pretensions that in *The Message in the Bottle* he has offered even a down payment on such a comprehensive theory. I do take him however to believe that that view of man embodied in the thought of Classical antiquity, in the Jewish and Christian theological-philosophical traditions, in the Continental, English, and American Enlightenment is derived from and developed out of premises that, as a matter of fact, we do no longer hold or are well on our way to finding suspect. For these reasons we must make a new beginning. Percy believes that the new premises may well be found in the phenomenon *Homo Symbolificus* and that at least one of the virtues that an investigation of this phenomenon may disclose is its power to account for man's deep, that is, his native, constitutional alienation as *Homo Symbolificus*. We find that Percy seeks an explanatory theory of language to account for two different phenomena: the fact that Helen Keller, in a few hours, and most of the rest of us, in months, break through into "the daylight of language" by discovering the one-word elliptical sentence, "[this is] water," discovering, in short, that things have names; and that having made this breakthrough, we humans are forever alienated from our environment, cast out of the Eden of mere organismic life into the world to suffer the "joys and the sorrows of symbol-mongering" (*MB*, 45). Thus we feel "bad in good environments and good in bad environments" (*MB*, 3) because symbols intervene between our experience and ourselves.

Let me now traverse a wide arc (to return at the end of this essay) over two hundred and fifty-three pages from the end of "The Delta Factor" to the beginning of "A Theory of Language" in *The Message in the Bottle*, in order more explicitly to connect the aims of the developed theory to the larger philosophical goals it is designed to serve.

There is a real injustice to Percy in this procedure, since even though it follows the logic of the book and, in a sense, the logic of the argument, it reverses the actual chronology of composition. Also Percy's most compelling treatment of language is set in the philosophically ample and relaxed setting of "The Delta Factor" amidst the concrete images of Helen Keller at the well-house, "the sadness of an ordinary Wednesday in Short Hills," and "the joys and sorrows of symbol-mongering" (*MB*, 45). Here, too, much of the argument is formulated in dialogue, that is, in the concrete representation of speech acts. Finally, in "The Delta Factor" we feel Walker Percy himself right there, in a first personal narrative passage such as this: "Would it be possible, I was wondering then in Louisiana, to use the new key to open a new door and see in a new way? See man not the less mysterious but of a piece, maybe even whole, a whole creature put together again after the three-hundred-year-old Cartesian split that sundered man from himself in the old modern age" (*MB*, 44). This pathos, this concreteness, this narrative and dialogue keep Percy close to his own incarnate reality as a speaker, himself often sad on ordinary mornings, and close therefore to the irreducible and radical truth about language which he sees.

However, if we are to take him seriously as a philosopher of language we must take him where he and we stand most to profit from what I have called his *profound* confusion, and for that we turn to "A Theory of Language." In this essay, we are warned in its subtitle, Percy has discovered that no explanatory theory of language exists and proposes what he calls a crude model of such a theory on the ground that something is better than nothing.

Bloomfield, Harris, and Chomsky, different though are their methods, offer no explanatory theory of language because, approaching the phenomenon "through a formal analysis of the corpora of languages," their analysis, Percy says, "abstracts both from the people who speak the language and the things they talk about" (*MB*, 299). Taking Chomsky as the example, Percy points out that "transformational grammar is not an explanatory theory of language as phenomenon but rather a formal description, an algorithm, of the competence of a person who speaks a language" (*MB*, 304). Percy then goes on to explain: "There is no evidence that this algorithm bears a necessary relation to what is happening *inside the head* of a person who speaks or understands a sentence" (*MB*, 304) [emphasis added]. I call attention to the words "inside the head" because it seems clear to me that, for Percy (though it is not clear that he appreciates this), even though the Chomskians allow for making the distinction between what is "outside the head" and what must be (logically) "somewhere else," they fail of an explanatory theory because they cannot connect what is "outside the head" with anything "inside" it. For Chomsky it would be grammar and syntax which are "outside the head" and a computerlike Language Acquisition Device or a preset restriction on the form of grammar (which would really have no logical relation to the cerebral cortex) which would be "somewhere else." For Percy and Geschwind, we learn in "A Theory of Language," the "somewhere else" would be the inferior parietal lobule "inside the head" (*MB*, 326–67).

B. F. Skinner and the learning theorists on the other hand do "offer a plenary model of language as a phenomenon, which meets all the specifications of explanatory theory" (*MB*, 303), but it is wrong, according to Percy. My suspicion is that Skinner's proposals count for Percy as an explanatory theory, although an erroneous one, because, bad as it is, the dyadic model of S→ $\boxed{s \rightarrow r}$ →R allows us to get "inside the head," which is a move in the right direction away from the ghostly, discarnate transformation rules of the Cartesians.

It needs to be observed here however that Skinner's model allows for the "inside the head"—"outside the head" distinction only by means of a pseudosubstitution. That is, on its face, sign and stimulus, signified and response seem to be logically homogeneous concepts.[2] A strict application of Skinner's principles however makes it clear that either *sign* is "reduced" to *stimulus*, in which case the hierarchical distinction between "inside the head"—"outside the head" vanishes; or *sign* and *stimulus* are logically heterogeneous, and Skinner's theory is only a very clumsy and covert version of the theory Percy himself wishes to advocate. In short, Percy seems not to have noticed that the appeal to the "inside the head" – "outside the head" distinction as a ground for distinguishing between a mere descriptive theory and a false explanatory one can be applied simultaneously to his two instant cases, Skinner and Chomsky, only in a logically most *equivocal* and therefore *profoundly* (in my above sense) confusing way.

For, applied strictly in Skinner's theory, "inside the head" would refer to the "hard-nosed" empirically located excitations traveling along neural paths in the cerebral cortex; "outside the head" would refer to such S→R structures closer to the body's surface or, extending "outward" from there in the empirically located environment. In Skinner's theory as he would like it to be, logically, "inside" and "outside" are of precisely the same order. This being so, "inside" and "outside" are indistinguishable, hence without sense. At most they refer merely to different "regions" of a homogeneous universe of S→R relations. For Percy this is an explanatory theory, but a wrong one because, though empirically grounded, it assimilates *signs* to *stimulus*.

Applied strictly in Chomsky's theory, "outside the head" would refer to "the corpora of language," which is logically irreducible to mere signs, hence to that which is logically homogeneous with events in the cerebral cortex. For Percy, this is a theory that *describes* languge as irreducibly *language*, as we all understand this notion commonsensically, but it *explains* nothing because it is unable to connect these irreducibly linguistic phenomena to anything definite in our brains, except through the medium of the black-box Language Acquisition Device, which stands to Chomsky's theory as the pineal gland stands to Descartes'.

We shall have to see whether, when he advances his own "crude" explanatory theory, Percy avoids the horns of the dilemma which he rightly deplores. But—grossly to simplify— Percy's unease with the structuralists and the behaviorists is due to the fact that the theories of both are abstracted from the irreducible phenomenon, speaking-meaning, hearing-comprehending meaning: the first from the body, speech organs, and brain of the speaker situated in the world saying what he means to his hearers about their mutual world; the second from the human mind, that is, the act (as opposed to the behavior) of speaking. Chomsky analyzes "speech" as if it took place only among gods; Skinner as if it took place only among *essentially* dumb brutes. There are really no speakers in either theory.

If I understand Percy aright, he wishes in his own theory to do away with this "either an angel or a brute" dilemma and to do this in an explanatory theory that does not scant the act of speaking. However, in due course, I shall try to show that he fails to do so because he *too* has been guilty of abstraction, by a failure to keep under his feet at every moment, however usefully he might analytically elaborate upon it, that ground which is the primordial setting out of which each man's reflection upon language is generated. He fails to locate his discussion in the radical linguistic (I would say, human) reality, the admittedly precarious, conceptually elusive, and ontologically ambiguous ground upon which each one of us uniquely stands; that is, Percy too disregards our power of authoring, authorizing, standing-by and owning-up to the words we speak in our own names.

A theory of language that is not generated out of and reintegrated to this phenomenon of speech avails us mainly confusion. Any act of reflection that does not allude to its own ontological radix antecedent to reflection will always issue in reflected dualisms that will not be healed. Thus, the study of language, wherever it may venture in the meantime, must, it begins to appear, start and finish in integration with the irreducible reality of speakers saying and meaning what they say about their ambient world and of hearers comprehending what is said and meant. Any discourse on *syntax* or *verbal behavior* which does not integrate the speaking acts or writing acts of its actually existent author is an incomplete and potentially incoherent account of language.

We have seen how both Chomsky and Skinner reject, ignore, or forget this: the one as a methodological bracketing out, from which the theory in all its lucid angelism cannot recover; the other as an alleged empirical finding upon which the thoroughly incarnate theory is held to be based. Given the deepgoing intellectual currents of the "old modern age," if a theory is not incoherent at the outset, as Skinner's, but merely *incomplete*, as Chomsky's, hence only potentially incoherent, it will become *actually incoherent* when it is interpreted by the denizens of that age.

Percy's ironic relation to the "old modern age" is not enough to save him from an even subtler form of the same blunder. The Ravening Particles cast up by its residual dualisms—matter or mind, things or thought, theoretical reason or practical reason, object or subject—these devour the very substance of reflection. When the idea of the search occurs to one, as it has to Percy, he had better be prepared to take with absolute philosophic seriousness: first, the irreducible equivocalness of an inquiry into language; second, the need to stake out, accredit, and dwell in a ground in his own personal ensconcement in the world; and finally the irreducible ontological hierarchy among things in the world and the logical heterogeneity of concepts.[3] The shrewd amateur's intuitive grasp of the fundamental issues, overlooked by the "serious" specialist who is really by definition a reductionist, even the novelist's natural eros for the concrete, will not protect him when he gets to the crux of these issues. He will have to go farther back—or down—"ontologically" before going forward.

The mystery of our human mode of being, of our lived irreducible unity in apparent duality, comes to focus, is deepened, and radicalized in the inherently equivocal status of language. Let us, then, look more closely at this, as prologomenon to the criticism of Percy's theory.

If I were to make a list of all of the things and of all of the sorts of things that there are in the world, say: rocks, Williston Bibb Barrett's funny knee, amoebas, Halley's comet, neural traces, the gross national product of Sri Lanka in 1971, the fastest one-hundred-meter footrace over run, black holes in space, a blackwhole in space, *The Tempest*, fantasies, my postcoital depression of June 2, 1975, logical entailment, *Don Giovanni*, the square roots of all the numbers from one to ten, people writing down words as I am here writing them down, people "thinking" about words as they write them down as I am "here" "thinking" about these words—*this* very word coming out of the end of my pen—as I write it down—if, I say, I were to make such a list, I would do so by using words as I have done here.

Imagine that I hand you my list, saying: "Here are all of the things and the sorts of things there are in the world." You might properly reply: "All of the things and the sorts of things there are in the world are not on this piece of paper; only their names. And that being so, you need to add two further names of things to the list, viz., *names of things* and *names of sorts of things*; or *proper names* and *class-terms*." Are the words I have just used to make the statement characterizing my list and your words used to take exception to that characterization of it, and to amplify it, among the things and the sorts of things on my list? If not, and I believe they are not, then what I have said to you and what you have said in reply are not among the things in the world; nor are they among the names of things in the world, not if the list is taken to be an exhaustive one, not if the limits of the list define the world. And, by the way, reader, do you notice anywhere among the words on this page, me, William H. Poteat, their author? No? Would, then, an attestation clause, signed by witnesses, help?

Here we see a few of the ways in which certain words used in certain ways with the authority of having been authored are funny sorts of things. The woman with whom I live hands me her grocery list: "Here's what we need for lunch," she says. At once a smart-ass and philosophically "profound," I say: "That may be what you need, but I intend to *eat* something for lunch." We are looking at the words on the list in two different, equally legitimate, equally revealing ways—though surely hers is the more ordinary way. The above words beginning with "We are looking at the words" are no part of the crossed transaction between me and the lady about what we respectively require for lunch. I want to say that *those* words, the words "We are looking at the words" are at one logical remove from *that* conversation even as what I am saying about the words being at *one* logical remove from it is at *two* logical removes. And I, William

H. Poteat, who am authorizing these words, claim these words as I author them while denying that I *am* them or am exhaustively *in* them, even though I can claim what I am claiming about the incommensurability of me and my words as beings or entities only *in* words by "owning" them as mine. And even, if in claiming these words as mine I own them, you are not likely to take offense either at my using the words or claiming them as mine, even though they are indeed yours and you may even claim them. And if no such dispute arises between us, it is neither because our relations are unusually genial nor because we don't know how to use the words *mine* and *own*, but rather because words are these strange sorts of things which are *there*, kind of in the world, and *there* for everybody, like space and time, and yet are there at all, *as* words, only when they are, in a way, the "private" property of a speaker who knows he owns them and admits to doing so; or will do so, or will deny doing so, if asked: "Do you really mean that?"

These are only a few of the strange, fascinating, and equivocal features of the act of speaking and writing words about speaking and writing. Because of these features, and others, Maurice Merleau-Ponty has been moved to say: "Language becomes something mysterious, since it is neither a self nor a thing. . . . [It] is neither a thing nor mind, but it is immanent and transcendent at the same time."[4] Percy understands all this and writes of it with originality, wit, polemical bite, and the ingenuousness of the true amateur who allows us to share in his wonder and to be edified by his naïveté. At the same time he writes from a background of sophisticated appreciation of some of the major writings on linguistics.

2

For all of this being so, however, between his reflections on the girl Helen Keller in an ecstasy at the well-house, in Tuscumbia, Alabama, in 1887, at the discovery that things have names through which he discovers "The Delta Factor" and his appeal in the last pages of "A Theory of Language" to the "human inferior parietal lobule" to account for this miracle, Percy acts out an intellectual drama that is as familiar as the history of the "old modern age." But Percy is a novelist who remains at once empathically close to and ironically detached from the alienated victims of abstraction, the "loss of the creature," the expertise, everydayness, and angelism that fill his novels. Yet he himself becomes a victim of that same abstraction when in his philosophical essays he loses his grip upon himself and thus upon the something that he is "onto." One of Percy's mentors Søren Kierkegaard might have applauded this way to "wound from behind" wherein even he who delivers the blow is himself wounded.

When we shall have examined in detail "A Theory of Language," we may come to suspect that the Martian whom Percy imagines looking pristinely at language among men on earth is in fact Walker Percy, and that Walker Percy is Williston Bibb Barrett in the Metropolitan Museum of Art where "the harder one looked, the more invisible the paintings became" (*LG*, 27). And so with Percy-Martian and the phenomena of speech. If only he had applied Dr. Thomas More's Qualitative Quantitative Ontological Lapsometer (*LR*, 226) to his own brain at the moment of wishing to view human speech from Mars, he would have immediately diagnosed that impulse as angelism!

In "A Theory of Language" Percy, obedient to Enlightenment philosophical injunctions, is looking very hard at language, but the harder one looks at the reflexivity of our relation to language, the more invisible it becomes. Language is man's singularity and therefore is a unique object of investigation; but any inquiry into speaking, hearing, and understanding is, like all inquiry, conducted in the medium of speaking, hearing, and understanding. It is therefore inherently and uniquely reflexive. That is why most readers of grocery lists think of groceries, not words, and why, as Percy says in "The Delta Factor," scientists who know a great deal about the world know less about language than about the backside of the moon. The phenomena of speech may be reflexively "observable," and speaking is certainly "observable behavior," but they are not observable as is the backside of the moon. Scientists as scientists are professionally committed to lucidity. Reflexivity is naturally opaque. The Ravening Particles—Cartesian dualism, the loss of the creature, the secret wish to "be useful to the behavioral scientist" (*MB*, 325), even while you suspect him—are "stealing the substance from [language] and viewer alike" (*LG*, 26).

B. F. Skinner and Noam Chomsky prize lucidity; that is why they prefer *Verbal Behavior* and *Aspects in the Theory of Syntax*, which are lucid, to accounts of speech phenomena which would make sense by coming to terms with the messy, opaque reflexivity of the speech about speech, which are not. Part of Percy's instincts, as he acknowledges in "The Delta Factor," are "on the side of the scientists in general and in particular on the side of the hardheaded empiricism of American behavioral science" (*MB*, 34); and that part of Percy is still at work insisting upon an explanatory theory of language. Thus in "A Theory of Language," he prefers the theory that refers to the "human inferior parietal lobule," because it will be more "useful to the behavioral scientist." However, Percy's own theory leaves the nature of the act of speech an utter mystery. This part of Percy harbors the same secret promethean longings for lucidity that Skinner and Chomsky harbor; and such lucidity is the animus par excellence of the Enlightened "old modern age," of which Dr. Thomas More with his Lapsometer is the diagnostician.

3

"A Theory of Language" proffers "a crude explanatory" theory of language on the assumption that none now exists and that something is better than nothing. Though Percy does not formulate his question as I do, I believe that I can articulate his perception of the problem. Here I am, he says, a dropout from the "old modern age," scarred by its dualisms. Commonsensically, I believe acritically in the singularity and uniqueness of my own acts of speaking and of comprehending speech. It is just as different as it could possibly be from the picture that is offered me by B. F. Skinner and his insufferable pigeons. And yet, no doubt about it, there has just got to be an ontological connection between things like those very carnal pigeons and my carnal body and brain, so that, if I am to make integral sense of the fact that I speak, that sense will have to acknowledge my body and brain situated in the world.

On the other hand, while Chomsky reinforces my acritical belief in the unassimilability of human languages, with their literally infinite variety, to a mere limited repertoire of signs and what they signify or stimuli and the responses they produce, he shows as little interest as Skinner in my singularity as the author and owner of my own spoken words. What's more, he propagates the same sad old dualism from the other side: an "upward" or angelistic reductionism.

If I can find an explanatory theory of language (I imagine Percy thinking), one that unites in one integral comprehension the different sorts of realities of body and brain, language acquisition, the phenomenon of sentence formation, and the act of a speaker authoring and owning what he says, while even so not being contained within or exhausted by what he says, then I shall have solid philosophical grounds—and I will offer them to you—for believing what I literally cannot help believing. I shall be able to affirm that the singularity of my acts of speech and yours are not *in* the world, as acts, even when our "words" are there. I shall heal the dualisms between thinking thing and extended thing by discovering a "third" thing, namely, my personal act of authorizing my own words. I shall, in disclosing how in acts of speech I at once appear in the world, yet remain less than fully disclosed to it, thereby provide the ground for a theory of man that will account for his alienation. And, lastly, then: "Mightn't one even speak of such a thing as the Helen Keller phenomenon, which everyone experiences at the oddest and most unlikely times? Prince Andrei lying wounded on the field of Borodino and discovering clouds for the first time. Or the Larchmont commuter whose heart attack allows him to see his own hand for the first time" (*MB*, 41).

So I imagine Walker Percy thinking down there in Louisiana.

Now, before taking the next step, I wish to issue, with some diffidence, since I shall not develop it at all, a necessary caveat regarding the concepts *explain* and *explanatory*. They are multiply ambiguous. What counts as an explanation is not one, two, or even half a dozen sorts of things. We suffer many different sorts of mental cramp; and that will count as an explanation which relieves it. Descartes' mental cramp could not be cured by reading Aristotle. Percy's, and my, cramp about language is not much relieved by reading Skinner, Chomsky, or Rudolph Carnap. And in claiming this I am not at all suggesting that you can relieve your mental cramp by just settling for any old explanation that makes you feel good. Mental cramp is a real, objective state and only that explanation which is specific to it will cure it.

The heart of Percy's crude model, as he calls it, both in its polemical implications for the other existing putative theories and in its constructive implications, is his distinction between a merely dyadic linear, cause-effect, stimulus-response, H_2SO_4 reacting to NaOH, energy exchange relation, on the one hand, while on the other hand he sets up a nonlinear, nonenergic phenomenon which is so complex that no simpler model than that of a triad will suffice to represent it—or as he has it in "The Delta Factor"—"a natural phenomenon in which energy exchanges account for some but not all of what happens" (*MB*, 39). With Helen Keller, water running over one hand while

Miss Sullivan writes the word *water* in her other, we are confronted by a phenomenon which cannot be understood dyadically, that is: no linear stringing together of the three terms *Helen*, *water*, and *"water"* by a sequence of arrows, in any order, can represent the "break through into the daylight of language." The simplest formula that will not *over*simplify the reality is the figure:

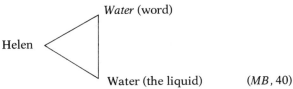

Helen

Water (word)

Water (the liquid)   (*MB*, 40)

The triangle is irreducible.

This distinction between dyadic and triadic relations is the fulcrum of Percy's argument. I shall animadvert to this in due course as the source of his *profound* confusion. For the moment, let me draw attention to the diagram above in which, being two dimensional, *Helen*, *water*, and *"water"* are all represented as *on a single plane*—on its face a trivial deficiency, but I think, one rich in potentiality for logical mischief. And the reason for this is that the dyad-triad distinction, *by itself*, is not sufficient to make Percy's point. The triad must be *interpreted* in a certain way, by Percy as he writes out his theory and thinks, "Does it work?", by me when I read it, wondering the same thing. If the imagination is bewitched for an instant by the visual metaphor of the diagram, trouble is in store. If the triad must be interpreted, then it can be *mis*interpreted, which means that Percy will have to superintend the working of his metaphor with the utmost delicacy. Even dropouts from the "old modern age" are routinely bewitched by visual metaphors.

Let us however show schematically what it is that Percy has hoped to do with the argument from the irreducibly triadic structure of the Delta Factor. Through the application of Delta it is possible to impeach Skinner's wrong explanatory theory. By claiming, too, that it provides the ground or the model for connecting to what goes on inside the cerebral cortex the syntactical and semantical elements of the language phenomenon (which phenomenon is taken seriously in different ways and in different degrees by Chomsky and the semioticists), it is possible to articulate a true explanatory theory. Finally, the triadic model will also provide a plausible way to think of language acquisition that neither reduces the process simply to operant conditioning, as in Skinner's *Verbal Behavior*, nor capitulates in despair to a black box theory, nor makes an implausible application of Peirce's theory of abduction as a solution of the problem of the LAD as with Chomsky.

Percy, I take it, is really making the following points: a theory of language has to take seriously the facts that people speak to one another about all manner of things in their mutual world; that they are able to do this because they follow (grammatical, syntactical, and semantical) rules which they "know" and upon which they are "agreed" without ever having been taught them or ever having made a contract about them; that had anyone been initiated into a different speech community, the same sorts of requirements for speaking would obtain, and the same human powers for meeting those analogous but different requirements would be available; and finally, that these extraordinary elaborations out of our merely organismic being must somehow be seen as comportable with the bodies, brains, and speech organs of carnal men in their ambient world. All of these are equally bedrock desiderata for an explanatory theory of language.

Therefore Percy says: "The main error of a generative grammar considered as a theory of language is that its main component is syntactical with semantic and phonological components considered as 'interpretations' thereof" (*MB*, 304). The crux, then, of Percy's theory of language insofar as it is to have the desired *explanatory* power is just here. He says: "For some time I had supposed that the basic event which occurs when one utters or understands a sentence must be triadic in nature (Percy). That is to say, sentences comprise two elements which must be coupled by a coupler (*MB*, 324). All seems quite innocent and regular, so far, even if not entirely clear. And then he continues: "This occurs in both the naming sentence, when semological and phonological elements are coupled, and in the standard declarative NP-VP sentence which comprises what one talks about and what one says about it" (*MB*, 324).

But then suddenly I begin to suspect that Percy and I use the word *sentence* differently. I know very well what it is like to speak a grammatical sentence in English about something in our mutual world; but what is it to "couple semological and phonological elements"? What do we gain by abstracting from the universe where speakers speak words about the world which others hear and understand? Then I remember a telling word above: the "*basic* event which occurs when one utters or understands a sentence must be triadic in nature" and feel the ground tremble ever so slightly. If the event we are talking about is more basic (say, located in the cerebral cortex) than people talking, listening, comprehending what is being said about what it is being said, then is it conceptually comportable with concepts like *sentence* and *sentence element* used in the ordinary, old fashioned way I had taken Percy to intend? I begin to see that Percy is taking concepts to be logically homogeneous which, it seems to me, are obviously heterogeneous; that where I would want to talk about ontological hierarchy or levels of being he, bemused, I would have a hunch, by the desire to "see man whole, a whole creature put together again after the three-hundred-year-old Cartesian split," slips in that familiar way by slow degrees toward the built-in monistic "downward" reduction of the "old modern age"—the very last thing he wants to do, and that I know. So perhaps I have him wrong.

But then the next thing I see is this diagram:

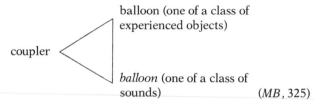

balloon (one of a class of experienced objects)

coupler

balloon (one of a class of sounds)   (*MB*, 325)

and I am told that this is a diagram of an event that occurs "inside both father and son" when a father utters the sound (why is it not a word that he utters?) *balloon* and the son looks and nods (*MB*, 324).

I stare at this diagram, cracking my head: "The coupler" (that's basic, I remember that) is inside the father. But the balloon is not inside the father; if it were, the boy would not have nodded; neither is *balloon*. The boy heard *balloon* because his father managed to get it outside. Yet the diagram, since it is drawn *on* a single plane, would suggest that the concept *coupler* means to me on the page, largely context-free—and the concepts balloon and *balloon*, as they stand there on the printed page are logically homogeneous. And yet obviously this is just not true, and, I think, "Oh, the treachery of triads!"

But, then, I say: "What an all-too-familiar mistake for us dropouts from the 'old modern age'—devoured as we are by ravening particles—abstraction, dualism, and reductionism. Walker didn't mean that and he and I both know it. So absolutely right and sure of himself when, in irony, he is spoofing the behavioral sciences, he suffers an attack of reductionistic amnesia while reading with Enlightened earnestness Geschwind's 'Disconnection Syndromes in Animals and Man.' He said it all, not quite accurately but with a fine sense for ontological hierarchy and for logical heterogeneity in his "The Delta Factor." He says: "Then what can one say for sure about the three elements of the Delta phenomenon? Only this: The boy in Delta is not the organism boy. The balloon in Delta is not the balloon in the world. The *balloon* in Delta is not the sound balloon." And then he adds: "An unpromising beginning" (*MB*, 44). But then perhaps he asks for too much.

And I find myself wanting to say a number of other things.

First, *balloon* is not "one of a class of sounds"—sounds, that is to say, that sound like "balloon." *Balloon*, the word, does indeed have a sound, sort of like *maroon* and *poltroon*, and, as having a sound, is a member of a class of sound-alikes. But it is a sound which, *as word*, is a member of the class of names. "Here is conceptual hierarchy," I say to myself.

Second, a sentence, unless you are going to start doing something really funny with it, is an irreducibly linguistic entity and its elements are linguistic entities. These elements, and the sentences that comprehend the elements, exist at all *only* for speakers, that is: people who hear words with their ears rather than with their auditory cortex, even though they would be up against it when it came to hearing if they *had* no such cortex: people who comprehendingly utter, that is speak, words with their mouths and own what they have said. A conceptual universe where *speaker* and *hearer* do not appear is one in which the concept *sentence* and therefore the concept *sentence element* have no meaning. "Here is conceptual heterogeneity," I think.

It is oversight of cases of this sort which leads Percy into puzzling claims like the following. He says: "Let us say nothing about the physiological or ontological status of the 'coupler.' Suffice it for the present to say that if two elements of a sentence are coupled,"—that is balloon and *balloon* of the above diagram—"we may speak of a coupler. Indeed, the behavioral equivalent of Descartes' *cogito ergo sum* may be : If the two elements of a sentence are coupled, there must be a coupler. The latter dictum would seem to be more useful to the behavioral scientist, including transformational linguists, than Descartes', because Descartes' thinking is not observable but his speech is" (*MB*, 325). There are several important philosophical contracts being negotiated in this passage, and, I believe, the ground for a good deal of litigation is being laid. I pass over in silence the questions as to the observability of Descartes' "thinking" and his "speech."

First, and in passing, it simply will not do to "say nothing about the physiological or ontological status of the 'coupler'" for it is only by specifying this that our conceptual orientation can be established to the diagram in which it appears, to the way in which *sentence, sentence element,* and *coupled* are understood to be functioning as concepts. Without this guidance we are, where the diagram is concerned, left with very close to the complete abstraction: black triangular figure on a white ground. And if reference is made to the words about the pointing father and the nodding boy as the exegetical device for interpreting the diagram, then we are once again openly faced with the question as to how the former is overlaid on the latter, which is to raise precisely the question about the ontological status of the coupler.

It seems clear to me that Percy emphatically does want, in the interest of his own argument, at least to say that whatever may be happening in the cerebral cortex and whatever neurophysiological events may be occurring in the "human inferior parietal lobule, which includes the angular and supramarginal gyri, to a rough approximation areas 39 and 40 of Brodmann" (*MB*, 326) as the *conditio sine qua non* of speech acquisition,— again, whatever happens there—the "coupler"—you, I, Helen Keller, Walker Percy, who go about naming things—has the status of a speaker, a symbol-user in the absolutely irreducible sense. If this is not his point, then he has capitulated entirely;

and if it is, then his argument leaves the mystery of the integration of the act of speaking with neurophysiological events—even triadic ones—in areas 39 and 40 of Brodmann no nearer explanation.

Percy, too, it appears, has left out the speaker! By failing to stay closely in touch with himself, the author, speaker, and writer-down of his own theory, he slips into the reductionistic amnesia of the "old modern age." This is the humiliation of drop-out critics! And in "The Delta Factor," I believe Percy, with some sadness, admits that this is so.

When, therefore, Percy asks: "What else indeed is the child up to for months at a time when it goes around naming everything in sight—or asking its name—than establishing these functional intercortical connections?" (*MB*, 326) we must reply: "Why, he is naming everything in sight." And we can underline the heterogeneity of concepts that are being taken to be homogeneous by observing that in the conceptual landscape where one finds *areas of Brodmann, intercortical connection,* and *inferior parietal lobule* one will look in vain for *child* and *naming.*"

Finally, a kindness to poor old Descartes from a dropout from the "old modern age": he was very careless when he promised to divest his mind of all his previous knowledge in order to begin with only the certain, since he forgot to rid it of Latin and of French. It therefore remained possible for him to say *Cogito ergo sum* and *Je pense donc je suis.* But when he uttered the words *cogito ergo sum,* I do not take it that Descartes had absconded, leaving behind only the sound of his voice on the wind. I believe he was openly and unambiguously a speaker speaking and not a coupler coupling. And confused (and *profoundly* confused, too) though Descartes often was, I think he would not have supposed as Percy would seem to have it (*MB*, 325) that the sounds (words) or the marks (words), *cogito ergo sum,* were really a disowned black box from which the "secret contents" in the form of a "behavioral equivalent" might one day be extracted. For, of course, there is no (merely) behavioral equivalent to the said or written-down authorized words, *cogito ergo sum*. There is however a behavioral equivalent to, for example, the sworn testimony of a young constable of Amsterdam, taken in January of 1641. Geulincx de Groot, by name, a Dutchman without any classical learning, he deposed: "Renatus Cartesius, a Frenchman, otherwise known as René Descartes, opened his mouth and out came the hideous sounds *cogito ergo sum*."

4

What then, in conclusion, am I saying about Percy's explanatory theory of language? Would he have been better occupied attempting other things? Not at all. The "Delta Factor" is a potent dialectical weapon against Chomsky, the transformationalists, the semioticists, and Skinner. It serves to put the language phenomenon back into the setting where it belongs, among human speakers and hearers; in doing so it clears the ground for new reflection on the human condition as Percy had hoped.

Admittedly, as he himself says, there is "very little to be sure of," but Delta does provide a better angle of vision and maybe more, yielding "a new world and maybe a new way of getting at it." And even if in the long run it were to turn out to be impossible "to arrive at an explanatory theory of language in any ordinary sense of the word" (*MB*, 323), it need not at all follow that we shall be condemned to revert to homunculus biology. The suggestion that such a reversion would be implied in this failure is but the bitter reflection of a disappointed child of the "old modern age" where total explicitness, as we were given meaninglessly and misleadingly to saying, is possible at least in principle.

Am I then saying that the integration of the "autonomous" phenomena of speech and language acquisition to what "goes on inside the brain" is impossible? I believe not; at least, I do not know that to be so. Percy, I think, has achieved an edifying and *profound* failure. This failure is especially likely to be edifying if we view him as the paradigm of the dropout from and critic of the "old modern age." He has shown us that a keen sense of ontological hierarchy and of the many valences which bind different concepts together in different ways will have to be carried into the research, along with Delta.

How, then does all of this bear upon Percy's hope that by reflecting upon man's breakthrough into the daylight of language he may come to see man of a piece, a whole creature put together again after he has been sundered from himself in the "old modern age"? How does it provide a clue for a new theory of man?

When we raise these questions on the far side of the confusions evoked by the conceptual equivocations of "A Theory of Language," they undergo a subtle change of meaning and weight. What has been perceived hitherto as Percy's philosophical naïveté suddenly can be appreciated as something intimately related to but quite different from mere naïveté, namely, the misexplication of Percy's profoundly significant intuition into the roots of our human being; Percy finds that our humanity is distinguished both by *our power to speak* and by *our alienation*.

In "A Theory of Language" Percy agonistically contends, and often unsuccessfully, with the dualism which threatens the reality of man's incarnate freedom by issuing in the dilemma: either angelism or bestialism. Despite his efforts, dualism prevails in this contest. Nevertheless, in his novels, in many of the essays in *The Message in the Bottle*, and preeminently in "The Delta Factor," Percy's profoundest and most original philosophical intuition is given. Here, free of the self-set demand for a philosophical rigor which, cultivated in the "old modern age," has a built-in gravitational drift toward dualism, Percy willingly gives himself over to the power of his imagination to make an unfamiliar juxtaposition of images.

The litany of questions in "A Delta Factor" begins with: "Why does man feel so sad in the twentieth century?" (*MB*, 3) and culminates with "Is there any other way to understand why people feel so bad in the twentieth century and writers feel so good writing about people feeling bad than in terms of the peculiar parameters, the joys and sorrows of symbol-mongering?" (*MB*, 45). The conclusion of these reflections, which have their own tonality and work their way with our imaginations by means of rhetorical strategies other than those of philosophical argument, juxtaposes *symbol-mongering* and *alienation*, a veritable Peircean abduction by Percy.

In *my* act of speaking (and this must always be articulated in the first person singular), in my act of laying claim to the tokens in our mutual native language to *say* something in my own name, while relying upon my body, brain, vocal cords, and tongue *in* the world, I perform the act by which these several strata are integrated to a meaning which *transcends* the world. In this act all dualisms are healed and my incarnate freedom becomes manifest. Yet the very incommensurability of the *act* of speaking with everything upon which it relies puts me in opposition to myself; in contradiction with myself; literally, speaking against myself. In my world-transcending act of speaking there appear both my incarnate freedom and my ontological unease—in every environment that might offer ease. Because I speak and insofar as I dwell in my own words I always have the feeling of being once-removed. My existence is always threatened by being merely ironical, by being lived in the subjunctive mood. As Percy writes in *Love in the Ruins*, "Only in man does the self miss itself" (*LR*, 36).

Symbolmongering and *feeling bad*: the model provided by this juxtaposition is, I believe, the very radix of Percy's imagination, the source of this profoundest reflection, given by him an absolutely original form, shaping everything he has written. It is singular: a more valuable contribution to the philosophy of language and philosophical anthropology than the particulars of the argument in "A Theory of Language." For it is the very stone ignored by the zealous philosophical builders. And as a model upon which to devise a new theory of man capable of expressing his finite freedom, it is heuristically more fecund and closer to our concrete being than models based upon oppositions and juxtapositions such as Buber's I-Thou versus I-It or Sartre's *en-soi* versus *pour-soi*, Marcel's problem versus mystery or Heidegger's *Sein, das Seiendes, Dasein,* with all of which it deserves comparison.

Here, in "The Delta Factor," Walker Percy has not surrendered his sovereignty to the "experts," he has not given in to the deep-going "old modern age" longing to force all one's serious claims into a rigorous and explicit philosophic medium. Here he has retained his hold upon the creature.

LEWIS A. LAWSON

The Fall of the House of Lamar

And, round about his home, the glory
That blushed and bloomed
Is but a dim-remembered story
Of the old time entombed.
—"The Haunted Palace" Edgar Allan Poe

"COME INTO MY CELL. Make yourself at home" (*Ll*, 3). With this genial invitation Lancelot Andrewes Lamar welcomes a visitor to what seems to be a "Center for Aberrant Behavior." Lance, as he is called, suspects that he already knows the visitor; he cannot be sure because the effort to remember requires more energy than he cares to devote to it. He thus appears to be another Percy protagonist who discovers that he understands his life about as well as he would understand a movie that he entered somewhere in the middle.

Lancelot, that is, appears to use the same introductory technique as the earlier novels: Binx Bolling returns to wakefulness from sleep, Will Barrett's past is gapped by amnesia,Tom More announces that he has come to himself wondering if "it" has happened. Certainly such a presentation of man's situation has been Percy's objective as a novelist; indeed, he has implied that it is the usefulness of fiction for phenomenological investigation that induced him to become a reader and—later—a writer of novels. Over and over, using slightly different phrases, he has identified the theme that compels him to write novels: [Concrete man, a stranger, transcending being, the point of view of one consciousness, the openness of an individual human existence] [comes to himself, finds himself, is put down, is located, is situated] [in a very concrete place and time, in a concrete situation, in a predicament, in a strange land, in a world].[1]

Rendered so abstractly, the theme evokes for the mind's eye a stark and sterile plain where walks a solitary soul, much like a painting by Dali or Chirico, say "The Great Metaphysicist." But embedded in a narrative, the theme loses its irreconcilable subject / object split; for Percy's earlier novels, while not exactly swarming with *Thou*s, do have at least one other being with whom the consciousness of the novel can enter into communion: Binx with Kate, Will with Sutter, Tom with Ellen. Readers occasionally complain that the concluding action of a Percy novel is insufficiently telling. Perhaps they look for the wrong kind of action: they are uncomfortable because the physical action is muted and ambiguous; but such readers fail to notice that, in the three novels before *Lancelot*, the metaphysical action has been unequivocal, the achievement of a bonding. This communion, it should be stressed, is not merely a guarantee against ordinary loneliness, but rather an essential to full consciousness; "consciousness, one suddenly realizes," Percy asserts in "Symbol, Consciousness, and Intersubjectivity," "means a knowing-with" (*MB*, 274). Or, again as he explains in "Symbol as Hermeneutic in Existentialism," "*L'enfer c'est autrui*. But so is heaven" (*MB*, 285). It would seem to follow that a being deprived of any communion with another being would suffer a defect of consciousness, which could result in severe mental disturbance.

Unlike the three earlier novels, which end but do not begin with a human bonding, *Lancelot* begins with an association of the consciousness with another being capable of understanding; for soon enough Lance acknowledges that he does remember his visitor, now Father John, but once Harry, a boy whose home was Northumberland, the next estate to Belle Isle, Lance's home. The two had been close friends up through their college days, so close that Lance thinks that their past is identical, that to see Harry is to see himself. He explains to Harry, "When I saw you yesterday, it was like seeing myself. I had the sense of being overtaken by something, by the past, by myself" (*Ll*, 5).[2]

The boys had been bookish. Lance remembers, "We knew each other by several names depending on the oblique and obscure circumstances of our lives—and our readings" (*Ll*, 9). As early adolescents they seem to have held the world in common by using the Arthurian legends as a focus; for Harry, Lance became Lancelot, while for Lance, Harry became Percival.[3] Then as adolescence became hard and insistent, their shared reading was *Ulysses* and *Tropic of Cancer*. There were other bonds of course: "We were honorable families" (*Ll*, 14).

In time, though, each family developed its characteristic mode: "The men in my family (until my father) were gregarious, politically active (anti-Long), and violent. The men in your family tended toward depression and early suicide" (*Ll*, 15). By the time the two boys were in college their respective family traits had overwhelmed them: Lance became popular and successful both in academics and in athletics, while Harry withdrew into solitary drinking and reading. In recollection Lance tries to make the fundamental distinction: "I was 'smart,' but never in your complex way of drinking and reading Verlaine (that was an act, wasn't it?)" (*Ll*, 15). Their reading no longer shared, Lance was still bookish enough to notice the specific book that Harry was accustomed to read; their world no longer shared, Lance was too well adjusted to his to understand that Harry's alienation could be symbolized by his reading a poet notorious for his conversion to Catholicism.

Later Lance recalls another puzzling stunt pulled by Harry: "you and I were riding down the river on a fraternity-sorority party and were passing Jefferson Island, which lies between Mississippi and Louisiana, was claimed by both states, and in a sense belonged to neither, a kind of desert island in the middle of the U.S., so you, drinking and solitary as usual, said to no one in particular: 'I think it would be nice to spend a few days in such a place,' pulled off your coat, and dove off the *Tennessee Belle* (that was an 'act,' too, wasn't it?)" (*Ll*, 60–61). Again the literary allusion embodied in the action reveals Harry's state of mind: like Huck Finn he is floating down the river, thus experiencing rotation, a savoring of the new as a deliverance from alienation; but when even that experience proves boring, like Tenente Frederic Henry, he dives into the river, fantasizes a rebirth, attempts to cross a zone into the authentic.[4]

It then occurs to Lance that the "act" might speak: "you, ever the one to do the ultimate uncalled-for thing—I never really knew whether it was a real thing or a show-off thing. And do you know, I've often wondered whether your going off to the seminary out of a clear sky was not more of the same— the ultimate reckless lifetime thing. Hell, you were not Christian let alone Catholic as far as anyone could notice. So wasn't it just like your diving off the *Tennessee Belle* to go from unbeliever to priest, leap-frogging on the way some eight hundred million ordinary Catholics? Was that too an act?" (*Ll*, 61). Of course it was an "act"—but not a "put-on"—instead *the* decisive act, the Kierkegaardian leap into faith.

After his ordination, Harry, now Father John, had gone to Africa as a medical missionary. But he had in time returned to New Orleans to serve as a "priest-physician. Which is to say," as Lance slyly puts it, "a screwed-up priest or a half-assed physician" (*Ll*, 10). Lance believes that the two concerns, one of the soul, the other of the body (including the mind), are fundamentally incompatible, hence any mixture of the two results, Lance thinks, in a grotesquerie. Feeling that either is irrelevant to his own condition, Lance reveals something of how warped his mind is. The priest, Lance suspects, has trouble with either one or the other; as he asks his visitor, "Have you lost your faith? or is it a woman?" (*Ll*, 61). Whatever it is, Lance suspects that it has disrupted his visitor's priestly function. It may be true that Father John is distressed that God through His church is doing no more to lighten the world's misery. But that does not mean that he has abandoned his Christian point of view. When he is first welcomed to Lance's cell, he is invited to make himself at home, take the chair, while Lance will hospitably sit on the cot. Rather, Father John indicates that he will stand by the window. His preferring to look out the window suggests that he intends to keep his sense of scale and proportion informed by the world at large, rather than allow it to be captivated by the isolation of that individual cell. Out the window is the mixture, the sacred and the profane, a cemetery and a movie house showing *The 69ers*. He is always seen through Lance's eyes as walking through the cemetery (never mind whether he can pray; he is not ignoring the eschatological fact that fundamentally defines a vision of life). Lance, on the other hand, rails at the obscenity of the movie and a bumper sticker exhorting MAKE LOVE NOT WAR, while being impressed by half a sign that proclaims, "Free & . . . ." His only conjectures about the remainder of the sign are "Easy" and "Accepted" (*Ll*, 4). Enraptured by the notion of freedom that became his upon the discovery of his wife's infidelity, he does not accept the paradox of man's estate, that he is free but responsible. No wonder that Lance likes to hear the girl out the cell window singing a mawkish song about freedom.

Although he disparages Father John's professional role, Lance nevertheless seemingly needs his old friend as a person: "seeing you was a kind of catalyst, the occasion of my remembering. It is like the first time you look through binoculars: everything is confused, blurred, unfocused, flat; then all of a sudden *click*: distance drops away and there is everything in the round, bigger than life" (*Ll*, 13). The priest, then, will serve as an intersubjective medium, a means through which Lance can retrieve and order the data of his past.

Lance already has an informing philosophy of history, a "sexual theory of history," to apply to the material thus retrieved: "First there was a Romantic Period when one 'fell in love.' Next follows a sexual period such as we live in now where men and women cohabit as indiscriminately as in a baboon colony—or in a soap opera. Next follows catastrophe of some sort. I can feel it in my bones. Perhaps it has already happened" (*Ll*, 35–36). In the beginning, according to Lance, the world that the boys shared was "a garden of delights." Perhaps he is alluding to the vision of Adamic innocence presented in the Bosch triptych, but if so he should recall that the final panel describes Hell. The onset of sexuality did not symbolize the lapse of innocence to Lance that it conventionally does; for an important distinction in his heritage provided an acceptable outlet for masculinity: there are ladies and there are whores. Lance recalls that he and Harry had gone to whorehouses together. Then he adds, with heavy irony: "I understand young men don't have to go to whorehouses any more" (*Ll*, 14). From his puritanical point of view, based on the double standard, all women are now whores.

There were, then, two realms in Lance's world: an Ideal and a Real. It follows that when Lance first sought a wife, he would visit the realm of the Ideal. There was, for Lance, an ethereality about Lucy Cobb: "Lucy was a virgin! and I did not want her otherwise" (*Ll*, 85). Thinking back of her, he attaches her to an inviolable southern past: "Lucy I loved too, but Lucy was a dream, a slim brown dancer in a bell jar spinning round and round in the 'Limelight' music of old gone Carolina long ago" (*Ll*, 119). Memories of her life, like those *bibelots* Lance displays for the Yankee tourists, evoke little but a taste for the quaint.

Lance married his Lucy and brought her back to Belle Isle,

with its one wing still in ruins from a mysterious fire over a hundred years before. In its decrepitude the house commented, like the House of Usher, Sutpen's Hundred, or Burden's Landing, upon the come-down of those who inherited it. In this house Lucy, who was, in effect, a ghost, albeit one who bore two children, simply disappeared, like one of those anemic Poe women. Lance describes the event: "Then she died. I suppose her death was tragic. But to me it seemed simply curious. How curious that she should grow pale, thin, weak, and die in a few months! Her blood turned to milk—the white cells replaced the red cells. How curious to wake up one morning alone again in Belle Isle, just as I had been alone in my youth!" (*Ll*, 84). Lance's response to Lucy's death reveals the fallenness of his condition. Bored and idle, while living upon the psychological capital of his tradition, Lance has been overwhelmed by the everydayness that so preoccupied Binx Bolling, and he can respond to another being not with passionate concern, with real feeling, but only with curiosity.[5]

With his mother, Lily (whose name suggests purity), Lance continued to live on at Belle Isle. He "practiced" law, recognizing himself the irony of his definition, for in his case it meant not command, but incompetence. He involved himself in civil rights advocacy, not apparently with any great sacrifice nor out of a sense of brotherhood, but rather of noblesse oblige. For diversion he did "a bit of reading and even some research and writing: the Civil War of course" (*Ll*, 59). In time, though, he found that his alienation had reached dreadful proportions: "During the last months I found that I could be moderately happy if I simultaneously (1) drank, (2) read Raymond Chandler, and (3) listened to Beethoven" (*Ll*, 144).[6] Despite all the false enthusiasms, though, Lance was dominated by public time, "the five o'clock whistle at Ethyl," for it heralded the latest TV newscast. "In those days I lived for the news bulletin" (*Ll*, 72), acknowledges Lance, almost literally displaying Heidegger's

Neugier, a greed for the new, an obsession for the merely interesting, for *Gerede / Geschreibe*, the shallow commentary of the mass media. Lance summarizes his condition quite aptly: "Do you know what happened to me during the past twenty years? A gradual, ever so gradual, slipping away of my life into a kind of dream state in which finally I could not be sure that anything was happening at all. Perhaps nothing happened" (*Ll*, 57). The ambiguity that Lance experiences is the third characteristic of a being's fallenness, a being's disowning of itself by immersion into the world of "them," so that his sense of his life's slipping away into dream is appropriate.[7]

Then Margot entered Lance's life, a year after his mother's death. With a fifth of Wild Turkey and a copy of *The Big Sleep*, naturally, in his briefless briefcase, Lance was hurrying "with no other thought in mind but to get past the tourists and the belles and the mud and watch the 5:30 news" (*Ll*, 72). Rounding a corner he caught sight of one of the belles, social aspirants provided as guides for the Azalea Festival, whose eye would not release his. With her hoop skirt and scent of orris root, "the right smell" for elderly southern gentlewomen, according to William Alexander Percy, Margot must have roused the image of the southern belle, the ideal past, for Lance.[8] Such ideality must have been strengthened at a subsequent meeting, when he found her among a field of two thousand other "lily-white" Colonial Dames, "listening to another Dame talking about preserving U.S. ideals and so forth" (*Ll*, 169). She becomes even more persuasive in her role when her speech reminds Lance of his mother.

Just as quickly, though, still at their first meeting, her image develops a second aspect. In the pigeonnier, to which she has invited herself for a drink, she quickly demonstrates that, though from Texas, she wears her southernness with a difference. She immediately steps out of the hoop skirt as if it were chaps and drinks, sans chaser, from the bottle. Margot must seem to Lance, then, to be the miraculous joining of the ideal with the real. When they had first spoken and shaken hands, Lance had noticed the substantiality of her hand, which had been pressing against the wall to cushion her spine: "her hand, coming from behind her, was plaster-pitted and big and warm" (*Ll*, 74). Soon, as they talk and drink, she lies down, invites him to join her, then measures him with the world's calipers: "Her fine leg, pantalooned and harlequined . . . rose, levitated, and crossed over my body. There it lay sweet and heavy" (*Ll*, 80).

Margot projects an image of realness in yet another way. To insure their privacy, Lance shoots the bolt and turns the ancient lock with an eight-inch key. As he remembered the scene: " 'My God, it sounds like the dungeon at Chillon. Let me see that key.' I lay down and gave her the iron key. She held it in one hand and me in the other and was equally fond of both. She liked antiques and making love. As she examined it, she imprisoned me with her sweet heavy thigh as if she had to keep me still while she calculated the value of the iron key" (*Ll*, 80). The action is both overtly and symbolically sexual. But her inspection of a tool should not be reduced to simply a sexual explanation, for her "calculation" of the key, and other subjects ("the little spiral staircase. Priceless!"), reveals that she has a mind that conceives of the serviceability of objects. As Lance recollected: "At heart she was a collector, preserver, restorer, transformer; even me and herself she transformed: to take an old neglected abused thing, save it, restore it, put it to new and charming use" (*Ll*, 81). Admittedly, Margot is mercenary—she could hardly be less, having been young and poor in West Texas— but beyond that she is capable of creating a world of immediate utility by her "*um . . . zu*" calculations.[9] The fundamental relation that a being has to its world is that of use, claims Heidegger; Lance seems to sense that hub-spoke image of *Dasein* as nucleus for its world, but only for woman-being: "Do you know the way a woman moves around a room whether she is cleaning it or just passing time? It is different from the way a man moves. She is at home in a room. The room is an extension of her" (*Ll*, 36). Margot is not, as Lance and his father have been, a lost subject defenseless in a distant world of objects; rather Margot is present in her world; she projects a sense of connection and touch that is not merely physical, but metaphysical.

Small wonder that Lance, bereft of a vigorous religious heritage (his father's Anglicanism being little more than a limp aesthetic reverie) and of the romantic splendor shed by Lucy, should reach for Margot worshipfully. Embodying many of the assertions in Sutter's notebook, in *The Last Gentleman*, Lance now views the genital as the only connection to escape in an everyday world, the "real thing," as another of Percy's sufferers, Kate Cutrer, in *The Moviegoer*, calls it. Reverently, before entering such a holy place, Lance pauses to regard "the warm cottoned-off place between her legs, the sheer negativity and want and lack where the well-fitted cotton dipped and went away. [He] kisse[s] the cotton there" (*Ll*, 81).

On their second meeting Lance begins to ritualize what may have been spontaneous in the pigeonnier. Having invaded the convention of the Colonial Dames, he takes Margot driving up the Trace. Again she bluntly initiates the sexual possibility: "'Let's go to bed'" (*Ll*, 170). And again there is that slippage from the appearance of traditional chastity to contemporary eroticism, for they go to a tourist cottage in Asphodel, in the "lily." Lance recalls their behavior:

> She undressed without bothering to turn out the light. . . . She stood naked before the mirror, hands at her hair, one knee bent, pelvis aslant. She turned to me and put her hands under my coat and in her funny way took hold of a big pinch of my flank on each side. Gollee. Could any woman have been as lovely? She was like a feast. She was a feast. I wanted to eat her. I ate her.
>
> That was my communion, Father—no offence intended, that sweet

dark sanctuary guarded by the heavy gold columns of her thighs, the ark of her covenant. (*Ll*, 170–71).

Once again alert to the directness, the openness, and the substantiality of her body, Lance has reason to feel that he can capture the real. His detailed description of his experience of desire has correspondences to Sartre's description of desire as "an attempt to *incarnate* the Other's body."[10] Thus what he wants to achieve is, through the reduction of himself to flesh, to caress Margot so that she experiences herself as incarnated flesh; then he, as Subject, can throw off his reduction to flesh and enjoy his appropriation of her not merely as object, but as subject trapped under his hand. Such a project always eventually fails, and one of the routes that such failure can take is into sadism. Lance embodies such a mutation in his later actions toward Margot and Raine.

But in the first blush of desire, Margot's body is certainly worthy of worship, of the bended knee; the genital becomes the ark, the locus of the sacred. As well, it is imagined as the transformation of the divine into flesh, the Eucharist. As such, Margot's body, with the singular goodness which it at first provides, is Lance's first, positive imagining of the Holy Grail.

For Lance, then, the combination is perfect. In appearance, Margot is the very picture of the lady, who, with her oil money, can restore and manage Belle Isle as well as any plantation mistress in the southern hagiography. In reality, she is his whore, complaisant to his sexual energy with the speed of a zipper. But perhaps she is too obliging:

> The truth is, it never crossed my mind in my entire sweet Southern life that there was such a thing as a lustful woman. Another infinite imponderable. Infinitely appalling. What hath God wrought?
> On the other hand, why should not a woman, who is after all a creature like any other, be lustful? Yet to me, the sight of a lustful woman was as incredible as a fire-breathing dragon turning up at the Rotary Club.

What I really mean of course was that what horrified me was the discovery of the possibility that she might lust for someone not me. (*Ll*, 129–30).

That dread possibility that she might be promiscuous occurred to Lance on their second meeting. Again, Lance responds to her hand, finding in her a miraculous meeting of styles—handshake, then fornicate. This time the forefinger tickles him, paddles the palm, as Iago says when he wants to paint Desdemona as the wanton; Lance is startled and asks if such manipulation has the same meaning in Texas as in Louisiana. Margot says it does not. They marry, and Lance contents himself with Binx Bolling's Little Way: "Drinking, laughing, and loving, it is a good life. Not even marriage spoils it. For a while" (*Ll*, 90). It never really occurs to him to wonder about the person whom he married; the body is sufficient: "on the floor, across the table, under the table, standing up in a coat closet at a party" (*Ll*, 90).

The person who is Margot attempts to assert sovereignty by the only way that seems available to her. Without a profession or without the justification that poverty provides, she cannot work outside the house. Thus she works inside the house, researching and commissioning its restoration, trying to remain in touch with that world of utility that she had possessed. With his personification of Margot only as a sexual organ, Lance describes their marriage glibly: "Later we lived by sexual delights and the triumphs of architectural restoration. Truthfully, at that time I don't know which she enjoyed more, a good piece in Henry Clay's bed or Henry Clay's bed" (*Ll*, 119). Lance does begin to understand vaguely that Margot suffered from lack of accomplishment, but he disparages her unique agony by incorporating it into a female type, which is subtly satirized by his male eyes: "Did you know that the South and for all I know the entire U.S.A. is full of demonic women who, driven by as yet unnamed furies, are desperately restoring and preserving *places*, *buildings*? women married to fond indulgent easy going somewhat lapsed men like me, who would as soon do one thing as another as long as they can go fishing, hunting, drink a bit, horse around, watch the Dolphins and Jack Nicklaus on TV" (*Ll*, 121). What he really says, of course, is that men say that women may do anything they like, as long as they don't interfere with male routine. As for Margot personally, "I could see her problem. Christ, what was she going to *do*? What to do with that Texas energy and her passion for making things either over or of a piece. What did God do after he finished creation? Christ, she didn't know how to rest. At least in Louisiana we knew how to take things easy. We could always drink" (*Ll*, 120–21). In truth, he really does not care what Margot is. Her last conversation with him is very much to the point: "'I'm nothing.'" Then she explains: "'That's what you never knew. With you I had to be either—or—but never a—uh—woman'" (*Ll*, 245).

Margot's resumption of her career at Merlin's Dallas-Arlington Playhouse, then, screams its intention: she wishes literally to act, to discover her own role. With Lance lapsed into constant drunkenness and frequent impotence, she could either be overwhelmed by Belle Isle or attempt to escape it. No wonder that, later, she will not go away with Lance, who, she must by then realize, carries Belle Isle within him, but rather plans to play Nora in the film-maker Jacoby's version of *A Doll's House*.

The tragedy of her attempt to make her life is that she instead makes another life. Lance unwittingly accepts the child, Siobhan, as his own, and Margot apparently is frustrated in her efforts to become someone. Eight years later she is trying still, having involved herself with a movie project, to be filmed at Belle Isle, about a planter named Lipscomb, who "gently subsides into booze and Chopin" (*Ll*, 153). It is a testimony of Lance's self-centeredness that he never acknowledges any similarity between himself and Lipscomb.

Certainly he is not blind to the behavior of others. He exudes pride in the acuity of his sight; he frequently resorts to implements or similes of vision to express himself, his own binoculars, telescopes, mirrors, Elgin's binoculars, television, movies, most especially: "The moment I knew for a fact that Margot had been fucked by another man, it was as if I had been waked from a twenty-year dream. I was Rip van Winkle rubbing his eyes. In an instant I became sober, alert, watchful" (*Ll*, 107). Lance, for all his bookishness, studiously avoids the much more apt literary comparison at this point: that other husband who, to prove his love a whore, demanded "the ocular proof."

The imagery of awakening may suggest the strategy earlier identified as Percy's characteristic method of starting a novel, Heidegger's *Befindlichkeit*, coming to oneself through feeling. But yet another aspect of the discovery scene is predominant, Lance's emotional state. Rather than experiencing "shock, shame, humiliation, sorrow, anger, hate, vengefulness" (*Ll*, 21), he is careful to reveal, as if proud that nothing need be extenuated, that he was aware of nothing but curiosity and interest.[11]

"What I felt was a prickling at the base of the spine, a turning of the worm of interest" (*Ll*, 21), he recalls. Then in his subsequent recital of his detective work in establishing the inescapable fact of Margot's infidelity he repeats the image "worm of interest" until it squirms with significance. The "worm" is primarily a description of his genital and suggests that Lance was now capable of tumescence. The worm will indeed turn, and a new style of behavior will occur. It thus becomes his lance, as he begins to envision himself as Sir Lancelot, "the Knight of the Unholy Grail" (*Ll*, 138).

The worm of interest thus becomes an instrument, a divining rod for carnal knowledge: "is all niceness then or is all buggery?" (*Ll*, 136). It first acts as a "magnet" to lead him to the factual proof of Margot's adultery. It ultimately guides him to conclude, to his satisfaction, that all is buggery. For when he invades his home, to apprehend his wife and her lover, he goes first to the room of Raine Robinette, the young actress. She, too, turns out to be aggressive: "She put her arms around my waist, locked her hands, and squeezed me with surprising strength" (*Ll*, 232). Then, lying down, she invites Lance to copulate with her, which is hardly surprising, in that her name, *rein*(s), suggests that Lance sees her (and by now all women) as merely a genital. When, however, he sees his daughter's sorority ring on the hand groping for his genital, he is reminded of Raine's corruptive influence on the sixteen-year-old Lucy, that Lucy may indeed become her sister. He has TV proof that Raine is a part of the buggery that goes on behind closed doors: "A little arrow of interest shot up my spine. I smiled and guided Raine's hand to me" (*Ll*, 235).

At this point in his narrative, Lance asks Father John: "You know why I smiled, don't you? No? Because I discovered the secret of love. It is hate. Or rather the possibility of hate" (*Ll*, 235). With slight modifications of terms, Lance is employing Sartre's scheme of "concrete relations with others." With the failure of sexual desire (which Lance customarily equates with "love"), sadism or "hate" (*Ll*, 235), as Lance calls it, sets in.[12] Then, to illustrate his meaning, Lance describes what he did next: "'Here now,' I said smiling, and tenderly pulled her body up, reaching around the front of her until my hands felt the soft crests of her pelvis. 'What?' she asked. 'Oh.' At first as her face was pressed into the pillow her lips were mashed down even more. I was alone, far above her, upright and smiling in the darkness" (*Ll*, 235).

Lance's objective is humiliation. As Sartre describes the event: "The sadist aims therefore at making the flesh appear abruptly and by compulsion; that is, by the aid not of his own flesh but of his body as instrument. He aims at making the Other assume attitudes and positions such that his body appears under the aspect of the *obscene*; thus the sadist himself remains on the level of instrumental appropriation since he causes flesh to be born by exerting force upon the Other, and the Other becomes an instrument in his hands. The sadist handles the Other's body, leans on the Other's shoulders so as to bend him toward the earth and to make his haunches stick up, etc." [13]

The worm has indeed turned. With insane contempt for all women, he buggers her, trying to discover the truth about evil, which must be "the great secret of life, the old life that is, the ignominious joy of rape and being raped" (*Ll*, 252). Raine thus would seem to personify Lance's second, contemporary sexual period, in which humans act as baboons; he determines to use his lance to probe the "heart of the abscess and let the pus out" (*Ll*, 236).

At the time of his discovery of Margot's betrayal, devoid of passion, Lance himself is little more than a beast, and he soon has an opportunity to see himself in that light. Passing through a room, he sees a figure: "He was watching me. He did not look familiar. There was something wary and poised about the way he stood, shoulders angled, knees slightly bent as if he were prepared for anything. He was mostly silhouette but white on black like a reversed negative. His arms were long, hanging lower and lemur-like from dropped shoulder" (*Ll*, 63–4). The reflection is that of a white simian, but Lance is too distanced from reality to make that interpretation of himself. Rather, he returns to his room to look into his own mirror, to be reminded of a Lancelot, disgraced not by his own actions, as the mythic Lancelot, but by actions committed against him. In his idleness, he has become, so he recognizes, a slob: "More like Ben Gunn than Lancelot" (*Ll*, 65).

At once Lance engages in ritual cleansing, then lies down naked on the cold bricks, as if to suggest that he is back in touch with gritty reality, after years of a "state of comfort and abstraction" (*Ll*, 66). At the same time he picks up a Bowie knife, drives it into the wall with one hand, then tries to draw it out with the other, in recapitulation of family behavior. The knife had been found among the detritus of history in the pigeonnier, had later been falsely reputed by Lance's grandfather to be one of Bowie's originals. Lance also probably contributes to the legend of the knife; during an early interview with Father John, he says merely that an ancestor had had a part in the "notorious Vidalia sand-bar duel in which Bowie actually carved a fellow limb from limb" (*Ll*, 18). In a later interview he attributes the same grisly action to his great-great-grandfather. Whatever the factual truth, the Lamar recourse to the Bowie becomes mythic truth, the kind that human beings base personal behavior on; Lance appropriates the myth to his own family in anticipation of his insane use of the Bowie on Jacoby.

With his fondness for casting himself as Lancelot, though, Lance should have perceived another meaning for the knife. According to Malory, when the sword in the stone appeared, Lancelot refrained from trying to pull it out, since only the purest knight in the world could accomplish the feat. Even in his love-madness, Sir Lancelot had known that he was sinful. But Lance, irrationally recognizing no sin in himself, tries the test and fails, yet does not abandon the Quest of the Unholy Grail. The morning after the discovery of Margot's original infidelity, at breakfast with her, Lance sets out to detect if she has also betrayed him the night before. During their conversation, he observes a fly on his wrist: "I watched him touch a hair. He did, crawling under it, everting and scrubbing his wings. As he did so, he moved the hair. The hair moved its root which moved a nerve which sent a message to my brain. I felt a tickle" (*Ll*, 88–89). That tickle, reminiscent of his paddled palm, mocks him by suggesting that his wife is still a whore. Also, just as Lance can see his own reaction to the fly mechanically—in terms of nerve ends and messages to the brain—so he can cope with outrage by reducing his own outrage over being cuckolded to a series of stimulus-response reactions. He does so, both when he gains the ocular proof and when he commits his own deeds.

Lance is single-minded in his pursuit of the exposure of his wife and her lover, whom he assumes still to be Merlin, allegedly the father of Margot's daughter. To that end, he hesitates at nothing; for, his southern honor having been traduced, any action is justified that will reveal the culprits. Despite his former championing of black dignity, he has no qualms about requesting shameful work from Elgin, the young black who is obligated to him. Elgin thus acts as a spy and, through his technical competency, provides the videotape that confirms the buggery in both Margot's and Raine's rooms. Self-consciously, Lance acts like his grandfather in being pleased with the performance of his "nigger," his slave (*Ll*, 181).

After he has seen his "Double Feature," Lance prepares to pass judgment and execute sentence upon the guilty. Raine and Dana, having corrupted his daughter, and Margot and Jacoby, the current lover, will not be spared. All the other inhabitants of the house are sent away, including, surprisingly, Merlin. Lance admits that he was astonished by his sparing of Merlin, and he tries to account for his decision, but his reasons (1) that poor Hemingwayesque Merlin is now impotent and (2) that he "liked" him seem evasive; perhaps, instead, being cuckolded by the same woman has created a bond between them. Then, with the approaching hurricane acting as natural comment upon Lance's whirling mind, he goes about his preparations. Jacoby had wanted a "'Lear-like effect'" for the movie about the planter. "'You know,'" he says to Merlin, "'mad king raging on the heath, wild-eyed, hair blowing.'" "'Yeah, right, Lear, okay,' said Merlin ironically, but Jacoby missed the irony" (*Ll*, 197). Just as crazy as Lear, though presenting a calm appearance, Lance had missed the irony that he was the real-life planter.

Unsealing the capped natural gas well under the restored wing of the house, Lance pipes the fumes throughout the house. As it gathers to an explosive density, he proceeds to execute his judgment by sodomizing Raine and killing Jacoby. A year later, talking to the priest, Lance attempts to make light of fornication: "fornication, anybody's fornication amounts to no more than molecules encountering molecules and little bursts of electrons along tiny nerves—no different in kind from that housefly scrubbing his wings under my hair" (*Ll*, 89). But he had not been so tolerant when he slipped into Margot's room to see that "great Calhoun" (or was it the "Clay"?) bed and "the strangest of all beasts, two-backed and pied" (*Ll*, 239). Then he had been particularly mechanically aware of his physical sensations after cutting Jacoby's throat with the Bowie knife: "I held him for a while until the warm air stopped blowing the hairs on the back of my hand" (*Ll*, 243).

Then Lance again acts in an astonishing way; rather than kill the creature who was charged with creating all his misery, he begins to talk with her. Even after feeling the flutter of eyelashes that only minutes before had paddled Jacoby's cheek, he begins to think of taking Margot away on a trip. As he lights the lamp, so that they can talk at length, the fumes are ignited. Over a hundred years before, the house had exploded, perhaps when the Cavalier spirit had become too expansive. Now it explodes again, Usherlike, in concert with the mind of a man whose honor-worshipping rigidity has driven him mad. Lance describes the effect of the blast: "I was wheeling slowly up into the night like Lucifer blown out of hell, great wings spread against the starlight" (*Ll*, 246). Lance is so Sartrean that he thinks of the presence of Others as hell; hence he insanely thinks himself like Lucifer in his splendid isolation. But Lucifer was cast out of heaven, out of communion with God, not out of hell. The presence of Others is also heaven, argues Percy, for Others can join the Self in an intersubjective bonding, a shared consciousness, the creation of reality.[14] *Lancelot* is thus fundamentally different from Percy's other novels, in that the protagonist perversely rejects any world but his own.

Lance's two inconsistent actions during his pursuit of "buggery," the sparing of Merlin and the apparent sparing of Margot, must receive attention at this point. As Lance arranges his recital of events of the previous year, he often draws a relation between them and events in the more distant past, both of which had destroyed his intensely personal idealizations of his experience. The discovery of Margot's infidelity, he says, was like the discovery of his father's involvement in graft. Thereafter, although he professes to be dispassionately seeking the truth of his wife's behavior, he seems frequently to be reacting, in fact, to that older set of events.

He begins to establish a model for the triangle of Margot, Merlin, and himself: his mother, his "uncle," and his father. The whole story of the older triangle may be a figment of Lance's imagination, of course; it nevertheless dominates his motivations at a layer deeper than he is capable of recognizing. The affair may be briefly reconstructed: his father, though descended from a line of honorable and active men, is incapable of living up to the family tradition; but in attempting to act, to succeed, he falls into dishonor; he then retires from the world into a fantasy of southern romanticism, leaving his wife prey to her own body and to the intruding male who can attend to its needs.

His father always reclining and poetizing and actually a party to his own betrayal, and himself too young to act as his mother's knight, Lance had suffered double disillusionment, father a weakling, mother a whore. No wonder that he would view the intruding male, Uncle Harry, as a rival, that he would remember Uncle Harry's gifts to him, candy-filled pistols and twenty-two bladed Swiss army knives, delightful toys for a child, but mocking symbols to an adult. In time, though, Uncle

Harry had been vanquished; as a young Comus knight, Lance had seen Harry as an old man with retracted genital.

When he had married Margot, Lance seems to have cast her in the role of southern matron. Then if she stooped to folly, does that not mean that he, like his father before him, has fallen into impotence? Hence he must restore that mother image to its chaste state, to demonstrate that he is capable of reactivating his manhood. Thus, when he discovers that Merlin is, like Harry, no longer a sexual threat, Lance can dismiss him.

The terms of Lance's motivation may be seen by the scene with the mysterious woman which he imagines on the night of the hurricane. Rather than being an apparition of Our Lady revealing a sacred site or charging the witness to some sacred task, the visitor is Our Lady of the Camellias, the personification not of chastity but of promiscuity. The figure reveals that Lance's mother was like Camille, alluding to the prostitute Marguerite in the several versions of Dumas' *La Dame aux camélias*, who lived only by and for love. Then, as in a dream, Lance sleeps; awakening he discovers that the figure has become his mother, who offers him the sword, the Bowie knife.

But is the knife to redeem her honor or to eliminate his rival? His encounter with Raine suggests the latter. Raine jostles him, perhaps reawakening in him the memory of the way that his mother had once grasped him. Then, when the drugged girl squeezes him, saying, " 'You're a big mother' " (*Ll*, 232), Lance's fundamental Oedipal motivation may be suspected.

The suspicion is strengthened when Lance approaches his wife's bed, which he sees as "a cathedral, a Gothic bed" (*Ll*, 237), fitting locus of Our Lady. As he slips up to it, he repeats an action that he had performed while sitting on Raine's bed; he puts "thumbnail against tooth" (*Ll*, 235). There he stands, peering at the bed, his adult description masking his childish action: he sucks his thumb. Then, after touching the bodies, in behavior unaccountable if adult, he gets in the bed with the "beast," to squeeze it. But when Jacoby points out that Lance is going to hurt Margot, not him, Lance releases his grip. Then they rise to fight, with Lance thinking of having "a mother's boy" at his mercy; then one mother's boy kills another (*Ll*, 241). In effect, then, Lance is trying to restore the past to a purity which it apparently never had. Rather than accept the past as it apparently was, undergo a repetition, so that his present can be built upon the authentic, he insanely acts out a past in the present.

Somehow uninjured and thought to be deranged by grief, Lance is placed in an asylum. He has apparently been there for a year when the priest first comes to visit him. Their meetings seem to take place over several days, during which only Lance's voice is directly heard. The priest's responses must be reconstructed from Lance's paraphrase of his speech and comments about his physical behavior. Slight as the response seems to be, Lance pays small attention even to that. He is never provoked into serious, extended thought by one of his friend's questions. Lance's domination of speech does not mean, however, that Father John is insignificant as a character. He poses a constant alternative to Lance's effort to reduce the range of possible relationships between men and women to sexual desire, ultimately to sadism / masochism. For always the priest attempts to pierce Lance's closed mind to offer a differing definition of love, as caritas, as the selfless recognition of another self. Rather than accepting the contention that "Man is a useless passion," he is testimony that Christ's Passion provides a model for all who would truly love.

Their opposed definitions of love constitute a basic tension in the novel. But their difference is not restricted to the way human beings handle one another, morals. Yet another contrast occurs in their perception of themselves in time. The priest seems at the end to be anticipating—more of the same. It may be, as Lance charges, that he has experienced a crisis of personal confidence, perhaps because ministering to the Africans had not been the grand exploit that he had expected. It may have been that his perception of evil had gotten lost among the social, economic, and political movements of that unstable continent. Or it may have been that he had not, as a physician, admitted that he must first of all heal himself. But whatever his own state of mind, the priest keeps an eye cocked to the outside, the graveyard; on the other hand, Lance never really appreciates the "outside," the burning of the levee bonfires on Christmas Eve as a ritual of watching and waiting for Christ's appearance or the All Souls' Day activities. And as Father John confronts the evil that Lance incarnates, he seems to grow stronger in his faith. He does pray in the cemetery; he does begin to dress like a priest, dressed up, not like Lee to surrender, but to do battle. His subsequent actions confirm his decision; he is to leave the asylum to become a parish priest in Alabama, where he will "preach the gospel, turn bread into flesh, forgive the sins of Buick dealers, administer communion to suburban housewives" (*Ll*, 256), in Lance's scoffing words. It will not be the grand exploit of converting pagans, but the infinitely more difficult task of fighting everydayness in Kierkegaard's Christendom.

Lance, on the other hand, views his life as an apocalypse, with himself as the agent of a steadily developing revelation. He asks his auditor why he was obsessed with knowing more, but he does not even pause for an answer, going on to detail his detective work. With the evidence gathered, he creates a sweeping generalization, a theory of history in which the forces of light (his "Third Revolution" or "new order") and the forces of darkness (the contemporary world) contend. The stripping away of "buggery" reaches the ultimate darkness, amidst the howling of the wind and the flashes of lightning, in the revelation of the great whore and the "beast," a description worthy of St. John the Divine. Then, having brought about the destruction of his immediate enemies, Lance envisions himself discovering the New Woman and recreating Eden somewhere east of Lexington, Virginia. The New Woman will be Anna, the occupant of the room next to Lance's, who has, according to Lance, been made innocent by being raped and forced to commit fellatio. It would be Anna, of course, "grace," one of the Godly remnant of Israel, whom Lance would see as worthy of joining him in his innocence in finding love among the ruins.[15] Even after Anna curses Lance for his boorishness, he madly forgives her, for, ignorant of the truth that he has discovered, she cannot, he assumes, appreciate his prophecy. He will bring about the millennium, and if God wants any of the credit He had better hop on the bandwagon.

Lance seems plainly to be suffering from severe insanity, perhaps paranoia, at the end. He may *think* that he is to be released; if he *is* actually to be freed, it is a profound comment on what passes for sanity these days. The priest clearly thinks that his old friend is mad; his looks show it. If those italicized responses are really the priest's, they are perhaps just such answers as we make to humor an irrational person. As for the last "yes," the only thing that the priest could tell Lance would be, "God help you."

So the bond between the two childhood friends is sundered at the book's end. One friend has revealed himself as a victim of arrested development, his dependence upon a notion of history as a series of great deeds as perverse as his obsession with the idealized image of his mother. In isolation he looks to a future, a utopia, which will be nothing less than the creation of his conception of the past; he will still be experiencing the empty tape slipping past the tape head, though. The other has evidently suffered from the present, perfect adjustment being neither possible nor desirable. But he gives no indication of returning to the past, to any more "acts" or great deeds, for deliverance from the present. Rather he will face the future, when it comes, with resoluteness and faith.

The two characters, Lance and Harry, each personify a tradition that Percy has often treated, the southern Stoic and the Christian. Moreover, the earlier treatments have revealed not merely the regional, but the personal significance of the traditions.[16] Hence the two characters invite attention to the two views of the world that have competed for Percy's allegiance.

The attractiveness of the Stoic attitude is felt by many traditional southerners, of course. For the Stoic code is an appealing refuge for those who still weigh conduct, especially in these days when trashy manners have been wonderfully and almost universally transmuted into the charismatic style. The code is even more intensely meaningful to Walker Percy, though, for being transmitted to him by William Alexander Percy. It is as close as the memory of a son who heard Senator Lamar and Robert E. Lee extolled as models of nobility by one who was himself an inspiration; it is as haunting as the scent of orris root. Lance Lamar is a part of Walker Percy.

The Christian tradition comes through Percy's fiction with no such nostalgic presence. Its fictional representatives have been caught up in paltriness as other folks. Indeed, if anything, they seem sometimes too easily able to live with it. But that, of course, may be their chief strength. That capacity is perhaps what Harry sought by his leap into the priesthood; with a family tradition of depression and early suicide, presumably occasioned by a strong family nose for paltriness, he could only live with the present by putting the past in its place. With his last name probably Percy, with his family home named Northumberland, like the home of the first southern Percy, with the family history of suicide, with his depression in his twenties, Harry is also Walker Percy.

There can be no synthesis of the two forces. Nor, indeed, has

Percy himself ever suggested that there could be. But his previous attempts to charm his Stoic ghost relied upon much softer incantations; Aunt Emily is a lofty, tough old patrician and Ed Barrett has a streak of noblesse oblige, before each is found incapable of transcending the paltriness around him. *Lancelot*, though, is a much more mordant portrait of the Stoic tradition than *The Moviegoer* or *The Last Gentleman*. Lance's father is not really a physical invalid, but rather a spiritual coward (Lance is silent on this point: did his father ease himself off the world's stage?), and Lance becomes a monster by feeding upon the legends of ancestors.

The ghost still beckons, then, inviting Percy to view the world as a set of fixed and immutable forms. And so tempting is its appeal that Percy has had to reveal, this time, just how lethal its influence could be. For the first time he has directly opposed the Stoic with the Christian. But the Stoic has not been vanquished; Walker Percy can no more stop being a southerner than he can stop being a Christian. As a southerner he will continue to despise the things that he as a Christian can live with. That tension has given us a brilliant sequence of fictions, *Lancelot* the most exciting yet, and it will give us more.

WILLIAM J. DOWIE

Lancelot and the Search for Sin

WHEN LANCELOT ANDREWES LAMAR, Walker
Percy's protagonist-monologist in *Lancelot*, thinks of himself
and his buddy J. B. Jenkins, the Grand Kleagle of the Ku Klux
Klan, as "sunk in life, soaked in old Louisiana blood and tears
and three hundred years of Christian sin and broadsword
Bowie-knife Sharps-rifle bloodshed and victory-defeat" (*Ll*,
101), his mind is fingering the pimple-become-volcano that is
at the center of the book's explosion. Time and again Lancelot's
mind circles back over the sins of yesteryear, its bold and decisive deeds, and the lack of sin and event today. It is Lance's
search for sin, his "unholy grail," that shapes the action of the
novel, and it is the failure of this quest that shapes the conclusion.

Although Lancelot's story can be laid out in a quite linear
fashion—remote southern history, childhood and his parents,
football stardom, Lucy Cobb, Margot, dream world, awakening, and events preceding his confinement—his own narration,
told from the cell of a New Orleans asylum, is fragmentary.
Like a man assembling a jigsaw puzzle, Lancelot picks up and
puts down the pieces of his past, trying to construct the frag-
ments into a whole. He is a detective sifting through clues to

recover and understand his personal history; and, although our curiosity is teased about the fateful events during the hurricane at Belle Isle, the real suspense is not about what happened in the past, but about what is happening in the present to Lancelot and his listener, Harry or Percival. It is suspense about what one is to do in the face of the contemporary situation.

Lancelot's past was split into two major segments by the letter *O*, his daughter's blood type and unmistakable evidence of his wife's unfaithfulness. Before the discovery, he had been living in a dreamworld of his own making; he had been sunk in the patterns of his ruined Louisiana aristocratic ennui. After he detects Margot's infidelity, Lancelot comes alive. "The moment I knew for a fact that Margot had been fucked by another man, it was as if I had been waked from a twenty-year dream. I was Rip van Winkle rubbing his eyes. In an instant I became sober, alert, watchful. I could act" (*Ll*, 107). The Rip van Winkle legend, which Percy has used before, repeats an archetypal pattern: he who was dead is now alive; Lazarus has been led out of the tomb; but with Percy, the pattern is usually precipitated by shock. Stung by the intolerableness of imagining his wife under the weight of another man, her mouth giving to another the familiar mews of pleasure's pangs, Lance bristles with excitement at the possibility of finding something unusual amidst the ordinariness of life. Could it be that sin, dismissed by contemporary society, actually exists? His skin prickles with interest. If he could know his wife's adultery in the most direct way, would he not know sin? Setting out on his quest for the unholy grail, Lancelot becomes a searcher like all of Percy's previous heroes; but he is the first to look for sin.

Until recently, sin was something the southern writer did not have to send his hero in search of. William Faulkner, Erskine Caldwell, Robert Penn Warren, and Flannery O'Connor portray characters who choose evil and are blamed for it. The whole southern tradition, Donald Davidson suggests, confronts us with "the ancient problem of evil and its manifestations"; and Davidson distinguishes it from the northern "assumption that there is no defect or irregularity in human nature and human affairs that cannot be remedied by the application of money, science, and socialistic legislation." By contrast, "for Willie Stark, for the Compsons of Faulkner's novels . . . there is no remedy in law or sociology, and no reward but the reward of virtue and the hope of heaven."[1]

The sources of the southern writer's sense of sin lay in the history of the region. Because of the clear injustice of one race's enslaving another, southern writers have been able to write about right and wrong. As Hugh Holman explains, "the southern writer has been uniquely equipped by his history to draw the symbol of guilt and to serve, himself, as an example."[2] Christian fundamentalism relies directly and literally on the Bible, and the Bible teaches there are commandments, and the violation of one of these commandments is a sin. Any good fundamentalist knows sin's reality, no matter what some jesuitical clergyman might say about the sinner's necessary knowledge, intention, and consent to the deed, or no matter what some psychiatrist might say about inner compulsion. Less pervasive than fundamentalism but nevertheless influential in the South was a Stoic tradition, originating in the planters of Virginia, which taught that in one's heart one knows what one ought and ought not to do. When fundamentalism's absolutism was accompanied in the southerner's postbellum consciousness by stoicism's ethic, the southern literary tradition (remembering slavery) was informed with a sense of sin and a knowledge of guilt.

With Percy, the guilt has run out. The older southern writers were close enough to the event of slavery to inherit the guilt, strain under it, and exorcize it by writing about evil as evil. But this condition no longer prevails, as Percy's flatly unemotional treatment of Negroes in his novels suggests. Elgin, the young black in *Lancelot*, has simply jumped over the whole history of slavery and the descendants of his race's enslavers by being smart and getting a scholarship to M.I.T. Such an example, regardless of its typicality, rather too conveniently suggests that injustice belongs to the dead past. As for segregation and the not-so-distant denial of civil rights, Percy suggests the white southerner's evolving attitudes. He portrays Lancelot Lamar as a liberal, guilt-motivated advocate of civil rights in the 1960s whose outlook changes to benign indifference in the 1970s. Lance, like most sympathetic white southerners, simply assumes that the battle for civil rights has been fought and won.

In fact, all of the conditions conducive to a sense of sin have changed. The overwhelming media influence of secular, unheroic America has penetrated and eroded the uniqueness of the South's consciousness. Fundamentalism has been compartmentalized into an *ism*, and a rural one at that. The Bible belt has been loosened, with the holy book now vying with *The Six Million Dollar Man* as a myth of morality. Stoicism has been eroded by psychological pragmatism and economic opportunism, with Marcus Aurelius giving way to Dr. Joyce Brothers and Dale Carnegie. Even the southerner's newspapers are filled with syndicated columns out of Chicago, New York, and Washington; and injustice no longer seems the responsibility of the South alone. The old South's righteousness and guilt have become homogenized into the same type of general smiling uneasiness experienced in the rest of the country.

This change is reflected clearly in Percy's early novels, which show almost no sense of or concern with sin. *The Moviegoer* was one of the first important southern novels in which this sense of moral evil was not felt. *Detached, flat, ironic,* and *curious* were adjectives used to describe the book's tone, in contrast to the more customary epithets like *gothic, brooding, southern, earth-fed* or *soul-searching,* much less *fury-driven*. All of

Percy's main characters have been wry and ironic observers of human conduct, but they neither judge nor are judged harshly, administering at most, as Binx Bolling phrases it, "a foot in the right place as the opportunity presents itself" (*Mg*, 218). Aside from a few lyric sexual tingles, the strongest emotions expressed by Binx Bolling and Will Barrett are boredom and curiosity. And, until the appearance of *Love in the Ruins*, could one have even imagined an apocalyptic novel in which hardly any blame is laid? Violence and destruction result from the various factions being trapped in their own abstractions, but the individuals hardly seem to be at fault.

Sin has been absent from Percy's work because he does not see it operative in the world about him. It is not that he is simply a novelist of manners. No, Percy is an observer of morals as well as manners. Yet the term *moralist* does not fit him because it implies a criticism of immorality that is absent in his work. Percy sees contemporary society not as immoral but as amoral, missing the moral dimension and so incapable of acting either morally or immorally.

Up until now, Percy has been satisfied with a detached, Horatian satire of the contemporary amorality. When he has criticized it more directly, it was through a secondary character like Sutter of *The Last Gentleman*. Now in the person of Lancelot Andrewes Lamar, named after the seventeenth-century Anglican divine, Percy unambiguously scourges the modern world's lack of moral responsibility, especially in the area of sex. Enraged by the sexual revolution that has hit his own wife, daughter, son, and mother, Lancelot Lamar lashes out at "the great whorehouse and fagdom of America" (*Ll*, 176). While one must be careful to distinguish the author from his protagonist, Lancelot's rhetoric is so strong about "this cocksucking cuntlapping assholelicking fornicating Happyland U.S.A." (*Ll*, 158) that Percy seems at once to be expressing his own outrage and, at the same time, parodying it.

Because of his Catholic background, Percy conceives of sin primarily as the subjective concurrence in an objectively evil act. But subjective concurrence demands freedom and core involvement, both of which Percy views as lacking in contemporary society. Percy sees the effects of objective sin; but he also sees that no one is able or willing to take responsibility for his own acts. "Not one in 200 million Americans is ready to act from perfect sobriety and freedom" (*Ll*, 157), observes Lance. He recalls a couple so bound by the surface patterns of their lives that it took a hurricane for them to "become free again to sin or not to sin" (*Ll*, 164). The hurricane poses such objective danger that it neutralizes their fear of admitting their hatred to one another.

Core involvement means that the person is integrally bound up with his act, emotionally as well as volitionally. However, modern psychology has so sliced up the human psyche that one seems less likely to have acted freely than to have acted out of a compulsion, from his shadow side, or because of his id's drives. As for emotional attachment to one's deeds, Lancelot notes that "people have fewer emotions these days" (*Ll*, 90). Merlin's actors can register fifteen emotions without having a single real feeling. In casting about for examples of obvious sin, Lancelot must reject Hitler, for "as everyone knows and says, Hitler was a madman" (*Ll*, 138). As for child beaters, they have "psychological problems and are as bad off as the children. It has been proved that every battered child has battered parents, battered grandparents, and so on. No one is to blame" (*Ll*, 139). Percy here is covering some of the same ground covered by Karl Menninger, M.D., in his *Whatever Became of Sin?* (1973), when Menninger traced the process by which sin became crime, and crime became illness. For a solution to its evils, the modern world has turned from the priest to the police to the psychiatrist. Menninger listed many of the things he considers sinful in contemporary society and urged "a revival or reassertion of personal responsibility in all human acts, good or bad."[3]

Although Percy would agree with the spirit of Menninger's exhortation, *Lancelot* shows that it would be naïve to make the problem one of will. Because of the limitations on human freedom, wholeness, and emotional depth, the connection between the doer and the deed has been snapped. Lance himself is both the channel of this message and the victim of it. He is more than capable of fathoming the depths of moral vacuity in people like Jacoby, Raine, and Troy Dana and lamenting it; and he desperately wants the moral connection mended. However, when it comes to taking responsibility for his own violence, Lance has a total emotional dissociation. He reflects on the moment before he committed murder, "As I held that wretched Jacoby by the throat, I felt nothing except the itch of fiberglass particles under my collar" (*Ll*, 253). He remembers "casting about for an appropriate feeling to match the deed"(*Ll*, 242) and not finding one. Lance is himself part of the no-feeling phenomenon he had described when he said, "This is an age of interest" (*Ll*, 138). One year after the murders, the closest Lancelot can come to admitting responsibility for his actions is to say that "something went wrong, because here I am, in a nuthouse—or is it a prison?—recovering from shock, psychosis, disorientation" (*Ll*, 108). Lance's moral sensibility is so slight that he knows "something went wrong" (not that he did something wrong) only "because" he is incarcerated. He is unable to call what he did a sin, preferring the more comfortable medical terms, "shock, psychosis, disorientation."

While Lance's frequent references to his "confession" may be taken literally as one seeking absolution from his priest, Lance's confession is the typically modern one of his own description, "Bless me, Father, for I have done something which I don't understand" (*Ll*, 155). Lance knows what it is that he did; he knows why he did it, but he does not understand the disparity between society's condemnation of the deed and his own emotional indifference to it. Percy has shown us the complexity of the difficulty in reestablishing moral responsibility through the irony of a hero who, though explicitly concerned about moral irresponsibility, is himself a victim of it. Lancelot Andrewes, the preacher, cannot practice what he preaches.

The list of sins in *Lancelot* differs somewhat from Menninger's, but the novel is plainly Percy's *Whatever Became of Sin*. Many of the wrongs in the novel are violations of the commandments. Lance's father is guilty of stealing. His wife lies to him (bearing false witness). Adultery is committed by Margot, Merlin, Jacoby, Raine, Uncle Harry, Lance's mother, and himself. Lance also violates the injunction not to kill. And Raine and Troy must answer to Christ's warning not to "lead astray a single one of these little ones" (Luke 17:1–2).

With all of these sins around, why and in what sense does Lancelot "seek" the unholy grail? Although Lance had been haunted all his life by the memory of his father's theft and the suspicion of his mother's adultery, these remained vague subterranean gnawing uneasinesses until the letter *O* (Percy's scarlet letter) set him on his quest for knowledge. Shaken by the intolerableness of Margot's unfaithfulness, Lance remembers a similar dislocation that took place when he discovered his father had stolen ten thousand dollars: "The old world fell to pieces" (*Ll*, 42). Disillusioned by the people he most needed to admire, Lance reflects, "How strange it is that a discovery like this, of evil . . . can shake you up, knock you out of your rut, be the occasion of a new way of looking at things!" (*Ll*, 51). His father's dishonesty, his mother's likely adultery, and his wife's infidelity challenge his assumption of the general beneficence of mankind. Lance had accepted without question the unchanging guise of niceness and blamelessness with which the world went on, but now he has to know whether it is all really niceness and blamelessness or buggery. "One has to know," says Lance. "There are worse things than bad news" (*Ll*, 131). He can make no further discovery about his parents' deeds, for they are lost in the irretrievable past; but Margot's are not.

The bad news Lance seeks, however, is more than the fact of Margot's unfaithfulness. He already knows that. He thinks that by actually seeing her in her adultery he will see sin. Even though his scientific frame of mind tells him that her actions are only molecules rubbing against molecules, would he not discover more in actual observation? Wouldn't he pierce to the heart of the intolerableness, wouldn't he find sin? After all, Lance thinks, if the best thing in life is sexual love, would not the equation be balanced if it were also the worst? This is the heart of the quest. "'Evil' is surely the clue to this age, the only quest appropriate to the age. For everything and everyone's either wonderful or sick and nothing is evil" (*Ll*, 138). But Lance assumes that, if only he can get beyond those closed doors, he will see the buggeriness of the buggery, the sinfulness of the sin, the raw culpability of their free and immoral act. And this knowledge will be revolutionary.

But the quest fails. Lance discovers nothing, he admits, at the heart of evil. "There is no unholy grail just as there was no Holy Grail" (*Ll*, 253). He does not see sin. He sees his wife's negative intermingling with Jacoby's negative; he sees his daughter in a three-way geometric pattern (diagramed, not described, in the book) with Raine and Troy Dana. So, not only does the Hollywood cinema fail to show sin as sin (as evidenced by the type of movie they are making), but even his and Elgin's (a scientist giving us the sheer facts) *cinema verité* also fails to show sin. Later, when Lance gets even closer to the deed and stands over his wife and Jacoby in bed, he senses only the "beastliness" of their act, nothing more. Why does Lance's quest fail so dismally and so abruptly?

Lancelot knew that he was going to blow up Belle Isle once he had seen the film of his wife's and daughter's bedroom activities. He plans the explosion carefully, sends away both daughters, Tex, Elgin and his parents, and even encourages Merlin, whom he's taken a liking to (after all, wasn't Margot dumping Merlin, too?), to leave as well. Through all this premeditation, Lancelot, quester after the unholy grail, does not even think to look for sin in his own actions, the only place where he could have hoped to find it.

Lance's quest is misdirected and hence doomed from the outset. In looking for sin in others, his wife and Jacoby in particular, Lancelot was looking for the impossible, for sin is a subjective occurrence existing only within an individual's psyche. Naturally Lancelot could never see sin. He saw but a negative image or a diagram—the inevitable vision from the outside. So taken up with his search for sexual sin in others, Lancelot misses the sinfulness of his own acts, sexual and violent. As he stands above Raine Robinette, about to enter her, Lance ruefully remembers the lost excitement of locker-room fantasies about Ava Gardner. His apparent flaccidity is rescued by the sight of his daughter's ring on Raine's finger and the erotic hate this sight stirs in him. "The possibility of hate rescued lust from the locker-room future and restored it to the present" (*Ll*, 235). Their intercourse is described by Lance without joy or guilt; neither during nor after it does he consider this act as a possible location for sin. Yet it was as much an act of adultery as Margot's—and with perhaps much less justification; for, after all, hadn't the man Margot married become an admittedly alcoholic dreamer who lately "had trouble making love" (*Ll*, 66) to her?

In his quest for sin, Lance is as uninterested in his murders as in his adultery. When he first grabs Margot and Jacoby in a bear hug, Lance's mind roams to historical speculation; "it seemed of no great moment whether I squeezed them or did not squeeze them" (*Ll*, 240). It is not just that his feelings are cold, but his intellect simply does not make the connection between what he is doing and the sought-for "sin." Through all of his meticulous preparation for the explosion, Lancelot has not one question about the morality of his own actions. He is incapable of self-knowledge, incapable of blaming himself, and therefore incapable of finding sin. Corresponding to the irony of Lancelot Andrewes preaching emotional involvement and practicing emotional detachment, we have the irony of Lancelot, the quester, looking for sin in the wrong place.

Percy saves the crowning irony of the novel, however, for the end. Just a little over a year after Lancelot's terrible deeds at Belle Isle, he is to be released. He crows gleefully to Harry-Percival, "I'm leaving today. They're discharging me. Psychiatrically fit and legally innocent. I can prove I'm sane. Can you? Why do you look at me like that? You don't think they should? Well, in any case, my lawyer got a writ of habeas corpus and my psychiatrist says I'm fit as a fiddle, saner in fact than he—the poor man is overworked, depressed, and lives on Librium" (*Ll*, 249–50). Lancelot's story then is one of crime and no punishment. Most probably he was deemed temporarily insane during the night of the hurricane. Now he is "psychiatrically fit and legally innocent" (*Ll*, 249). Psychiatry and law have no more means for holding a man responsible for his horrors (four people were killed by Lance's hand) than calling his behavior "aberrant" and detaining him until he has recovered from "shock, psychosis, disorientation" (*Ll*, 108). Dostoevsky at least gave Raskolnikov, who also was judged temporarily insane, eight years in Siberia. Percy in letting Lancelot off so easy seems to be implying that the sanctions of society on such behavior are almost nonexistent. Not only is Lancelot unable to hold himself responsible for his actions, but society is equally impotent to deal satisfactorily with human evil.

Since he fails to find his grail, how does Lance plan to deal with morality in the future? He determines simply to avoid the whole question of moral responsibility when considering the masses and to use a clear and frank language that describes deeds not motivation. There will be "whores," "ladies," "thieves," "honorable men" in his self-declared new dispensation. General Lee and General Forrest will know one another instantly amidst a convention of Buick salesmen on Bourbon Street because they will instantly recognize in each other a high, old, Stoic code of honor and courage. In his efforts to simplify, to find some clear method of dealing with the intolerableness of the modern world, Lancelot abandons the befuddling complexity of the human psyche. People will be their deeds and their deeds will conform to his categories, he concludes, thus objectifying and ultimately dehumanizing mankind. He decides to play God and divide mankind into the sheep and the goats, left hand and right hand. Thus he is guilty of supreme hubris. Lancelot reassures Harry that he will not need violence in his new order, for he has found that if you say something with conviction, people will usually believe you. He sheathes his sword, but does not discard it.

When Harry-Percival agrees with Lancelot's "it's your way or mine," Percy has limited the theme of his novel considerably. In the past he has been accused of copping out in his endings, but in *Lancelot* he takes an unequivocal stand. There are only two real responses: Lance's new found code of the heart, an oversimplifying hearkening back to the old pagan view of virtue for virtue's sake, encouraging others to accept this code, and waiting for (or perhaps instigating) something to happen to stop the madness of the modern; and the priest's way.

We have spoken little of this silent figure who himself has undergone changes during Lancelot's monologue. At the start of the novel, Lance had noticed his friend refuse to say prayers for the dead at the request of a woman in the graveyard. Later Percival is seen kneeling and praying by one of the tombs. He has also clarified his own future. Instead of continuing as a priest-doctor, he will go back to being a priest, content to minister to the needs of the poor in Alabama (like Val in *The Last*

Gentleman). Percival (the name's similarity to "Percy" deserves mention) reverses the process that Karl Menninger had described. He abandons medicine and turns back to faith. His way is believing in the Christian God, continuing to mediate in his small way that God to his people, hanging onto the complexities of sin's subjectivity, resisting Sodom in his own person and encouraging those around him to do the same, but forgiving them when they do not. His way is the "God-bless-everything-because-it's-good-only-don't-but-if-you-do-it's-not-so-bad" attitude that is mockingly rejected by Lance. Percival's choice is at once an alleluia, a prohibition, and an absolution —a combination incomprehensible to Lance.

However, in the face of Lance's ranting and raving, the priest's way quietly becomes the true thematic center of the novel in its final pages. From the start Percival had considerable stature because of the amount of affection, trust, and admiration bestowed on him by Lance, who is not lavish with such things. He is the first person Lance would speak to in over a year; and Lance talks compulsively to him as a defendant addressing his judge, as a patient confiding in his doctor, as a penitent baring his soul to his confessor, and as a friend reminiscing with a friend, even though Lance admits, "I don't know why I want to talk to you or what I need to tell you or need to hear from you" (*Ll*, 85). In chastising Percival for leaving the United States for Biafra, Lancelot muses, "if you'd been around to talk to . . ." (*Ll*, 106). He doesn't finish the sentence, but the implication is that things might have been different.

Percival's silence involves tremendous concentration and interest as he keeps coming back to Lancelot's cell just to listen. His silence is an active one, a time of assimilation and decision. In a time when talk is cheap, Lance respects his friend's silence despite his efforts to provoke Percival out of it. Lance taunts him about being a spoiled priest, about the ludicrous changes in the Church with nuns in pant suits wriggling their asses to guitar music during mass, and about the Church's failure and its need for a new Reformation. Harry-Percival's silence in the face of these accusations does not imply consent, but rather consideration and ultimately confidence in his own way. When he does speak, his words carry an intensified power because of the preceding silence and because of their strategic location at the end of the novel. Percival is given the last word. When a man utters thousands of words, his message is likely to be lost in the clutter; when another man listens to the first's every word and then answers in thirteen words of his own, his message sticks. Percival usurps the novel.

His answers to Lancelot's questions are clear and firm. He establishes their lines of agreement and their differences. He agrees with Lance's condemnation of Sodom, so Percy closes the door on the modern American do-your-own-thing sexual utopia. But that is "all" they "can agree on" (*Ll*, 257). Percival does not share Lancelot's rage, and he does not approve Lancelot's deeds in the past or in the future. What is it that he would like to tell Lancelot at the end but does not? That Lance's way will not work. It has been tried before, by the Romans and the Old South, and it has failed. The sword, which Lance intends to have recourse to if nothing apocalyptic happens, is wrong. Lance in his outrage at the speck in his wife's eye has missed the plank in his own.

In *Lancelot*, Percy has written a disturbing book. His perspective on the modern world is a self-imposed narrow one, for as Lance says, "Have you noticed that the narrower the view the more you can see?" (*Ll*, 3). Lancelot's cell becomes a symbol of our need to get a more oblique, more partial view of the world in order to understand it. As such, the cell is an instrument of recovery like Binx's movies, Will's telescope, and Tom's lapsometer. However, all of the previous protagonists were absorbent characters, sponges. Lancelot is sharp, clear, and decisive, a lance. Thus Walker Percy, M.D., uses the most drastic of medical treatments, the knife, to expose the moral stagnation of American life. Since his instrument is itself infected, however, it is offered not as a cure but only as a corrective. Percy retains an ironic distance from Lancelot's blindness to his own evil; and he uses the priest-doctor Percival as a guide to a more healthy future.

CLEANTH BROOKS

Walker Percy
and Modern Gnosticism

IT IS DANGEROUS to impute to one man ideas
that belong to another, and as one reads the pages that follow,
this may seem to be precisely the course that I am pursuing.
But that is not at all my intention. Although in *The Moviegoer*
Percy refers to "the peculiar gnosis of trains" (*Mg*, 184) and in
Love in the Ruins writes of "Gnostic pride" (*LR*, 64), I am not
aware that he has ever mentioned gnosticism itself in any of
his writings. Nor is it necessary, for what I have to say, that he
should have done so. After all, why should any modern writer
mention an ancient heresy of the first centuries of the Christian
era?

Gnosticism, however, is far from dead. There is plenty of
hard evidence that it pervades Western civilization. Consequently, the study of it, far from being a subject of merely anti-
quarian interest, could be indispensable for an understanding
of the great intellectual movements that have convulsed our
own century. Such at least is the contention of Eric Voegelin,
whose monumental five-volume series, *Order and History*, is
being published by the Louisiana State University Press. If
Percy never mentions gnosticism, neither has he, so far as I
know, ever mentioned Voegelin and may never have read him.

But again, that possibility does not figure in my present design which amounts to no more than pointing out some highly interesting, and I think, significant parallels between the writings of these two men. Yet if the parallelisms are genuinely significant, the readers of either Percy or Voegelin may benefit from the widened perspective effected by the cultural context of each writer's work.

The basic resemblance between Percy and Voegelin that first struck me was the fact that both writers see modern man as impoverished by his distorted and disordered view of reality. As for Percy, I noticed it first in his novels. There, since he is a genuine novelist, the view is simply implied. It is, of course, spelled out in the essays that make up *The Message in the Bottle*. A comparable account of man's distorted perspective and an account of how it developed is the very theme and subject matter of all of Voegelin's writings for the last thirty years.

In all of Percy's novels the hero inherits what amounts to an orthodox Christian view of man and his relation to reality, but the world inhabited by the hero is dominated by ideas that are powerfully twisted away from any orthodox view. In the first three novels the heroes finally achieve, despite the age they live in, a religious apprehension of their own stance in the world. In the fourth novel, however, the protagonist is maddened by what he sees as the ineffectuality of Christianity in a world he finds intolerable. Vowing to take matters into his own hands, Lancelot becomes a modern gnostic.

As I have remarked, the essays collected in *The Message in the Bottle* spell out Percy's estimate of the situation in which modern man finds himself. In the very first essay, Percy argues that a "theory of man must account for the alienation of man" (*MB*, 23), but points out that the dominant ideas of the twentieth century do not and cannot. That is because they define alienation as a phenomenon located in this time and place, rather than recognize it as the necessary condition of man. But the anthropology of Judeo-Christianity has always seen alienation as man's essential condition. That tradition accounts for alienation through the doctrine of the fall. According to this doctrine there occurred at the beginning of human history a separation or alienation of man from God, an alienation that accounted for, as Percy sees it, the "homelessness of a man who [in this world] is not in fact at home" (*MB*, 24). Moreover, the Judeo-Christian scheme provided, in its own terms, ways and means for man's becoming reconciled with God; but it did not promise him any heaven on this earth. The bliss of perfection and peace was to be recovered elsewhere, in eternity, and not in the world of time.

By contrast, the modern view regards man as only "a higher organism satisfying this or that need from its environment" (*MB*, 24). Man thus can be made happy by a more perfect adjustment to his environment. Through the efforts of our marvelous technology, man can now hope to make radical modification of his environment and so perfect his adjustment to it.

Our scientists and humanists, therefore, have erased the notion of the Fall and have promised to take Man back to Eden; that is, to the perfect environment from which the Judeo-Christian account claimed that he had been expelled. But the new Eden will be real, no mere fable. It will be a place—as Percy rather sardonically puts it—"where scientists know like the angels, and laymen prosper in good environments, and ethical democracies progress through education." (*MB*, 24).

Unfortunately, however, this promised utopian Eden remains unrealized. Man remains alienated. As Percy explains in "The Delta Factor,"

> The scientists were saying that by science man was learning more and more about himself as an organism and more and more about the world as an environment and that accordingly the environment could be changed and man made to feel more and more at home.
> The humanists were saying that through education and the appli-

cation of the ethical principles of Christianity, man's lot was certain to improve.

But poets and artists and novelists were saying something else: that at a time when, according to the theory of the age, men should feel most at home they felt most homeless.

Something was wrong. (*MB*, 25)

Percy's view is that on this issue our poets and artists and novelists have been dead right. On earlier pages of this essay he asks a number of searching questions:

Why has man entered on an orgy of war, murder, torture, and self-destruction unparalleled in history and in the very century when he had hoped to see the dawn of universal peace and brotherhood? . . .

Why have more people been killed in the twentieth century than in all other centuries put together? . . .

Why do young people look so sad, the very young who, seeing how sad their elders are, have sought a new life of joy and freedom with each other and in the green fields and forests, but who instead of finding joy look even sadder than their elders? (*MB*, 3, 4, 7)

Percy has his own way of answering these questions. His readers will already know, or by further reading of his work, can learn, what his answers are. What I want to do now is to turn to Voegelin's description of the way in which modern man conceives of himself.

Like Percy, Voegelin interprets the various powerful drives of the modern age as heading up in a belief that utopia can be achieved. A perfect society of one sort or another is the goal, according to Voegelin, of all the modern manifestations of gnosticism. But in this matter they inherit from the ancient gnostics, who are their forebears in unbroken continuity. Like the modern scientists and humanists, the ancient gnostic cults sought to erase the idea of any fall of man. They could not agree with what was proclaimed in Genesis, namely, that the creation was essentially good—that it was the handiwork of a good God, who, in viewing his handiwork, had pronounced that "it was very good."

On the contrary, the ancient gnostics held that the creation was the work of a demon—of a cruel demiurge. The world—with its mutability, sexuality, wickedness, and violence—is woefully imperfect, but man has the potentiality to be perfect if he does not confound himself with this imperfect world. Man had the misfortune to be placed in this flawed world not by his own error, but by an evil god. His task then is to extricate himself from this evil world, partially at least by throwing off the bonds of his own evil flesh. Then he can get back, in spite of the obstructions set up by the demiurge, to the true god and achieve the more perfect order for which he was originally designed.

Two crucial aspects of gnosticism are worth emphasizing here: (1) Man the creature is not responsible for the evil in which he finds himself. He has a right to blame it on someone or something else. The assumption that "In Adam's fall/We sinned all" is to the gnostic pure nonsense. And (2) man's salvation depends upon his own efforts. He must rely not upon faith but on gnosis, the secret knowledge that makes it possible for him to evade the snares and entanglements of the demon and to reunite his soul with the divinity from which he had come.

These two traits, Voegelin points out, continue to characterize gnosticism, even in its present-day secularized form. Dissatisfied with the nature of reality, man can now the more confidently hope that, with his increasing knowledge, he can remake the world to suit himself. As Voegelin puts it, what is common to the profusion of "gnostic experiences and symbolic expressions" is "the experience of the world as an alien place into which man has strayed and from which he must find his way back home to the other world of his origin." The divine spark within him is "an alien in this world and the world is alien to it."[1]

The continuity of gnosticism from the ancient gnostic sects of the classical world on down to modern manifestations of this kind of speculation was worked out as early as the first half of the nineteenth century, largely by German and French scholars. That history is highly interesting, but it can have no part in this abbreviated essay. More to my purpose here are the names of some of the modern thinkers whom Voegelin regards as gnostics and their different formulas for eliminating modern man's sense of alienation.

It will be interesting, for example, to compare with Voegelin's view what Percy has to say about Karl Marx. Man has always been alienated, Percy writes: "By the very cogent anthropology of Judeo-Christianity . . . human existence was by no means to be understood as the transaction of a higher organism satisfying this or that need from its environment, [either] by being 'creative' or enjoying 'meaningful relationships.'" Rather, human existence was to be understood "as the journey of a wayfarer along life's way" (*MB*, 24). Not so for Marx. For him, as Percy puts it, "the experience of alienation was . . . an inevitable consequence of capitalism" (*MB*, 24). So Marx hoped to get rid of capitalism, and expected that man's alienation would subsequently disappear; without capitalism, man could be beautifully adapted to his environment and reconciled with himself.

According to Voegelin, "Marx is a speculative gnostic." Marx has convinced himself that he has penetrated the secret of history and therefore knows the way in which it must go. The perfect society of the classless state will be achieved through "the revolution of the proletariat and the transformation of man into the communist superman."[2] But, according to Voegelin, like all gnostic utopians, Marx misrepresents the nature of man and for his own purposes deforms the nature of reality.

Or consider Georg Friedrich Hegel. Martin Luschei writes that Percy once told him that "After twelve years of scientific education . . . he felt rather like Kierkegaard when he finished reading Hegel: 'Hegel, said Kierkegaard, explained everything under the sun, except one small detail, what it means to be a

man living in the world who must die.'" Furthermore, Luschei
quotes, with reference to Percy's reaction against abstraction,
Kierkegaard's statement that Hegelian idealism had abolished
"'individual man,'" for "'every speculative philosopher'" had
confused "'himself with humanity at large.'"[3] In short, as Percy
puts it with an amplitude that will cover Marx, Hegel, and
many another philosopher, German philosophy had for a long
time suffered from an "old interior itch" which turns too heav-
ily to abstraction and as a consequence lets "the world slip
away" (*MB*, 33).

Voegelin would add further names—not limited to the German philosophers and thinkers who had let "the world" and
reality itself "slip away." In fact, he would define the "old interior itch" as gnosticism itself. "All gnostic movements," he
writes, "are involved in the project of abolishing the constitu-
tion of being, with its origin in divine, transcendent being, and
replacing it with a world-immanent order of being, the perfection of which lies in the realm of human action." But specifically, what does Voegelin say about Hegel? For him, Hegel is
another of the moderns who have, by willfully ignoring certain
elements of humanity, promulgated a deformed conception of
reality. Voegelin says, among other things, that the "factor
[that] Hegel excludes [from reality] is the mystery of a history
that wends its way into the future without our knowing its end.
History as a whole is essentially not an object of cognition; the
meaning of the whole is not discernible."[4] Nevertheless, Hegel's
interior itch set him to constructing a history of man that was
"fully comprehensible."

One could go on with Voegelin's rollcall of other great gnostics of later times—Hobbes, Comte, Nietzsche, Freud, Heidegger, *et al*. But I am here not writing an essay so much as setting
down notes for an essay to be written. I shall limit myself therefore to only one more example, one that is the more interesting
because it is highly problematic.

Saint Thomas More wrote of a utopia—indeed, coined the word. Does Voegelin regard him as a gnostic? Well, no; but his treatment of More is very interesting.

> In his Utopia [Voegelin writes] More traces the image of man and of society that he considers perfect. To this perfection belongs the abolition of private property. Because he had the benefit of an excellent theological education, however, More is well aware that this perfect state cannot be achieved in the world: man's lust for possessions is deeply rooted in original sin, in *superbia* in the Augustinian sense. In the final part of his work when More looks over his finished picture, he has to admit that it would all be possible if only there were not the "serpent of superbia." But there *is* the serpent of superbia—and More would not think of denying it.[5]

Is the protagonist of *Love in the Ruins*, Dr. Thomas More, a descendant of the Saint—is he a gnostic? Well hardly, but Percy has been very careful not to make him a saint, and, even more important, not to make him merely the embodiment of an abstract idea, even of an idea to which Percy is himself devoted.

Dr. Thomas More is a Roman Catholic, but Percy does not present him as a model of Christian piety. More enjoys bourbon whiskey—Early Times is clearly his favorite brand—and he is strongly attracted to a pretty girl—almost any pretty girl. He admits that he is a "bad Catholic." He says that he is like the saint's second wife, a woman "who believed in God but saw no reason why one should disturb one's life [for Him], certainly not lose one's head" (*LR*, 384).

In his novel, Percy has made the issue more complicated still—and thereby rendered his protagonist more thoroughly human—by having him invent the lapsometer, an instrument for making miraculous diagnoses of the human psyche, with the promise of reshaping humanity and, with it, the world. When More says, near the end of the novel, "I still believe my lapsometer can save the world," he sounds rather like a gnostic himself. But the saving clause that follows—"if I can get it right" —and, still more, the sentence that follows in which he tells

what he considers is wrong with the world, together indicate
that he is no utopian (*LR*, 382–83). He has no ambition to create a new Adam. Apparently his modest ambition is to help
with a highly necessary repair job on the old Adam, who now
suffers from "chronic angelism-bestialism that rives soul from
body and sets it orbiting the great world as the spirit of abstraction whence it takes the form of beasts, swans and bulls,
werewolves, blood-suckers, Mr. Hydes, or just [a] poor lone-
some ghost locked in its own machinery" (*LR*, 383). (René Descartes, thou shouldst be living at this hour—to witness where
thy classic riving of soul from body has left the modern world.)

Dr. More's vocation is that of a healer—so is Dr. Percy's—
which is one way of saying that both are in the human repair
business and that neither is a quietist or a defeatest, waiting
for the civilization to collapse. But then, of course, neither is
Eric Voegelin. There is a difference between (1) trying to put
back together a world that is "broken, sundered, busted down,"
and (2) junking the world in favor of a fool-proof model that
you have thought up in your own head.

All right, all right, the skeptical reader may say, but is there
any positive justification for raising in Dr. Thomas More's case
the complicated issue of gnosticism? I think so, and the best
way to show it is to listen to More's talk. He may be a "bad
Catholic"—he may, for example, have let eleven years elapse
before coming again to his father-confessor—but his theological orthodoxy is genuine, and he is himself quite conscious that
it constitutes his anchor against the undertow of the powerful
currents of modernity. What do we hear him saying—and what
are some of the things said to him?

More says of the connection between revolution and totali-
tarianism: "Students are a shaky dogmatic lot. And the 'freer'
they are, the more dogmatic. At heart they're totalitarians:
they want either total dogmatic freedom or total dogmatic un-
freedom, and the one thing that makes them unhappy is some-

thing in between" (*LR*, 233). (Voegelin's "metaxy" is the "in-between state"—between the animal and the divine, between the immanent and the transcendent—which is the peculiarly human realm.)

More, speaking of his first wife, remarks that "What she didn't understand, she being spiritual and seeing religion as spirit, was that it took religion to save me from the spirit world, from orbiting the earth like Lucifer and the angels, that it took nothing less than touching the thread off the misty interstates [Voegelin's metaxy again] and eating Christ himself to make me mortal man again and let me inhabit my own flesh and love her in the morning" (*LR*, 254).

More is addressed by a revolutionist as follows: "Let me put it this way, Doctor. You know what we're going to do. We're going to build a new society right here" (*LR*, 300). This state-ment has what Voegelin would call the genuine gnostic ring: the speaker's absolute confidence that he knows the true state of affairs, an equal certainty about the soundness of his mo-tives, and a genuine relishing of his sense of power.

The same accent is to be heard in what a revolutionary pro-fessor says to More, though his speech also exhibits the not un-common gnostic ruthlessness. The professor is voicing his praise of a certain (mythical) Latin-American dictator. He says, "He's the George Washington of Ecuador, the only man beloved north and south and the only man capable of uniting the country." When More asks whether he "didn't kill several hundred thou-sand Ecuadorians who didn't love him," the professor is at no loss for a reply: "Yes, but they were either fascists or running dogs or lackeys of the American imperialists. Anyhow, the ques-tion has become academic" (*LR*, 326).

In this general connection, it will be interesting to cite More on the subject of what he calls "angelism," which, as I interpret it, arises from the human being's impatience with the limita-tions of the mortal mind—impatience with perceptions mediated through the senses, the progress of thought from the known to the unknown, and dependence upon common sense and reason. A man who has fallen into "angelism," Dr. More tells us, "will fall prey to the first abstract notion proposed to him and will kill anybody who gets in his way, torture, execute, wipe out entire populations, all with the best possible motives and the best possible intentions, in fact in the name of peace and freedom, etcetera" (*LR*, 328). Angelism, then, is essentially gnostic and potentially violent. Thus Voegelin's account of twentieth-century gnosticism in action includes, along with those of milder gnostics, the names of very violent ones like Stalin and Hitler. The point is that a gnostic impatience with human limitations can easily convert into a hubristic denial of one's own limitations and an amoral disregard for ethical systems demanding decency in the human community.

That seems to be what happens to Lancelot Lamar.[6] In *Lancelot* the protagonist says of his own quest: "So Sir Lancelot set out, looking for something rarer than the Grail. A sin" (*Ll*, 140). But Lance discovers only "buggery" (*Ll*, 136), not sin. (Of course, he fails to look within himself.) His basic assumption is that "Original Sin is not something man did to God but something God did to man" (*Ll*, 222). In other words, Lance, like an ancient gnostic, would blame God—or a cruel demiurge —for the world's imperfections, rather than take any of the blame upon himself.

Lance sees his task as dissociation from and purification of this evil world. He decides: "I cannot tolerate this age. What is more, I won't. That [when he destroyed Belle Isle and four people in it] was my discovery: that I didn't have to" (*Ll*, 154). Instead, "There is going to be a new order of things and I shall be part of it" (*Ll*, 156). He will begin a "new Reformation," a "Third Revolution" in America, the first having been "won at Yorktown," the second "lost at Appomattox" (*Ll*, 220). Lance then believes both principal tenets of gnosticism—that man is not responsible for evil and that his salvation depends on his own efforts.

At several points in *Lancelot* Percy juxtaposes Lance's answers with Christianity's. Lance himself explains his extremism in terms of the church's apparent defection: "I cannot tolerate this age. And I will not. I might have tolerated you and your Catholic Church, and even joined it, if you had remained true to yourself. Now you're part of the age" (*Ll*, 157). The church, in Lance's gnostic vision, has confounded itself by being a part of this world. In the book's ending, Lancelot and the priest Percival agree, not on that issue, but on the absoluteness of their own alternative visions: Lancelot says, "One of us is wrong. It will be your way or it will be my way." And the priest answers *"Yes"* (*Ll*, 257).

The ending of *Lancelot* is ambiguous, but I think that Percy juxtaposes the speaker and the auditor, the gnostic and the Christian, in order to suggest that we are indeed in an either/or situation. *Either* we accept alienation as our necessary condition—acknowledging the world's evil condition and helping to ameliorate it, but never presuming to believe that we can eliminate it—and live in faith, *or* we will find our own theories inviting and condoning the Hitlers, the Idi Amins, and the Lancelots of the world.

There is hardly need to go on—and anyway a mini-essay has strict limits. Clearly Percy and Voegelin are more than superficially alike in their diagnosis of the present state of the culture. Modern man has a distorted notion of what he is and therefore a deformed conception of reality. For a succinct account of the modern situation and how it developed, one might well look at the Introduction to Voegelin's *Science, Politics, and Gnosticism*. But I am not using this essay to ask Percy to adopt Voegelin's terms or to suggest to Voegelin that in his studies of modernity he give more attention to some of the special problems so brilliantly dramatized in Percy's novels. I would consider it presumptuous to offer counsel to either man. My intention is only to suggest to Walker Percy's readers that the basic themes of Percy's novels are certainly not to be regarded as the privileged crankiness of a somewhat eccentric Roman Catholic intellectual; and they are not merely the private and special insights of an important novelist. But they have a close relation to a powerful and searching criticism of the modern world, of which Voegelin is clearly the major exemplar but which in the last decade has begun to claim the attention and the endorsement of an increasing number of modern scholars.

TED R. SPIVEY

Walker Percy
and the Archetypes

WALKER PERCY belongs among a small group of writers in our time who have done something for modern American literature that many people thought would never be done. He and novelists like Saul Bellow, Flannery O'Connor, and J. F. Powers—to name people from three regions—have given to contemporary American fiction an intellectual and even a philosophical tone lacking in classic modern writers like Hemingway and Fitzgerald. Percy and writers like him have become intellectually involved with European thinkers and novelists and have used insights gained from this involvement without losing their own native genius for writing fiction. They have not cut themselves off from their ethnic and regional traditions but rather have followed these traditions back to their sources in the Old World. They have derived benefits from being Jewish or Catholic or even Episcopalian that other and perhaps greater writers of the American past often did not know. Thus Percy cannot be pigeonholed as, say, a Catholic novelist. Instead, Percy is a novelist of profound intellectual curiosity and sensitivity. He feels himself more closely aligned with the continental novelists, for "the European novels are more philosophical, more novels of ideas"[1] than English and American novels are.

The ideas in Percy's novels are basically Kierkegaardian, but the novels are not simply a framework for presenting the Danish philosopher's ideas. Instead, Kierkegaard is, for Percy, as Emerson was for Whitman, a kind of flame that brought the author to a boiling point. When one writer influences another the way Kierkegaard influenced Percy, it is not because one gives and the other takes certain ideas. It is because the older author brings the younger author face to face with one or more of the archetypes. It is Kierkegaard's encounter with the archetypal mythic quester, his "knight of faith," that helped to shake Percy out of his mental fixation on the general laws of science. Ideas usually inspire men and women to generate more ideas, but archetypes set flowing a stream of images in the psyches of artists who are receiving a torch from their masters.

The work of neither Percy nor Kierkegaard reveals an understanding of the theory of the archetypes. One of the subtlest of literary and philosophical psychologists, Kierkegaard arrived too early on the modern scene to encounter archetypal psychology. And Percy's serious knowledge of depth psychology does not go very far beyond Freud. He greatly respects Freud, having once elevated him, in his own words, "far beyond the point that even [Freud] would place himself."[2] But an understanding of the relationship between modern depth psychology and the visionary experiences of certain modern artists who have been influenced by it is missing in Percy. Perhaps, though, it is best that the artist-thinker not have a clear picture of what he is doing while he is doing it. At the Oracle of Delphi a priestess spoke the message of the gods but others translated it.

What is important is that Percy and Kierkegaard reveal that they have encountered the power of the archetypes. Both began their serious literary work as thinkers who were not content to settle for a view of life from the angle of general laws, but who insisted on preserving, along with general laws, a sense of the mystery of individual life. They came up early in their careers against that problem suggested by T. S. Eliot's now well-known term *dissociation of sensibility*. Both Kierkegaard and Percy show in their work that if man clings to reason alone and the systems that reason inevitably spins out, then he will stifle imagination and the sense of individual mystery and in time destroy reason too. They also know that if one holds imagination as higher than reason, as some Romantics did, he may well become lost without a guide in a world of visions without meanings. For Kierkegaard the answer was to set out on a quest for God with belief that he would be successfully guided through the modern desert of empty thought systems. Thus he could indict Hegelian idealism and nineteenth-century institutional Christianity as systems that sought to imprison the mind and the soul. Because he refused to surrender his reason, he saw clearly when other nineteenth-century philosophers reacted with repressed, tangled emotions.

But Kierkegaard had problems that relate to his own time as well as to our time. He encountered the realm of archetypes, and it is this encounter that gives his writing that peculiar and haunting force missing in the dead language of so much prose prophecy of the last century. Kierkegaard's chief problem was that he was seized, or possessed, by several of the archetypes; and it is this seizure which accounts for the fanaticism, the hypersensitivity, and the murkiness that inform some of his best writing. Walker Percy has intuitively grasped this seizure, and the protagonists of his novels, who in a sense begin their quests as twentieth-century Kierkegaards, are aware of their own seizures. A quester goes into the realm of the archetypes to experience their power and to know deeper levels of human awareness thereby. But if he is seized and held by one or more archetypes, he is in danger of losing the very power he sought to gain or even of losing his powers of reason and imagination.

And what is particularly important for Percy's fictional protagonists is that their quest for archetypal powers is an effort to overcome an inherited partial possession by archetypes that hold everyone in the protagonists' society.

Before examining the quest for archetypal power and the danger of archetypal possession in Kierkegaard and Percy, a definition of archetypes must be framed. The theory of archetypes is as old or older than Plato and as new as C. G. Jung. As one who formulated a theory of the archetypes for our century, Jung seeks simplification by occasionally calling archetypes "primordial images." At other times he speaks of "instinctual images," which are not intellectually invented but which are always present in the conscious and the unconscious thought patterns of men in all historical periods and in all regions of the earth. In the book Jung began work on at the end of his life, *Man and His Symbols*, he particularly emphasizes the importance of the anima and the animus, the wise old man or woman, the shadow, and the self. Above all he emphasizes the mandala. Jung points to the many different forms individual archetypes take in different cultures, but his main emphasis is always on the power of archetypes to release the energies of the individual psyche.

As for possession by an archetype, Jung is continually giving the example in his work of the conventional middle-aged man who suddenly throws up everything and runs off with a beautiful young girl, his mind and soul possessed by her image. The archetypal interpretation of this story is that the personality of an individual is caught up, sometimes totally but sometimes partially, in a fixation on the image of the "eternal feminine," an image Jung calls the archetypal image of the anima. Archetypal encounter is a different matter. The individual on this quest or pilgrimage encounters anima, animus, wise old man, hero, shadow, and other such patternings and is not possessed or bewitched and held up on his journey. Instead this individual moves past the dangers of destruction inherent in archetype possession. This quest toward archetypal encounter is the movement that is the basis of the universal story called *myth*. There are dangers, suffering, even the agony of personality dissolution, but there is the encounter with ever deepening psychic powers until there is a breakthrough to a new personality with expanded consciousness and deepened creative energies. Thus Mircea Eliade defines the "initiatory schema" of myth and ritual as "comprising suffering, death, and resurrection (=rebirth)."[3]

When we find a novelist like Percy who, guided by Kierkegaard and Dostoevsky, writes of mythic protagonists on pilgrimages in contemporary America, we must turn to Jung and to the solid work of people in various fields for a deeper understanding of Percy's meanings. There is, besides Jung, the Eranos Round Table in Switzerland, which for many years brought together men and women in many different disciplines to discuss psychology, mythology, religion, and related subjects. In America, during recent years, Mircea Eliade, Joseph Campbell, and others have incorporated in their work both the old and the new materials of psychology, mythology, and religion. Even the laboratory work of controlled experiments with LSD, done by psychologists in California, indicates that Freudian, Jungian, and other interpretations of experience exist in the unconscious mind. Finally, British psychiatrist R. D. Laing gives full credit to Jung for his work: "Jung broke the ground here but few have followed."[4] Laing also discusses the theory of archetypes and of the mythic journey in terms of the schizophrenia of the 1960s, the decade in which Jung died and Percy published his first novel.

In *The Politics of Experience* Laing speaks of the archetypes and of the basic mythic theme of death and rebirth: "True sanity entails in one way or another the dissolution of the normal ego, the false self completely adjusted to our alienated social reality; the emergence of the 'inner' archetypal mediators of divine power, and through this death a rebirth, and the eventual re-establishment of a new kind of ego-functioning, the ego now being the servant of the divine, no longer its betrayer."[5] Binx Bolling in *The Moviegoer* is almost an exact fictional statement of Laing's insight. As the novel opens we see him fairly well adjusted to what everyone around him calls "the good life of contemporary America"; but Laing would call it "our alienated social reality"—because we are alienated from what he also calls "'inner' archetypal mediators of divine power." For Laing, archetypes are symbols that, when they emerge, bring with them a kind of creative power traditionally called divine. When these symbols are missing in one's life, the kind of despair we today call angst—which Kierkegaard, as one of the first modern psychologists, analyzed so well—becomes so deeply embedded in the individual's life that it is not even noticed. Jung too saw the encounter with archetypes as an encounter with creative energies that lift the human out of everyday boredom and apathy, those casual symptoms of genuine despair, and set him on a path moving toward personality integration.

Binx Bolling learns to face his own despair and begin what he regards as a search for God: "What do you seek—God? you ask with a smile," Bolling writes in his notebook. He goes on to answer himself by writing that Americans have already "settled the matter for themselves" because "polls report that 98% of Americans believe in God and the remaining 2% are atheists and agnostics—which leaves not a single percentage point for a seeker" (*Mg*, 13–14). But simple belief, Bolling sees, would not change anything for him. "The only possible starting point: the strange fact of one's own invincible apathy—that if the proofs were proved and God presented himself, nothing would be changed. Here is the strangest fact of all" (*Mg*, 146). Only some kind of affirmation or commitment will do, Bolling sees. And because he sees and affirms God, he becomes in a contemporary sense a quester seeking the creative powers of the universe that are mediated through the archetypes. It is true that Bolling only makes a beginning; certainly both he and Percy reveal a metaphysical diffidence not found in either Kierkegaard or Dostoevsky. But any seeker who questions the attitudes and the values of the society he lives in and who begins a search for the living power of what has been called the divine does encounter within himself the archetypal quester and is aided by the power of this symbol. Thus, as he searches, Bolling encounters this archetype and is aided by it.

Bolling moves at the beginning of the novel from his static position at Kierkegaard's aesthetic level of cultivating pleasurable sensations in business, reading, and casual love-making. His life of sensations is summed up by his pleasurable contemplation of the images of the moving-picture screen. At the end of the novel Bolling would seem not to have changed much, but his whole life in fact is turned in a new direction because he has encountered not only the archetype of the quester but also the archetype of the anima, that symbolic manifestation of the eternal feminine. The change in Bolling is revealed in a passage near the end of the novel when he observes a young man from the North going to New Orleans, his head filled with images of sexual pleasure. He is Bolling's double, as it were, one who has set out on a search for an archetypal female beauty in New Orleans even as Bolling has sought the ultimate pleasure in a great movie palace of Chicago. But Bolling is different from his double in that he is now in the process of being dispossessed of the anima archetype. All of his conscious pleasures and particularly his moviegoing are but projections of this one entanglement with the feminine. Part of Percy's genius as a novelist and much of his value as a philosopher of the contemporary mythic quest is that he can depict the struggles of a protagonist partially possessed but gradually being freed from archetypal possession. Bolling's movement beyond possession is feeble, but then so is contemporary man's. To write any other way would be to fabricate myth, which is a common enough fad in our times, or to write religious propaganda, which has never had any appeal except to the dullest of readers.

Bolling's movement from anima possession to anima encounter is seen in his relationship with the one woman in his life who is not totally connected with those fantasies of endless pleasure that always surround the anima-possessed psyche. He flees to Chicago to lose himself in the movie palace that he calls a great Urwomb, symbol of his desire for total immersion in the feminine, which is the goal of the journey of the anima possessed; but he is at the same time taking a journey of encounter with the woman that he will marry. The movement toward a deepened encounter with the feminine is a journey out of anima possession, and it means struggle and pain mixed with joy, whereas the journey into anima possession is a continual grasping at sensations that lead the bewitched psyche to a final surrendering of all ties with the world around him. Anima encounter, or animus encounter if the quester is a woman, leads to an enriching of all of one's experiences in this world because one is continually discovering the complementary "other" of oneself that is hidden in the psyche and symbolized by an image of the opposite sex. Benign anima and animus figures appear in the dreams, fantasies, and actual experiences of men and women moving on the journey of individuation. But those moving toward deeper anima or animus possession are giving up more and more of both the powers in their own souls and the good that is in the world around them in order to become more deeply involved in the life of sensations related to the anima or the animus. "All for love," or "the world well lost," to use the words of Dryden's other title of his play about anima possession, is the eternal rallying cry of the anima-possessed individual; or, when the anima image is projected onto other images associated with the pleasures of the remembered womb, the cry may then become, as in Bolling's case, "all for movies and the rest of the world be damned." When the world has been thrown over for the sensations of the archetype of anima or animus, these figures in dreams, fantasies, and actual experiences become threatening and destructuve. Then the anima figures become witches that devour the soul.

Percy loves the world too much to abandon it to the dim memories of the womb, but he will not surrender the anima archetype either. His protagonists therefore must encounter the anima and not be possessed by it or by a substitute for it (*e.g.*, the movies). Literature, since the Romantic Movement, has produced two extreme types of artists: one who clings to one or more of the archetypes and sinks into isolation and madness and the other who thinks he has escaped madness by denying the archetypes altogether and clings to what he takes to be the "real" world, but the dullness of his "realistic" art can also cause madness or at least disguise madness. The greatest artists since 1750, however, have let go neither the archetypes nor the world, but they have struggled to keep both. Nobody sums up the problem better than Goethe, who has his Faust exclaim: "Zwei Seelen wohnen, ach, in meiner Brust," which is to say, "Two souls, alas, dwell in my breast." One soul clings to the earth with a lover's lust, Faust says, and the other flies up to heaven, abode of the divine powers. Not to surrender either soul is the mark of an artist's greatness, but what strategy is needed to hold the two together? Faust made a deal with the archetype of the shadow, symbol of the destructive powers of the universe and, as he learned, this brings its problems. Faust encountered the power of the shadow in hopes of using it for his own benefit, but he found that he became destructive to those he should have served. Faust is unable, like a classic mythic hero such as Orestes, to placate the powers of destruction so that they find their proper sphere without becoming dominant in the community. In his first three novels, Percy did not pit his archetypal quester against the shadow. In the fourth the hero is possessed first by the anima and then by the shadow. I will suggest toward the end of this essay that if Percy is to continue his journey into the realm of archetypes, he must deal with encounter, not possession. But before Percy can successfully depict the encounter with the shadow, an event that might make him a major world novelist, he must on a deeper level invoke the powers inherent in that archetype Jung calls the main archetype—that is, the mandala or self.

Archetypally speaking, Percy's first two novels are one, or one might say *The Moviegoer* lays the foundation for *The Last Gentleman*. In this second novel the protagonist, Williston Barrett, has already made the choice to seek God that Bolling makes at the beginning of *The Moviegoer*. Of Barrett, Percy says at the beginning of the novel: "Thereafter he came to see that he was not destined to do everything but only one or two things. Lucky is the man who does not secretly believe that every possibility is open to him" (*LG*, 4). Both Bolling and Barrett begin their pilgrimage with a quest for God, which sets powers loose within their souls that begin to free them from possession by the archetypes. But Barrett's involvement with the centrality of inner guidance is much deeper than Bolling's, and thus his working out of the details of his journey is a much more complex matter. As his journey proceeds, Barrett becomes more deeply involved with the truth of the chief archetype, the mandala, which Jung has thus characterized: "It is what is called ultimo exquadra the square in the circle, or the circle in the square. It is an age-old symbol that goes right back to the prehistory of man. It is all over the earth and it either expresses the Deity or the self; and these two terms are psychologically very much related. . . . It expresses the fact that there is a center and a periphery, and it tries to embrace the whole. It is the symbol of wholeness."[6] Anyone familiar with archetypal symbolism will be immediately aware of the poverty of this type of emblem in Percy's work. Yet the truth of the mandala resides in the actions of both Bolling and Barrett. They center their minds on the guidance of the inner creative power and thus are led to encounter the archetypal powers that are held in balance by the center, symbolized in the mandala by the center point. Without overt mandala symbolism, that psychic center nevertheless suggests the controlling or master power holding together those powers symbolized in the mandala by four or multiples of four.

Symbols that have imaginative impact arise spontaneously out of voyages into individual psyches, and Percy knows that these voyages must now be begun slowly and with great care because of our psychic poverty. Archetypal encounter, if it is real, must be limited. If Percy were "rich in symbols" at this point in history (when other novelists readily "paste" myths and symbols onto threadbare plots), it would be a sign that no true journey had been attempted. To plunge deeply into the "forest of symbols," to use Baudelaire's phrase, is too dangerous for the limited voyager of today. Like Percy's protagonists, the journeyer who walks into the forest proceeds haltingly.

That Percy was fully aware of the contrast between his voyager and the mythic journeys of earlier times is seen in Barrett's contrasting himself with an Apache youth at the beginning of *The Last Gentleman*: "When he was a youth he had lived his life in a state of the liveliest expectation, thinking to himself: what a fine thing it will be to become a man and to know what to do —like an Apache youth who at the right time goes out into the plains alone, dreams dreams, sees visions, returns and knows he is a man. But no such time had come and he still didn't know how to live" (*LG*, 11). In an age like ours when knowledge is more prevalent than imaginative experience, we think too highly of ourselves in the areas of science and technology, and yet we long for visionary experience. We are mesmerized by the images of earlier archetypal encounters. Thus among "born again" Christians, chanting devotees of Krishna, and believing astrologers, archetypal possession is everywhere. Why journey into the soul when one can easily slip into the apparel of a holy man?

Barrett thinks only briefly of the Apache youth and sets forth on a quest for visions of his own. Yet how characteristically modern that he should think of himself as somehow inferior to the Apache. He does not have any clear-cut idea of what he should do, but as his journey continues he is given directions concerning tasks he must perform. Instead of being like the Apache who knows what to do once he has had visionary experiences, he is more like Parsifal, who must continually admit to a failure of knowledge. Percy's Barrett is in many ways like a medieval knight beginning a quest. Percy calls him the last gentleman because he is the last of a long line of gentle knights helping ladies in distress. But he is also a beginning. He is Kierkegaard's knight of faith, and he is a modern shaman in the making.

Barrett suffers from amnesia caused in part, we might say if we viewed him through psychoanalytical eyes, by the repressed pain of his life. His illness also includes epilepsy, and of his health Percy has said: "The reader is free to see him as a sick man among healthy business men or as a sane pilgrim in a mad world."[7] How fitting that the year this remark was published (1967) was also the year of the publication of Laing's *The Politics of Experience*. For Laing the sign of the voyager is his seeming "insanity," and he reminds the reader that our sanity (that of average "sane" people) is not "true sanity." He goes on to say: "Their madness is not true madness. The madness of our patients is an artifact of the destruction wreaked on them by us and by them on themselves. Let no one suppose that we meet true madness any more than that we are truly sane. The madness that we encounter in patients is a gross travesty, a mockery, a grotesque caricature of what the natural healing of that estranged integration we call sanity might be."[8] Laing ends his work on the same note:

In this particular type of journey, the direction we have to take is *back* and *in*, because it was way back that we started to go down and out. They will say we are regressed and withdrawn and out of contact with them. True enough, we have a long, long way to go back to contact the reality we have all long lost contact with. And because they are humane, and concerned, and even love us, and are very frightened, they will try to cure us. They may succeed. But there is still the hope that they will fail.[9]

In Laing's view then many are called to the voyage leading to the archetypal powers we associate with the shaman, who undergoes the transformation of his psyche through a visionary relationship with archetypal images. That Laing is speaking in the tradition of shamanistic experience going back to the most primitive peoples can be seen in a study of any one of many scholars in the field of shamanism. As an indication of this fact, here are two quotations from Mircea Eliade's *Myths, Dreams and Mysteries* which illustrate both Laing and Percy on the subject of the archetypal voyage: "The future shaman marks himself off progressively by some strange behavior: he seeks solitude, becomes a dreamer, loves to wander in woods or desert places, has visions, signs in his sleep, etc. Sometimes this period of incubation is characterized by rather grave symptoms." Concerning the supposed insanity of the future shaman, Eliade says:

In the first place, it is not correct to say that shamans are, or must *always* be, neuropaths: on the contrary, a great many of them are perfectly sound in mind. Moreover, those who had previously been ill have *become shamans just because they succeeded in getting well*. Very often, when the vocation reveals itself in the course of an illness or an attack of epilepsy, the initiation is also a cure. The acquisition of the shamanic gifts indeed presupposes the resolution of the psychic crisis brought on by the first signs of this vocation. The initiation is manifested by—among other things—a new psychic integration.[10]

In relationship to Percy I must emphasize the statement concerning epilepsy, one of Barrett's problems. Seen in the light of shamanistic experience, Barrett's journey into the South can be seen as part of his "getting well," a process that brings with it certain powers that are archetypal, or shamanistic, and which makes him "saner" than those around him because he is slowly achieving a measure of "psychic integration" while others are disintegrating. He can, for instance, turn away from his intensive ego-centeredness to take an active role in aiding those like Kitty and Sutter Vaught who are floundering in their psychic fragmentation.

An understanding of the making of the shaman in many different cultures is helpful for an understanding of the archetypal experience of any writer, but the development of that experience—if it is true and not fabricated experience—must take place in the framework of one's own culture. An Apache youth and a young Indian prince like Gautama Siddhartha, who became the light of Asia, must achieve archetypal experience through their own traditions; similarly modern man, as C. G. Jung many times observed, cannot go deep within himself by dressing up in the clothes of foreign mythologies. Wisely, Percy chooses Kierkegaard as shaman or a fictional starting point for portraying archetypal experience because Kierkegaard himself encountered the first archetype of our culture. This archetype of the quester—the one who rejects easy solutions to human problems in a society that has denied the lived experience of its religion—is necessary to begin the voyage.

Both Percy and Kierkegaard satirize an easy Christianity and the new idealistic systems that have tried to replace religion in decline, systems that promise easy and painless solutions to problems that are simply repressed and forgotten by those who accept them. In Kierkegaard's day it was Hegelian idealism that offered a system of rational spirituality one could accept without the pain of archetypal encounter or the need to make an either/or choice. For Kierkegaard the real movement into archetypal territory comes with acceptance of the experience of the quester in a psychic wasteland and with making the either/or choice of obeying God—the leap of faith, the Dane called it. Kierkegaard published in 1843, at age thirty-two, his most basic works, *Either/Or* and *Fear and Trembling*, the first dealing with the necessary choice of the quest and the second with painting pictures of the knight of faith.

The picture Kierkegaard paints of the knight of faith in *Fear and Trembling* is of a man who can live comfortably with all of the feminine aspects of life because he has successfully encountered the anima archetype. Yet Kierkegaard says in *Fear and Trembling* that he must "admit that in my practice I have not found any reliable example of the knight of faith."[11] Kierkegaard himself was not the knight of faith because, when he set out on his own journey, he did not go anywhere. Although he preached faith, he could not himself find the faith to overcome archetypal possession. When he encountered the power of the anima archetype, he reacted in a way typical of many nineteenth-century poets and philosophers: he rejected the eternal feminine, an action which is as much an indication of anima possession as is abandoning oneself to the life of the feminine, as many twentieth-century poets do. On October 11, 1841, Kierkegaard made his final break with his fiancée Regina Olsen and thereafter developed his doctrine of the single one. "In order to come to love," he said of his renunciation of Regina, "I had to remove the object." Martin Buber in his essay on Kierkegaard called "The Question to the Single One" gives this quotation and adds his own comment: "Creation is not a hurdle on the road to God, it is the road itself."[12] Yet no more beautiful picture of one who accepts creation exists in nineteenth-century literature than Kierkegaard's of his knight of faith: "He takes delight in everything, and whenever one sees him taking part in a particular pleasure, he does it with the persistence that marks the earthly man whose soul is absorbed in such things. He tends to his work." Then: "On his way he reflects that his wife has surely a special little warm dish prepared for him, e.g., a calf's head roasted, garnished with vegetables."[13] I quote at length this picture of the knight of faith because Kierkegaard's vision is a perfect statement of Barrett's encounter with the anima on his journey into the South in *The Last Gentleman*.

That Barrett is himself a knight of faith is seen in the fact that he, unlike Kierkegaard, who has only glimpses of the archetypes, can perform certain acts of service on his way to a fuller realization of the archetype of the hero, or cosmic man, as Jung sometimes calls this archetype of creative power. Barrett's first important task, after encountering the anima in the form of Kitty Vaught, is accomplished with the antihero archetype foremost in the eyes of those around him. He is called to save Jamie Vaught from dying outside the Church. As he is dying, Jamie can nod assent to the basic truths of religion because of his belief in Barrett and Barrett's own tacit acceptance of these truths. Barrett's "saving" of Jamie has not been overt, or "heroic," but indirect. Barrett performs an act of spiritual aid by bearing Jamie's burden of loneliness and allowing Jamie to communicate without words his own belief. Father Boomer's explanation of the "truths of religion" that Jamie accepts are a Christian statement of the truth of the mandala: "'Do you accept the truth that God exists and that He made you and loves you and that He made the world so that you might enjoy its beauty and that He himself is your final end and happiness, that He loved you so much that He sent His only Son to die for you and to found His Holy Catholic Church so that you may enter heaven and there see God face to face and be happy with Him forever'" (*LG*, 403).

Barrett must also struggle against the death wish of Sutter Vaught, who is suffering from mythic identification. Mythic identification happens readily to those who become involved with the heroic stories of man, as did Don Quixote, and who do not see that one cannot choose on his own to act out the role of any of the archetypes. But if one hopes not to lose his mental balance through mythic identification in a delightful way like Don Quixote or in a dangerous way like Faust, all he can do is to seek an ever closer identification with the divine center, or the "self" as Jung calls it. The Hindus teach that the lotus—the chief form the mandala takes in the Far East—is the sun within, that is, the basic cosmic energy at the center of the individual and the cosmos. But those who approach the archetype from the outside, without concentrating their minds on the center —whose power upholds and unites the two, the four, and the multiples thereof—will tend to identify, as Sutter does, with the archetype of the hero. In other words, they see myth from the outside.

Myth seen from the inside is the quest for personality, or psychic integration; that quest entails encountering along the way the power of the archetypes, which themselves perform service to others as their energies are released within the soul. The sign that heroic actions are the result of archetypal encounter is that the true hero is never separated from love, that unifying power which always protects the sanity of the true quester. By trying to set himself up as a hero instead of seeking that integration that activates the hero archetype within himself, Sutter is condemned to isolation and cynicism; thus he seeks to "redeem" his seeming failure by suicide. Sutter is like his nineteenth-century forebears Kierkegaard and Nietzsche, who too were idealists possessed by the hero archetype. Kierkegaard became in his own eyes the great exposer of a phony "Christendom" and Nietzsche became Zarathustra, a prophet of power and a denier of antipower. They both set out on journeys like Percy's Sutter, but theirs ended in bitterness, destructiveness, and madness. Sutter's journey too would have ended so, were it not for Barrett's love, alloyed though that love is with a desperate need for friendship. Thus when Sutter encounters the depth of Barrett's concern for his life, he is checked in that destructive madness that so often accompanies archetypal possession.

Love in the Ruins continues Percy's epic of man freeing himself from archetypal possession. Dr. Thomas More is caught up in the web of both the anima and the hero archetypes. He is in certain ways both Sutter Vaught and Binx Bolling, and the novel is in part the story of his freeing himself in order to encounter the power of the archetypes. But *Love in the Ruins*, unlike *The Last Gentleman*, is not primarily a book about archetypal pilgrimage. To analyze it as such would be to miss much of the wit of Percy's comedy of manners. It is as if the author were taking a kind of holiday from the more serious occupations of his life. And rightly he should because his satire has something important to say about such matters as the sexual revolution and the cult of psychiatry, about white suburbs and black revolutionaries. Yet *Love in the Ruins*, with its apocalyptic theme, also contains a suggestion of Percy's next serious fictional encounter with the archetype.

In Percy's latest novel, *Lancelot*, there is movement toward shadow possession. The protagonist in his insanity reveals the influences of a shadow destructiveness. Lancelot, who was first possessed by the anima with its womblike, mother-haunted vision of a past southern community of glory and pleasure, moves into possession by an archetype of the hero. As his name suggests, he is as archetypally possessed as his namesake. He will, like Don Quixote, take up his lance and create again the good of the remembered past by destroying the enemies who are decimating the old order. But the good society cannot be created by an act of the will, and to try to do so is to be at best pathetically humorous to those who look on. In setting, Lancelot, in contrast to the character Percival, who listens to his ravings, Percy has performed another remarkable service for modern man. He has outlined the two approaches possible for the person who sees the emptiness of our pseudoculture. One is Lance's way of destruction and the other is Percival's way, which is to do simple parish work and to "forgive the sins of Buick deal-ers" (*Ll*, 256). Like Parsifal, Percival is with those in Percy's earlier novels who see that they must begin in the simplest ways to take upon themselves the burdens of the Christian cult which stands at the center of what is left of our old Western culture.

It is extremely important that the priest will *forgive*, be-cause one cannot forgive who does not love. And love cannot be an act of the conscious will but instead is a gift given to those who follow the path of pilgrimage, which leads again and again to the shadow powers. Those who overcome these destructive powers not once but many times receive the love and creative power necessary for the re-creation of culture, becoming thus culture heroes in that they allow the hero archetype to work through them. And as Percy suggests, the two ways into the fu-ture are that of the one who allows the archetypes to seize and carry off his personality and his humanity, and that of the one who through pilgrimage grows into that state of individuation, as Jung called it, in which one becomes human, individual, creative, and loving.

I have already suggested that Percy must bring his fictional characters of the future into a profounder relationship with the shadow than he has already done if he is to continue his explo-ration of archetypal territory. The shadow has been appearing with greater frequency in modern literature since 1945. Mann, Golding, Powers, O'Connor, Gary, and Cheever are only a few of the novelists who have invoked the shadow in fiction of the postwar era. In the life and literature of our time there is a fas-cination with images of destruction, so much so that one might suspect that possession by the shadow is becoming widespread, an event our civilization has not witnessed since the late Mid-dle Ages, though we have seen something of it in the religious madness of the sixteenth and the seventeenth centuries and in the political madness of the Nazis. Certainly Lancelot is possessed by the shadow. But today more than ever we need pilgrims who will face and overcome the power of the shadow archetype. This pilgrim is that shaman who can encounter archetypes without being possessed by any one of them. Perhaps Percy is now ready to write about him.

The rise to power in our time of the archetype of destruction poses the question of what form art itself will take. Possibly the novel really is dead, as some critics have been saying for several decades. Or possibly what is dead is a certain kind of novel—the novel, I would suggest, of the tragic ego. Whether it was *Moby Dick* or *The Golden Bowl*, *The Sun Also Rises* or *The Sound and the Fury*, the novel that held the attention of the good reader for a hundred years was the novel of the tragic ego. The tragic egos of contemporary literature lack the ability to struggle against archetypal powers, even as Goethe's tragic Faust struggled to maintain his own personality while being used by the shadow. The result in much literature today, including, finally, *Lancelot*, is that archetypes like the anima and the shadow often overcome human personality. Without a vision of personality, works of literature cannot serve the deepest needs of man, and they eventually become relegated to the level of artifacts in a museum. The renewal of literature begins when individual works deal with protagonists who, through encountering the archetypes, undergo a deepening of personality. The subject of myth essentially is the growth and development of personality through encounters with suprahuman powers. Now the ego is so swamped by archetypal images that it cannot cope with them; therefore the forms of tragic art have broken down. But Percy and novelists like him are not tragic artists. They write comedies, in the Dantesque sense of the word, stories with happy endings. We are used to such stories being fabricated for our daydreams, pseudomyths of no archetypal significance. But the stories of Percy and others do have archetypal power, and because they do there is hope that we might with the help of new-found shamans be moving out of the tragic phase of our civilization. The furies of the apocalypse must still do their work, but the comic artist must look beyond the end of the world, and with the shaman he must take those steps that lead beyond tragedy to a new, lasting comedy. Walker Percy without doubt is one of those who travels on that journey of man that goes beyond tragedy.

ABOUT THE AUTHORS

CLEANTH BROOKS is Gray Professor of Rhetoric Emeritus, Yale University. He has been a Rhodes Scholar and cultural attaché to the American Embassy in London (1964–1966) and is a member of the National Institute of Arts and Letters. His significant contributions to modern criticism include *The Well-Wrought Urn, Modern Poetry and the Tradition, William Faulkner: The Yoknapatawpha Country*, and *Toward Yoknapatawpha and Beyond*. With Robert Penn Warren he is co-author of such introductions to the study of literature as *An Approach to Literature, Understanding Poetry*, and *Understanding Fiction*.

PANTHEA REID BROUGHTON, an associate professor of English at Louisiana State University in Baton Rouge, holds a Ph.D. from the University of North Carolina, Chapel Hill. She is the author of *William Faulkner: The Abstract and the Actual*, coauthor of the textbook *Literature*, and has been a Fulbright lecturer. Her articles on Faulkner, Agee, McCullers, and Coleridge have appeared in *Southern Review, Mississippi Quarterly, Southern Humanities Review, Twentieth Century Literature*, and *Wordsworth Circle*.

WILLIAM J. DOWIE, is an assistant professor of English at Southeastern Louisiana University. He received a Ph.D. from Brandeis University. He has published articles on Walker Percy, J. R. R. Tolkien, Joseph Conrad, and William Blake in *Novel: A Forum on Fiction, The Heythrop Journal*, and *Innisfree*. Cornell University Press's *J. R. R. Tolkien, Scholar and Storyteller*, edited by Mary Salu and Robert T. Farrell, includes an essay by him. As a long-range project, he is investigating novels of this century that share identical themes with texts from other disciplines.

WILLIAM LEIGH GODSHALK, professor of English at the University of Cincinnati, received his Ph.D. from Harvard in 1964. He is the author of *Patterning in Shakespearean Drama, The Marlovian World Picture*, and *In Quest of Cabell*. He has edited James Branch Cabell's *Beyond Life* and Ellen Glasgow's *Voice of the People*. Among his other publications are essays on Shakespeare, Marvell, and Walker Percy.

JANET HOBBS has taught English and journalism at the North Carolina State University, Raleigh. She holds an M.A. from Virginia Polytechnic Institute and State University. She is now the editor of the *Western Wake Herald*. Her articles have appeared in various North Carolina newspapers and magazines.

J. GERALD KENNEDY, an associate professor of English at Louisiana State University, holds a Ph.D. from Duke University. He has written a biography of the frontier traveler and man of letters William Darby and has been a Fulbright lecturer in France. He has published numerous articles on Poe and nineteenth-century fiction in such journals as *American Transcendental Quarterly, Topic, American Literature*, and *Studies in the American Renaissance*. In 1974, he began work on "The Sundered Self in the Riven World" by discussing the basic approach with his colleague, Walker Percy, in the office next door.

LEWIS A. LAWSON received his Ph.D. from the
University of Wisconsin (1964). A former Fulbright lecturer, he
is a professor of English at the University of Maryland, where
he specializes in modern American and southern literature.
His essays on the presence of Kierkegaard in the recent American novel have appeared in *Contemporary Literature, Texas
Studies in Literature and Language, CLA Journal,* and *Journal of
the American Academy of Religion.* His essays on southern literature have appeared in *Renascence, Literature and Psychology,
Texas Quarterly, Southern Literary Journal, South Atlantic Bulletin, Mississippi Quarterly, American Indian Quarterly,* and *Southern Quarterly.*

THOMAS LECLAIR is an associate professor of
English at the University of Cincinnati. He received his Ph.D.
from Duke University in 1972. He has published essays on contemporary fiction in *Contemporary Literature, Twentieth Century Literature,* and *Critique,* and reviews for *New York Times
Book Review, New Republic, Saturday Review,* and *Commonweal.*

MARTIN LUSCHEI, professor of English at California Polytechnic State University in San Luis Obispo, took
an M.F.A. in English at the University of Iowa and a Ph.D. in
American Studies at the University of New Mexico. His interest in Walker Percy led him into his only serious venture into
criticism, *The Sovereign Wayfarer: Walker Percy's Diagnosis of
the Malaise.* Professor Luschei has published a novel, *The Worst
Season in Years,* and is currently at work on another.

RICHARD PINDELL is an assistant professor of
English at the State University of New York at Binghamton.
He received his Ph.D. from Yale University in 1971. He has
published both stories and essays, including an article on *The
Moviegoer* for *Boundary 2.* He has recently completed a novel
and is now finishing a book on the spirit of place in British and
American, especially southern American, fiction.

WILLIAM POTEAT is chairman of the Department of Religion and professor of Religion and Comparative Studies at Duke University. His essays on language and meaning have appeared in *Philosophical Quarterly, Philosophy and Phenomenological Research, Journal of Religion, Mind, Cahiers de Lumen Vitae: Psychologie de la Religion*, and *University of Maine Law Review*. He coedited (with T. A. Langford) *Intellect and Hope: Essays in the Thought of Michael Polanyi* to which he also contributed: "Myths, Stories, History, Eschatology and Action." He is now at work on a book, *Polanyian Meditations: In Search of a Post-Critical Logic*.

TED SPIVEY is a professor of English at Georgia State University. He holds a Ph.D. degree from the University of Minnesota. He is the author of two books on myth and modern literature entitled *The Renewed Quest* and *The Coming of the New Man*. He has published numerous articles on English and American literature of the nineteenth and twentieth centuries.

WELDON THORNTON, who received his Ph.D. from the University of Texas in 1961, is a professor of English at the University of North Carolina at Chapel Hill. His research interests involve Anglo-Irish literature and modern British and American fiction. His publications include *Allusions in Ulysses: An Annotated List, J. M. Synge and the Western Mind*, and articles on Joyce, Faulkner, Synge, and others.

SIMONE VAUTHIER holds her doctorate from the Sorbonne Nouvelle and is a professor of English at the Université des Sciences Humaines de Strasbourg. Among her various essays, published in French, American, and German periodicals, are more than a score of articles on the literature of the American South. She has written before on Percy and also on William Gilmore Simms, Robert Penn Warren, John Peale Bishop, James W. Johnson, Shelby Foote, Reynolds Price, and Madison Jones.

MAX WEBB is an assistant professor of English at Louisiana State University. He received his Ph.D. from Princeton University. He is working on a book to be entitled "The Masks of Ford Madox Ford" and has published articles on contemporary and Edwardian writers in *Southern Review, Journal of Popular Culture, English Literature in Transition*, and *Mississippi Quarterly Review*.

NOTES

Webb

1. Martin Heidegger, *An Introduction to Metaphysics*, trans. Ralph Manheim (New Haven: Yale University Press, 1959). The question is the opening sentence of the text.

2. Though Walker Percy and his brothers addressed William Alexander Percy as "Uncle Will" and Walker sometimes refers to him as "my uncle" (*MB*, 4), William Alexander Percy was actually a first cousin to Walker's father Le Roy.

Luschei

1. George Bluestone, *Novels into Film* (Berkeley: University of California Press, 1961), 1, 22–23.

2. Walker Percy, "From Facts to Fiction," *Writer*, LXXX (1967), 27.

3. For a full treatment of this interpretation, see the third chapter of my book *The Sovereign Wayfarer: Walker Percy's Diagnosis of the Malaise* (Baton Rouge: Louisiana State University Press, 1972), 64–110.

4. Gabriel Marcel, *Metaphysical Journal*, trans. Bernard Wall (Chicago: Gateway Editions, 1952), viii. -

5. The second chapter of *The Sovereign Wayfarer* offers a lengthy analysis of the existentialist sources of his ideas which there is no need to repeat here.

6. "The majority of men," wrote Kierkegaard, "are curtailed 'I's'; what was planned by nature as a possibility capable of being sharpened into an I is soon dulled into a third person." Søren Kierkegaard, *The Journals of Kierkegaard* , trans. Alexander Dru (New York: Harper Torchbook, 1959), 248.

7. Søren Kierkegaard, *Fear and Trembling and The Sickness Unto Death*, trans. Walter Lowrie (Princeton: Princeton University Press, 1968), 62

8. Gabriel Marcel, *The Mystery of Being* (Chicago: Gateway Editions, 1966), I, 67–68.

9. The film rights to *The Moviegoer* have been held by a succession of

302 *Notes*

owners. Most recently Karen Black and Kit Carson bought them, but still (as of this writing) there is no movie of *The Moviegoer*. (Editor's note: Percy himself reports that "the *rumor* is that she will start filming in early 1979." Walker Percy to Panthea Broughton, March 31, 1978.)
10. Bluestone, *Novels into Film*, 2, 63.

Hobbs

1. Søren Kierkegaard, *Fear and Trembling and The Sickness Unto Death*, trans. Walter Lowrie (Princeton: Princeton University Press, 1968), 186–87. Kierkegaard's use of *aesthetic* in terms of a stage of existence does not carry the usual connotations of the term *aesthetic*.
2. *Ibid.*, 79.
3. Søren Kierkegaard, *Concluding Unscientific Postscript*, trans. David F. Swenson and Walter Lowrie (Princeton: Princeton University Press, 1968), 288.
4. Kierkegaard, *Fear and Trembling*, 79.
5. Kierkegaard, *Sickness Unto Death*, 187.
6. *Ibid.*, 168.
7. *Ibid.*, 192.
8. *Ibid.*, 159.
9. Søren Kierkegaard, *Concept of Dread*, trans. Walter Lowrie (Princeton: Princeton University Press), 128.
10. In "The Man on the Train" Percy defines repetition in his own terms and admits that his definition is an alteration of Kierkegaard's: "the rider . . . voyages into his own past in search for himself" (*MB*, 95). Percy goes on to say that "we need not consider here Kierkegaard's distinction that true religious repetition has nothing to do with travel but is 'consciousness raised to the second power'" (*MB*, 96).
11. Richard Lehan, "The Way Back: Redemption in the Novels of Walker Percy," *Southern Review*, IV (1968), 312.
12. Kierkegaard, *Fear and Trembling*, 50.
13. *Ibid.*, 131.
14. *Ibid.*, 59.

Pindell

1. Nathaniel Hawthorne, *The Complete Novels and Selected Tales of Nathaniel Hawthorne*, ed. Norman Holmes Pearson (New York: Modern Library, 1937), 529.
2. Frederick D. Wilhelmsen in his introduction to *The End of the Modern World* by Romano Guardini (Chicago: Henry Regnery Co., 1968), 6.
3. The photograph to which Percy alludes, "a sharpshooter's last sleep," is one of the most famous of the Gettysburg photographs and surely the most interesting. It was taken on July 6, 1863, three days after the battle not by Matthew Brady but by Timothy O'Sullivan, a photographer in Alexander Gardner's camera crew, and not on Little Round Top but in Devil's Den. Gardner's own story that he returned some four months later to this spot and found the undisturbed skeleton and the rusting rifle is sheer fiction concocted for publicity purposes. The subject was almost surely not a sniper—his rifle-

musket was the wrong weapon for a sharpshooter—but an ordinary infantry-man, probably of either the 1st Texas or the 17th Georgia. The photograph was staged in that the body was carried from a place forty yards away and posed in the den. See William A. Frassanito, *Gettysburg: A Journey in Time* (New York: Scribner, 1975), 186–92.

4. The location of Val's place in Alabama connects with the presentation there of language-learning. It was in Tuscumbia, Alabama, in a well house, the summer of 1887, that Helen Keller discovered "water." As his essay, "The Delta Factor," attests, that event is an epiphany point in Percy's own odyssey.

5. See André Leroi-Gourhan quoted in Joseph Rykwert, *On Adam's House in Paradise* (New York: Museum of Modern Art, 1972), 21: "Such archeological evidence [as there is] would seem to justify the assumption, that from the higher paleolithic period onwards there was an attempt to control the whole spatio-temporal phenomenon by symbolic means, of which language was the chief. They imply a real 'taking charge' of space and time through the media-tion of symbols: a domestication of them in a strict sense, since it involves within the house and about the house, a controllable space and time."

6. Frederick Brown, *Père Lachaise: Elysium as Real Estate* (New York: Viking, 1973), 9.

7. As Percy is undoubtedly well aware, there is evidence that the build-ers of the Bomb were hooked on the aesthetics of it and thus saw humanistic scruples as threats to their artistic and scientific autonomy.

8. Quoted by Geoffrey H. Hartman, *The Fate of Reading* (Chicago: University of Chicago Press, 1975), 272. The quotation is the epigraph for Daniel Boorstin's *The Image: A Guide to Pseudo-Events in America* (New York: Athe-neum, 1962).

9. John Carr, ed., *Kite-Flying and Other Irrational Acts: Conversations with Twelve Southern Writers* (Baton Rouge: Louisiana State University Press, 1972), 51.

10. Carlton Cremeens, "Walker Percy, the Man and the Novelist: An In-terview," *Southern Review*, n.s., IV (April, 1968), 184.

11. Andre Gide, *The Counterfeiters* (New York: Modern Library, 1927), 316. With its odd "blasted planet" landscape, the presentation of language, and the mentions of Adam and Jesus (Val's slang epithets and Will's profan-ity amount on one level to name-dropping) the visit to Val's stages fully in the O'Connoresque manner a grotesque version of John 1:1 & 14: "In the begin-ning was the Word, and the Word was with God, and the Word was God. . . . And the Word was made flesh, and dwelt among us . . . full of grace and truth."

Of Walker Percy's four novels, the influence of Flannery O'Connor shows far and away the most strongly in *The Last Gentleman*—as strong, at least, as Guardini's or Eliade's or even Heidegger's or Kierkegaard's. She died during the writing of *The Last Gentleman*, and I am tempted to see in the visit to Val's a tribute to her memory. She seems so fully there: her evangelical Ca-tholicism, her backwoods hardscrabble haunts, her deadpan weirdo kind of grotesque, her orthodox religious correlative; and the scene of Val feeding the hawk strongly suggests the famous photograph of Flannery O'Connor feeding her peafowl.

12. Here Percy may be following Geoffrey Gorer, *Death, Grief, and Mourn-*

ing: A Study of Contemporary Society (Garden City: Arno Press, 1965), 128: "At present death and mourning are treated with much the same prudery as sexual impulses were a century ago."

13. Martin Heidegger, *An Introduction to Metaphysics*, trans. Ralph Manheim (Garden City: Doubleday Anchor, 1961), 133. I have changed the word *alien* in the translation to the more literal *unhomely (unheimlich)*.

14. Mircea Eliade, *The Sacred and the Profane: The Nature of Religion*, trans. Willard R. Trask (New York: Harcourt, Brace & World, Inc., 1959), 91.

15. Walker Percy, "Virtues and Vices in the Southern Literary Renascence," *Commonweal*, LXXVI (May 11, 1962), 181.

16. Saul Bellow, "On Boredom," *New York Review of Books*, XXII (August 7, 1975), 22. These reflections are made by Charles Citrine in Bellow's novel, *Humboldt's Gift* (New York: Viking, 1975).

17. When asked once if he worries when he is afflicted by "writer's block," Percy replied: "No. I remember something Franz Kafka wrote. He had a motto, '*Warten*,' written on the wall over his bed. *Wait.* You don't have to worry, you don't have to press, you don't have to force the muse, or whatever it is. All you have to do is wait. And that's true." Cremeens, "Walker Percy: An Interview," 289.

18. The phrase is from the sculptor David Smith, describing one of his own ideals of form.

Vauthier

1. For a detailed treatment of the narratee's functions, see Gerald Prince, "Introduction à l'étude du narrataire," *Poétique*, XIV (1973), 178–96. This is an expansion of the author's earlier "Notes towards a Categorization of Fictional 'Narratees,'" *Genre*, IV (March, 1971), 100–105.

A word on the terminology and method of this paper: I find the concept of *diegesis* as used by Gérard Genette (see in particular *Figures III* [Paris, Seuil, 1972]) very helpful. *Diegesis* refers to the space-time universe of the story, *diegetic* and *intradiegetic* to that which belongs, *extradiegetic* to that which does not belong to that universe. Since *metadiegesis* designates an inner story, the universe of Sutter's notebook is metadiegetic and so is the allocutor he addresses, often an image of his sister Val, although both Sutter and Val are intradiegetic characters, in the general narration. In this case diegesis and metadiegesis are continuous, unlike the Cass Mastern episode in *All the King's Men*. The words *author* and *reader* are used to refer to the writer's and the reader's "second selves." See Wayne Booth, *The Rhetoric of Fiction* (Chicago: University of Chicago Press, 1961), 138. To call the impersonal narrative instance a narrator and refer to him as an animate being is of course only a convenient figure of speech, one of the many images of critical discourse. Finally, although for brevity's sake I only give one illustration or two, all the devices I have selected for analysis are represented in the text with a certain frequency.

2. Simone Vauthier, "Narrative Triangle and Triple Alliance," *Les Américanistes: French Critics on Contemporary American Fiction*, ed. Christiane and Ira Johnson (Port Washington: Kennikat, 1978).

3. Emile Benveniste, *Problèmes de Linguistique Générale* (Paris: NRF, 1966), 241–42.

4. Ian Watt, "Realism and the Modern Form," *Approaches to the Novel*, ed. Robert Scholes (San Francisco: Chandler Publishing Co., 1961), 65.

5. Roland Barthes, "Analyse textuelle d'un conte d'Edgar Poe," *Sémiotique Narrative et Textuelle*, ed. Barthes *et al.* (Paris: Larousse, 1973), 34; see also Barthes, *S/Z* (Paris: Seuil, 1970), 101.

6. For Bibb see *The Narrative of the Life and Adventures of Henry Bibb* (1849); rpt., New York: Negro Universities Press, 1969; on Barrett, read Clement Eaton, *The Freedom-of-Thought Struggle in the Old South* (New York: Peter Smith, 1964), 133; I am indebted to Walker Percy for the information on Williston (Walker Percy to Simone Vauthier, March 21, 1975). Yet the information was there for everyone to see, not in some dry "Who's Who," but in William Alexander Percy's *Lanterns on the Levee* (Baton Rouge: Louisiana State University Press, 1974).

7. Martin Luschei, *The Sovereign Wayfarer: Walker Percy's Diagnosis of the Malaise* (Baton Rouge: Louisiana State University Press, 1972), 117.

8. Let anyone attempt to count the occurrences of "the engineer" and he will notice how easy it is to let one slip by, precisely because the word now and then works as a shifter.

9. Claude Levi-Strauss, *La Pensée Sauvage* (Paris: Plon, 1962), 242.

10. James Joyce, *Ulysses* (London: Penguin, 1973), 209–10.

11. Lewis A. Lawson, "Walker Percy's Indirect Communications," *Texas Studies in Literature and Language*, XI (Spring, 1969), 899.

12. The suggestion has been made by Martin Luschei, *The Sovereign Wayfarer*, 167.

13. Benjamin de Mott, "The Good and the True," *Book Week* (June 12, 1966), 2.

14. The designating process in *The Last Gentleman* brings to mind that of Voltaire in *L'Ingénu*. In this, the most novella-like of his *contes philosophiques*, Voltaire persistently refers to his hero as "l'ingénu" (a word which bears some phonetic resemblances to "the engineer"), and occasionally as "le jeune homme," "notre captif," etc. It is interesting to note too that he often plays with appositions to the name of the heroine—in a way which is sometimes arresting in French (*e.g.*, "l'heureuse et désolée Saint-Yves"). Wayward as it may seem to compare Catholic novelist Walker Percy and the archenemy of the Church, both are concerned with embodying in their fiction a certain conception of man—however different—and of his relation to the world into which he is thrown. Both view their protagonists with a philosophical detachment which does not exclude sympathy for their very ingenuousness.

15. Walker Percy, "Naming and Being," *The Personalist*, XLI (Spring, 1960), 153.

16. A fictional narrator does not reproduce speech in the way a newspaperman reproduces a statesman's utterances; one might distinguish between narrators who pretend they do and narrators who do not bother to keep up the pretense. With the demurrer, one can, I think, use the words *reproduce*, *relay*, and the like. For a historical survey of the criticism on Free Indirect Style and related views on Indirect Style, Direct Style, and Free Direct Style, see Gérard Strauch, "De quelques interprétations récentes du style indirect libre," *Recherches Anglaises et Americaines*, VII (1974), 40–73. I have borrowed the criteria mentioned by Strauch: oblique/nonoblique, introduced/nonintroduced (Free Direct Style being both nonoblique and nonintroduced) as well as his criterion of literal/nonliteral, although the question of literality raises again special problems in a work of fiction. The French "style indirect libre"

is usually translated as "free indirect style," but I have preferred to render *style* by *discourse*.

17. Barthes, *S/Z*, 51.

18. French linguists are paying more and more attention to the dispositif énonciatif; see Claude Coulomb, "Dispositif énonciatif et stratégie narrative," *Recherches Anglaises et Americaines*, VII (1974), 171–89.

19. John C. Pline, *Library Journal*, XCI (June 1, 1966), 2877; de Mott, 2.

20. Walker Percy, introduction to "The Last Gentleman: Two Excerpts from the Forthcoming Novel," *Harper's Magazine* (May, 1966), 54.

21. "Plus transparente est l'instance réceptrice," says Genette, "plus silencieuse son évocation dans le récit, plus facile sans doute, ou pour mieux dire plus irrésistible s'en trouve rendue l'identification, ou substitution, de chaque lecteur réel à cette instance virtuelle" (*Figures III*; Paris: Seuil, 266). The figure of the narratee is certainly much less visible in *The Last Gentleman* than it is in *The Moviegoer* where it serves among other things as a device of distancing.

22. Walker Percy, "Two Excerpts," 54.

23. Mikhail Bakhtine, *La Poétique de Dostoievski*, French translation (Paris: Seuil, 1970). "Le narrateur romanesque est, en termes clairs et analogiques, le créateur mythique de l'univers romanesque," Wolfgang Kayser, "Qui raconte le roman?" *Poétique*, IV (1970), 509.

24. The impression of a circulation of meaning is certainly enhanced at the level of the narration by the beginning of the story, which seems to have started before we listen in, and the ending, which raises unanswered questions.

25. T. S. Eliot, "Ash Wednesday," *Collected Poems, 1909–1962* (New York: Harcourt, Brace, and World, 1962), 92. The phrase "the silent Word" is also Eliot's.

Broughton

1. Walker Percy to Panthea Broughton, March 31, 1978.

2. Mircea Eliade, *The Sacred and the Profane*, trans. Willard R. Trask (New York: Harcourt, Brace & World, 1959), 63.

3. *The Cathedral Daily Missal: The Roman Missal Adapted to Everyday Life* (St. Paul, Minn.: E. M. Lohmann, 1961), 719. A more literal translation of the Latin would read that it is through an "arcane admixture" of His divine power (*arcána sui núminis admixtióne*) that the water becomes regenerative.

4. Percy to Broughton, March 31, 1978.

Kennedy

1. William Barrett, *Irrational Man* (New York: Doubleday Anchor, 1962), 80, 82, 83.

2. René Descartes, "Meditation VI," *Meditations on the First Philosophy*, trans. John Veitch, in *The Rationalists* (New York: Dolphin Books, 1960), 165.

3. See Carleton Cremeens, "Walker Percy, the Man and the Novelist: An Interview," *Southern Review*, n.s., IV (April, 1968), 282.

4. Arnold Toynbee, *A Study of History* (London: Oxford University Press, 1939), V, 376–439; VI, 49–132.

5. *Ibid.*, VI, 118.
6. Frank Kermode, *The Sense of an Ending* (New York: Oxford University Press, 1968), 14.
7. Toynbee, *A Study of History*, VI, 170–71.
8. Herman Hesse, *Steppenwolf*, trans. Basil Creighton, rev. Walter Sorrell (New York: Modern Library, 1963), 63.

Godshalk

1. For a discussion of this matter in another context, see my essay, "Walker Percy's Christian Vision," *Louisiana Studies*, XIII (1974), 130–41.
2. Compare the intersection of Interstates 10, 12, and 59 east of New Orleans, which somewhat resembles the present landscape of the novel; and see Percy's headnote to *Lancelot* where he details the "imaginary terrain" of that novel.
3. Compare *The Message in the Bottle* (New York: Farrar, Straus & Giroux, 1975), 109: "Like Thomas More . . . he is the most cheerful with Brother Death in the neighborhood."
4. This and the following statement are taken from "A Dialogue between Arthur Kopit and John Lahr" printed without pagination as part of Kopit's *Indians: A Play* (New York: Bantam Books, 1971). The emphasis is mine.

LeClair

1. Bradley R. Dewey, "Walker Percy Talks About Kierkegaard: An Annotated Interview," *Journal of Religion*, LIV (1974), 282.
2. Søren Kierkegaard, *The Present Age*, trans. Alexander Dru and Walter Lowrie (London: Oxford University Press, 1940), 163.
3. Søren Kierkegaard, *Attack Upon "Christendom"*, trans. Walter Lowrie (Boston: Beacon Press, 1956), 159.
4. Fyodor Dostoyevsky, *The Brothers Karamazov*, trans. Constance Garnett (New York: Random House, 1950), 787. The devil is also portrayed as a salesman in Walter M. Miller, Jr., *A Canticle for Leibowitz* (New York: Bantam Books, 1976), which Percy has written about.
5. Dostoyevsky, *The Brothers Karamazov*, 776, 779, 789.
6. Søren Kierkegaard, *Training in Christianity*, trans. Walter Lowrie (Princeton: Princeton University Press, 1944), 71.
7. Søren Kierkegaard, *Fear and Trembling and The Sickness Unto Death*, trans. Walter Lowrie (Princeton: Princeton University Press, 1968), 51.
8. John Barth, "The Literature of Exhaustion," *Surfiction: Fiction Now and Tomorrow*, ed. Raymond Federman (Chicago: Swallow Press, 1975), 21.
9. "The Sustaining Stream," *Time*, February 1, 1963, p. 82.
10. Carlton Cremeens, "Walker Percy, the Man and the Novelist: An Interview," *Southern Review*, n.s., IV (April, 1968), 275; the following three quotations are from this interview and appear on pages 280, 282–83, and 275.
11. John Carr, "Rotation and Repetition: Walker Percy," in John Carr (ed.), *Kite-Flying and Other Irrational Acts: Conversations with Twelve Southern Writers* (Baton Rouge: Louisiana State University Press, 1972), 40.
12. Cremeens, "Walker Percy: An Interview," 279.
13. Bruce Cook, "To Walker Percy, Man's Prognosis is Funny," *National Observer*, May 24, 1971, 17.

Thornton

1. The essays are not arranged chronologically in the book, nor are the dates of original publication given. The essays are reprinted in *The Message in the Bottle* substantially but not precisely as they were originally. In some instances sentences or even paragraphs have been added to (less frequently, deleted from) the earlier versions.

2. The distinction Percy expresses here by *triad(ic)* and *tetrad(ic)* is expressed in later essays (1972 *et seq.*) by the terms *dyad(ic)* and triad(ic). This is a change of terminology, not of idea, brought about by Percy's following the usage of C. S. Peirce. For Percy's own explanatory note on this, see "Toward a Triadic Theory of Meaning" (*MB*, 167*n*). The potential confusion for the reader of *The Message in the Bottle* is compounded since the essays are neither dated nor chronologically arranged.

3. I have quoted Percy at length here, to present these crucial points in his own words. But I must confess my difficulty in following him when he says that the word *blue-dollar* has "the same ontological status as the bird." I suspect that this contention involves an impasse, such that those of Percy's own philosophical persuasion will agree with him, those of a different camp will disagree, but neither will find much "explanation" of how a word is simultaneously sound and symbol.

4. One other effect of Percy's serious if tentative suggestion that the locus of man's capacity for meaning lies in "the human inferior parietal lobule . . . to a rough approximation of areas 39 and 40 of Brodmann" is to give pause to the readers of *Love in the Ruins*, because of the analogy with Dr. More's lapsometer, which works on various Brodmann areas to produce contentment and wholeness of personality. In that novel the machine is, we had thought, an object of Percy's trenchant satire, but we find now that Percy's attitude may be less clear-cut than first appears.

Poteat

1. Blaise Pascal, *Pensées*, trans. W. F. Trotter, with Introduction by T. S. Eliot (London: J. M. Dent and Sons, 1948), Fragment 71.

2. I do not argue here from Langer's distinction between "sign" and "symbol" upon which Percy relies. My premise is the more radical contention that "sign" is logically heterogeneous with "stimulus." If true, then *a fortiori*, "symbol" and "stimulus" are heterogeneous.

3. The concepts of logical heterogeneity and of ontological hierarchy are complementary. Two concepts are logically heterogeneous when the repertoire of concepts with which they function is different, *e.g.*, *heart* in anatomy and in contract bridge. Ontological hierarchy refers to the fact that an inventory strictly limited to the physical-chemical properties of what we antecedently know to be a machine could not include the principles of mechanics, *i.e.*, the principles in terms of which we would understand what it is for something to *be* a machine. Such an inventory of the printed letters on a page equally could not include conventions of spelling, grammatical or syntactical rules. Metals and letters are ontologically—that is, as to the nature of their being—subordinate *as entities* to the machines and sentences which they jointly respectively comprise, subject to mechanical rules and spelling conventions, grammar and syntax.

4. Maurice Merleau-Ponty, *Consciousness and the Acquisition of Language* (Evanston, Ill.: Northwestern University Press, 1973), 5–6.

Lawson

1. The theme is Heidegger's conception of *Dasein's* experience of *Befindlichkeit* and Sartre's conception of *pour-soi's* conflict with the *en-soi* which is its past. Percy's various treatments of the theme are to be found in the Abádi-Nagy, Brown, Bunting, Carr, Cremeens, and Dewey interviews and in Percy's essays, "From Facts to Fiction" and "Notes for a Novel About the End of the World."

2. The reasoning behind his interpretation might be either Sartrean or Heideggerian. For Sartre the past is the objectified *pour-soi*, so that seeing Harry, so closely aligned with his past, might remind Lance of himself, but of a hardened self, no longer available. For Heidegger, our possibilities are always out in front of our actualities; thus if Lance is thinking of himself as free possibility, he might mean that seeing Harry reminds him of what he cannot deny, his actuality.

3. Because *Lancelot* is narrated entirely from Lance's point of view, an interpretation of *Lancelot* first of all must clarify what actually seems to have happened. Hence, statements which may appear only to review incidents and situations actually offer either an acceptance or a rejection of the narrator's interpretation.

4. The Huck Finn and Frederic Henry examples are found in "The Man on the Train," collected in *The Message in the Bottle.* As Percy's classic treatment of everydayness and alienation, the essay is most useful to anyone reading *Lancelot*.

5. See Martin Heidegger, *Being and Time*, trans. John Macquarrie and Edward Robinson (New York: Harper & Row, 1962), 214–17.

6. Lance Lamar's bourbon is more expensive that Tom More's—he drinks Wild Turkey, not Early Times. With an inclination to Chandler, he has better taste than the man on the train, who reads Erle Stanley Gardner. With his feeling for Beethoven, he aligns himself with Tom More, rather than with Ed Barrett, whose worst moments are accompanied by Brahms. The intention here is not to produce a trivial footnote, but to emphasize the fact that through such constant characterization of the trivial Percy has stressed the efforts his *Dasein* makes to avoid being overwhelmed by the malaise.

7. Heidegger, *Being and Time*, 217–19.

8. William Alexander Percy, *Lanterns on the Levee* (Baton Rouge: Louisiana State University Press, 1973), 8.

9. Heidegger, *Being and Time*, 95–102. In *The Moviegoer*, on the bus back from Chicago, Binx distinguishes between two ways of relating to things: the college boy is an idealist, seeing the real world as a shoddy degeneration from transcendental forms and alienating himself as he distances himself from the world around him, while the hardware (happy choice!) salesman is at home in his world because he conceives of it as a complex of tools ready to his hand with which he has a personal connection. Binx says that the salesman is a metaphysician, albeit that his metaphysics don't go far enough. The salesman can be seen as metaphysician as soon as one accepts that there is no such thing as essence or the thing-in-itself. Instead, existence is essence (thus

what it appears to be is what it is); therefore, the necessary first approach to the world and to metaphysics is through being in touch with things.

10. See Jean-Paul Sartre, *Being and Nothingness*, trans. Hazel E. Barnes (New York: Philosophical Library, 1956), 389.

11. See Heidegger, *Being and Time*, 210–24.

12. Sartre, *Being and Nothingness*, 398–99.

13. *Ibid.*, 402–403. "The Other" requires a masculine reference in French.

14. See *The Message in the Bottle*, especially "Toward a Triadic Theory of Meaning," "Symbol, Consciousness, and Intersubjectivity," and "A Theory of Language."

15. See "The Man on the Train," *The Message in the Bottle*, 84. Percy adapts Ortega's description of the romantic who wishes to find Arcadia among the ruins to fit his conception of the alienated man.

16. See Lewis A. Lawson, "Walker Percy's Southern Stoic," *Southern Literary Journal*, III (Fall, 1970), 5–31, and Jim Van Cleave, "Versions of Percy," *Southern Review*, n.s., VI (October, 1970), 990–1010, for Percy's employment of family background in his first two novels.

Dowie

1. Donald Davidson, *Still Rebels, Still Yankees* (Baton Rouge: Louisiana State University Press, 1957), 178.

2. Hugh Holman, *The Roots of Southern Writing* (Athens: University of Georgia Press, 1972), 13.

3. Karl Menninger, *Whatever Became of Sin?* (New York: Hawthorn Press, 1973), 178.

Brooks

1. Eric Voegelin, *Science, Politics, and Gnosticism*, trans. William J. Fitzpatrick (Chicago: Gateway Editions, 1968), 9.

2. *Ibid.*, 23, 92.

3. Martin Luschei, *The Sovereign Wayfarer: Walker Percy's Diagnosis of the Malaise* (Baton Rouge: Louisiana State University Press, 1972), 6, 32.

4. Voegelin, *Science, Politics, and Gnosticism*, 99–100, 105.

5. *Ibid.*, 101.

6. This essay was written before the appearance of Percy's latest novel, *Lancelot*. It was the editor of *Stratagems for Being* who later suggested to me that I should make some allusion to *Lancelot* since Percy had presented in the character of Lancelot Andrewes Lamar the complete twentieth-century gnostic, a millenialist through and through who was confident that he knew how to reform a corrupt world and was willing to kill if he could not cure.

I am convinced that Professor Broughton is right, and I have proceeded not only to adopt her basic interpretation but to incorporate in this essay the specific wording that she tentatively offered. The concluding pages of my short essay are therefore best regarded as a sort of collaborative effort of the editor and myself.

Spivey

1. Barbara King, "Walker Percy Prevails," *Southern Voices* (May/June, 1974), 19.

2. *Ibid.*, 22.
3. Mircea Eliade, *The Sacred and the Profane*, trans. Willard R. Trask (New York: Harcourt, Brace & World, 1959), 196.
4. R. D. Laing, *The Politics of Experience* (New York: Ballantine, 1976), 168.
5. *Ibid.*, 144–45.
6. Richard I. Evans (ed.), *Conversations with Carl Jung and Reactions from Ernest Jones* (Princeton: Princeton University Press, 1964), 62–63.
7. Ashley Brown, "An Interview with Walker Percy," *Shenandoah*, XVIII (Spring, 1967), 7.
8. Laing, *The Politics of Experience*, 144.
9. *Ibid.*, 168.
10. Mircea Eliade, *Myths, Dreams and Mysteries*, trans. Philip Mairet (New York: Harper & Row, 1960), 75, 77.
11. Søren Kierkegaard, *Fear and Trembling and The Sickness Unto Death*, trans. Walter Lowrie (Princeton: Princeton University Press, 1968), 49.
12. Martin Buber, *Between Man and Man*, trans. Ronald Gregor Smith (London: Routledge & Kegan Paul, 1947), 52.
13. Kierkegaard, *Fear and Trembling*, 50.